TECH-FREE VACATIONS FOR YOUR ***BUSY LIFE***

LISA RICKWOOD

BALBOA.PRESS
A DIVISION OF HAY HOUSE

Balboa Press books may be ordered through booksellers or by contacting:

Balboa Press
A Division of Hay House
1663 Liberty Drive
Bloomington, IN 47403
www.balboapress.com
844-682-1282

Print information available on the last page.

ISBN: 978-1-9822-7343-9 (sc)
ISBN: 978-1-9822-7344-6 (hc)
ISBN: 978-1-9822-7342-2 (e)

Library of Congress Control Number: 2021917569

Balboa Press rev. date: 03/23/2022

For all those who color "outside the lines,"
break boundaries, and escape the pace.

Thanks to my supportive and loving husband, sons, and friends,
without whom I could not be the woman I have become.

CONTENTS

Preface ix

Introduction xi

Chapter 1 Serene Mini-Holidays 1

Chapter 2 Mental Relaxation 39

Chapter 3 Rejuvenating Rituals 75

Chapter 4 Cozy Home Retreats 107

Chapter 5 Quick Escapes 145

Chapter 6 Fun and Creative Pursuits 181

Chapter 7 The Great Outdoors 217

Bibliography 265

PREFACE

Tech-Free Vacations for Your Busy Life came to be because the timing was right, and the message was crucial for people to read at this point in history.

Since 2003, when my first book, *Escape the Pace: 100 Ways to Slow Down and Enjoy Your Life*, was published, I've witnessed an increasingly fast pace of life. The first book touched on ways to slow down and relax. However, it was published years too soon; people didn't understand its value until after the rise of the digital age.

With the advent of more sophisticated technologies and social media, our lives have become more complex and stressful. As much as we are connected digitally, we may be disconnected because we are distracted by technology and not living in the present moment.

My path for creating a simpler, less chaotic life began in 1999 with the sudden death of a new employee in a store I co-owned with my husband. This employee was with us for only four days, and on his last day, he suffered a massive heart attack and passed away before he fell to the ground. This experience forever changed me, and I suffered from post-traumatic stress disorder and other health issues for a year before researching and discovering positive ways to improve my mental, emotional, spiritual, and physical health. The research led me to become a columnist, facilitate workshops and seminars, appear online and on television, in magazines, and eventually write my first book. This experience also led to me becoming a Certified Professional Co-Active Coach and Global Career Development Facilitator. I already had a degree in visual art with a minor in social sciences, and the skills, abilities, and experience I gained were helpful to support clients with challenges.

I am passionate about helping people go from "chaos to calm" and assisting them in making the most of their lives. Before the global pandemic, I witnessed the rapid increase in the use of technology, and yet it helped us navigate these turbulent times. However, as we lived through this global threat, we rapidly grew exhausted from using technology. There needed to be a more balanced approach to integrating these tools into our busy lives.

One of the best ways to break from the hectic pace of life and technology is to engage in fun, relaxing interests alone or with others. Engaging in non-technological activities creates a buffer from the stress and anxiety that technology and operating at breakneck speeds can cause. There are many benefits to escaping the pace, and you need to read on to learn how to put them into practice. Everything in nature takes a break, so why shouldn't you?

INTRODUCTION

"Escape the pace. Life's not a race." –Lisa Rickwood

Do you remember carefree moments in your life when you did not possess a digital device? When you were young, played outdoors, and enjoyed nature with family and friends?
Did you play in the park, ride your bike, spend time outdoors, take walks or hang out with friends, or go camping?

I remember when technology didn't rule our lives—it was a simple way of living.

For example, when I was a child, I'd visit my grandparents in town. I lived in the country, and there were no children in my area—and I would play with the neighbors' children in the cul-de-sac. We would be outdoors all day, using our imaginations and playing games such as: "hide-and-go-seek," "Nicky Nicky Nine Doors," (where you and a group of friends would knock on random strangers' doors and run away; the goal was to knock on nine doors), "road hockey," and other games. We'd be outdoors from morning until night, and we didn't have our parents tracking us on cell phones because they didn't quite exist.

I remember hiking and exploring, riding my bike into town to swim at the big outdoor pool during the summer, camping with friends, having bonfires, and exploring the outdoors. The days seemed to last and last, and we had so much freedom; our parents couldn't reach us for many hours.

The changes started happening in the late 1960s and later trickled into our classrooms with the advent of the *Apple* computer. I went from being in grade seven and having minimal knowledge about personal computers to utilizing computers in high-school classrooms. Computer science was a popular class and challenging because people had to use a more archaic system—DOS (disc operating system), long before Bill Gates devised the Windows platform.

I knew I was balancing between the analog and digital worlds. The simple world was disappearing with the unprecedented advancement of technology.

As a member of an often ignored generation, *Generation X,* many of the technological advances that have happened were due to the influence of *Generation X.*

Generation X (sometimes called "Bust") refers to people born between 1965 and 1980. This generation was often referred to as *"The Forgotten Generation"* because only a small number of people were born. *The Baby Boomers* (*post-war*) generation and the *Millennials* often received more attention in the news.

The *Gen X* lifestyle often consisted of two-parent households, higher divorce rates, an obsession with materialism, and technological advances. While today's media and marketers may "snub" this demographic, these were the people who were highly influential and dramatically shaped our society over the last few decades and currently today.

The founder of Amazon, Jeff Bezos, grew up "right in the middle of the growing tech era." He was born in 1964. Sergey Brin and Larry Page, co-founders of Google, were born in 1973. Twitter founders Evan Williams, Biz Stone, and Jack Dorsey were born in the early 1970s.

Elon Musk was born in 1971 and founded SpaceX, Tesla, and a few other companies.

There are too many influential people to mention, but they represented *Generation X*—entrepreneurial, risk-taking, and inspired by technology.

While *Baby Boomers* may have been responsible for founding the Internet in 1969, Generation X took the discovery and made it relevant to our lives, and subsequent generations have built on this.

I lived through advances, including CDs for music and storage, cellular phones, personal computers, and the Internet. I stood on the precipice of a simple world and viewed the other side of the mountain, where there were advances in technology and a more complicated world.

I remember the carefree days, and when I told my children about my childhood, they would often give me the *"I feel sorry for you"* look as I mentioned life before smartphones, the Internet, and social media. I didn't know any better. I thought it was a pretty great life.

My children were raised without smartphones in elementary school, with maybe too much video gaming but many outdoor adventures. As a full-time working mother, I would spend as much time with my children as possible, and this happened outdoors; I believed it was critical to immerse them in nature.

My best friend and I would take our sons on long, arduous hiking trips, and our boys didn't complain; they would bounce rocks off the side of a cliff, take off their shoes and dip their toes in the ocean, look for "cool" sticks and shells...

As my sons got older, I made it a point to spend precious time outdoors with them, and we'd hike, swim, relax in portable hammocks, have picnics, drive to other towns, and explore our environment. The boys had lots of memories that didn't involve technology.

Having had the opportunity to experience the world on the verge of a technological revolution and seeing the aftermath, I must say there are positive and negative views of this adventure. Technology is a tool meant to simplify and improve our lives as it enables us to do more than we could ever dream of; we have yet to see what it can do for us. Technology is like a hammer—it may tear down or cause damage or be used to grow and build great things. We need to be aware of how to utilize it in our lives.

One of the great benefits of technology is that it was sophisticated enough to assist us all around the world when we experienced the worldwide pandemic. We were forced to self-quarantine and had to practice socially distancing from each other, so we used technology more to maintain our social lives—we stayed connected to our family, friends, colleagues, and more. Video conferencing, emailing, texting, and phoning helped us navigate this unprecedented historical time. Had this occurred 40 or 50 years earlier, it would've been - a challenge to humanity.

The downside of this experience is many of us became "burned out" from video calls, emailing, and how we stayed in contact with others. There was an unhealthy focus on technology, and this also included me.

Like many in the world, I heard the news by the *World Health Organization* on March 11, 2020, that deemed a virus to create a global pandemic. Things were changing so fast that I wasn't practicing healthy habits. I was exercising and eating well but was failing in terms of my health because I was reading and scrolling on my smartphone for hours (my "*Digital Wellbeing*" app indicated hours of online use) and I was mesmerized by changing news. This news addiction wasn't healthy. I knew other people were also locked in this vicious 24/7 digital information overload cycle.

This book is not about slamming technology; it's been critical in allowing some of us to keep working and has been an important tool to provide us with the human connection. Whether you like it or not, technology will continue to play a role in our lives.

It's important to view technology as just tools and not let it overtake our lives. We may become unbalanced if we spend hours focused on blue screens; if unchecked, this activity leaves us feeling tired, stressed, and overwhelmed. We must be aware of our actions and understand that taking digital breaks can create more balance in our lives.

Arianna Huffington, CEO of Thrive Global, offers this great quote:

"Disconnecting from our technology to reconnect with ourselves is absolutely essential."

We need to practice escaping the pace regularly to create a relaxing buffer and help us feel energized. One of the best ways to do this is to create a tech-free vacation every day—a mini-escape without carrying the weight of the world on your shoulders. Take this moment to ignore the news and the problems and worries you may be experiencing. This mini-vacation allows your body, mind, and spirit to relax and recharge.

Except for humans, everything in nature takes breaks, pauses, and slows down. Watching videos, responding to every smartphone notification, checking social media until the wee morning hours, and at blue screens until our eyes feel like sandpaper is not a healthy approach to life.

We have all found ourselves immersed in technology, and using it for work, entertainment, and socializing. Yet, many of us feel exhausted by its constant use.

This book focuses on spending time outdoors in nature because fresh air and open spaces are beneficial for us mentally and physically. There's much research around the benefits of being in nature; this makes sense as our evolution revolved around spending time outdoors, hunting, and gathering food for our families and villages. It is not natural to spend our lives indoors 24/7 under artificial lights and air conditioning.

If you live in a city, you probably spend a lot of time indoors, and it may be a challenge to get outdoors; most cities have parks and green spaces available to enjoy. It's worth the effort to find time to escape outdoors to enjoy "green scenery" instead of "blue light."

Escaping the pace isn't about ditching technology. It's about creating a more balanced approach to living that includes time away from blue screens and more time in nature and engaging in hobbies and activities that make you feel good. Taking a "tech-free vacation" is possible every day and may take as little as five minutes.

HOW TO USE THIS BOOK

As you read this book, use it in a way that works for you. You may open up a page, read and pursue an activity on that page, or start reading the book from beginning to end. Take your time and read through and record ideas of what you'd like to do. Earmark the pages, write notes in the book, use it to inspire you to "escape the pace" in a way that works for you.

WHEN PLANS CHANGE

One of the biggest challenges of living during the 21st century is that life moves fast, and change occurs more frequently. As a result, we may spend more time online, using technology to keep up with the constant changes. All this compounds and adds to our mental stress, and we may feel the need to disconnect and relax temporarily. The best way to do this may be with a tech-free vacation.

While it may be easy to get outdoors and walk, hike, and engage in other activities, some indoor mini-vacations may be more of a challenge.

For example, if you enjoy visiting coffee shops, restaurants, indoor concerts, antique shops, and other indoor venues, you may decide these are great ways to escape. Still, you discover closures or restrictions, so you may have to change your plans.

I remember planning to have lunch with a close friend, and the restaurant wasn't open to people sitting inside but was allowing people to order and take food. Since the restaurant was near the ocean and had favorable weather that day, my friend and I grabbed our lunches and headed to the beach. The visit ended up being more memorable than sitting in the restaurant as we were seated on battered old driftwood logs overlooking a sandy beach. Seagulls were flying, and there were sounds of crashing waves, a sailboat in the distance, and children running along in the sand. It was a moment to remember.

Being creative and adaptable is essential as we live and thrive during unprecedented times. While there are many great ideas for mini-vacations mentioned in this book, you may need to add your spin on these ideas and be flexible with your great escapes. You may need to call ahead to ensure places are open, check on regulations or rules, and have an open mind. When you tap into your creative, problem-solving mind, you create more options for yourself.

One of the best things you can do is create a personal list of great tech-free vacations and keep that list at hand so you can review it regularly. Then, you have ideas when you have a day off, a few free hours, or need a moment to slow down, relax, and recharge.

THE INSPIRATION FOR THE BOOK

The inspiration for *Tech-Free Vacations for Your Busy Life* has challenged me to think differently in recent years. Since I wrote my first book, *Escape the Pace: 100 Fun and Easy Ways to Slow Down and Enjoy Your Life*, I felt the pace of life keep accelerating, and people appeared to be more stressed and overwhelmed trying to keep up with everything. As a working mother and career professional, I also felt the pressure of growing demands.

People complained about how technology was impacting their lives. They would mention their tech-addicted children getting lost in online gaming or social media. I also heard people say how technology changed their jobs or eliminated some positions due to technological advances.

I felt the impact of a changing workplace and a heavy reliance on technology. Before the spring of 2020, I facilitated in-person workshops, met with and coached people, and enjoyed an office environment. Then, my position changed from seeing people in person to instructing numerous online webinars from my home. After several months of creating and delivering online content to clients, I felt exhausted, burned out, and overwhelmed. I knew something needed to change, and this was when I began researching ways to take technological breaks.

During this challenging time, I wanted to create a buffer from technology. One of the best ways to counterbalance the use of technology is to get outdoors in the natural world. I found gardening to be one way to embrace this concept.

I grew a small garden when my children were young, but as they became teenagers, I stopped gardening as my life was busy. Over the years, I thought about having a garden.

In 2020, I decided to resurrect my interest and grow a vegetable garden. After working in front of a computer screen all day, I would change into my gardening clothes and tend to this garden. It was a great escape to be outdoors in the sunshine, prepping plants for growth. I walked 20 feet to the garden during harvest season to grab fresh tomatoes, snow peas, carrots, and lettuce to make a healthy, delicious lunch.

The garden was one of many mini-vacations I started to engage in to add more fun, creativity, and balance to my life. I also revisited my passion for art and took photographs of landscapes, plants, and insects. The pictures were beautiful, and I transferred them to large canvases, added oil paint, and created a one-of-a-kind, multi-media painting series.

I considered writing this book because I felt positive effects as I engaged in these activities. Spending time outdoors and being physically active lowered my stress levels and increased my happiness. I felt more connected to nature and experienced more joy in my life, which inspired me to consider writing this book. More people need to know about the importance of taking techno-breaks and enjoying the power of mini-vacations no matter how little time they think they have to spare.

MY LIFE

The idea of inventing mini-vacations started when I was young. I used to think about adventures I could do on seven acres of pristine land my parents owned in the Okanagan in British Columbia. Being in nature was my sanctuary from the challenges and struggles of growing up. Whenever I had felt sad or frustrated and had time, I escaped outdoors and engaged in a mini-vacation.

Creativity was an essential part of my life, so I worked hard and managed to win art scholarships to attend university and obtain a visual art degree. I continued down the creative path, attending large gift shows, selling art, and exploring ways to be innovative.

As an entrepreneur and working mother, I needed simple ways to relieve the anxiety and exhaustion of being a co-owner of a 2,000-square-foot, high-end men's retail store and juggling the demands of raising young children.

I started exploring healthy ways to relax and destress. The research eventually led me to become a local columnist for a newspaper and a magazine, and the experience and feedback from readers inspired me to write my first book.

I was asked to be a speaker at numerous events, featured in media such as *Breakfast Television* and magazines including *Woman's World*, newspapers, blogs, online websites, and interviewed as far away as New Zealand.

In 2007, I became a Certified Life Coach and author and created a website, www.escapethepace.com. After a few years, I coached clients across North America and decided to gain more knowledge in the career development field. My curiosity led me to get certified as a Career Development Practitioner, and I've since been helping clients successfully navigate through life and career changes.

If you enjoy the book, email me your thoughts or escape ideas to: info@escapethepace.com. I always love to hear what you're doing to bring more escapes into your lives. If I don't respond immediately, I may be escaping the pace, so please be patient as I will get back to you as soon as possible.

Happy escaping,

Lisa Rickwood — Chief Escape Artist (CEA)

CHAPTER 1

Serene Mini-Holidays

Whether you thrive on constant activity or enjoy a slower pace, there will be times when you want to take short, relaxing mini-holidays where no one expects anything of you, and you have a moment to rest and recharge your body, mind, and soul.

These mini-vacations may happen at home, work, while you travel, or when you are out in nature. The trick is they should be calming and help you de-stress and relax.

TECHNOLOGICAL ESCAPE PLAN

> "There's no Wi-Fi in the forest, but I promise you will find a better connection." —Ralph Smart

Our lives have merged with technology for quite some time. While we work, we may connect to the Internet and digital devices to complete our tasks. When spending time at home, we may watch TV, doom scroll (scroll through online feeds and focus on negative news), review and respond to social media, play video games, and research online.

There are many challenges with technology. One issue is the constant bombardment with notifications and distractions from emails, texting, social media, and more. While there are benefits to having this information and connection with others, it is also distracting and makes us less productive.

We lose a lot of time scrolling on social media and viewing others' lives, the latest news events, and updating our status. We get sad and depressed due to focusing on negative-based news. The need for constant connectedness makes us anxious. We feel like we have to check our email and texts, thus becoming exhausted. Sometimes we need a technological break.

A positive way to improve your relationship with technology is to break from it by creating boundaries. This practice is healthy and allows you to have strong connections with family and friends. One of the best ways to take a break from technology is to spend time outdoors. Nature is a buffer and antithesis to technology. As soon as you're outdoors and not on a blue screen, you feel your stress and anxiety dissipate—fresh air, exercise, open space, a change of scenery—nature is magical.

It doesn't matter whether you take a short outdoor walk, a long hike, go camping, ride a mountain bike, kayaking or relax in a hammock. The effect of the outdoors is one of the best ways to decompress from technology.

Turning off notifications allows you to avoid the distractions of "dings" and fully live in the present moment.

Another trick to handle the effects of technology is to delete items that waste your time: social media apps, mobile games, news apps, and other apps that may have "empty" content. Try eliminating something that takes your time. If it's gone for a few days and you don't miss it, you probably don't need to bring it back.

For the websites and apps you still have, you may want to set a time limit for yourself and set up your device to stop working when you reach your "limit." For example, you might limit your viewing time to one hour of social media per day. You might also stop using your mobile device up to one hour before your bedtime.

When you start putting boundaries on time you spend with technology tools, you'll discover you have more time and are less distracted. It won't be easy to create this habit when you first try taking breaks. You might feel anxiety and distraction, but if you keep focused on minimizing screen time, you'll begin to enjoy the break from technology.

Immediate benefits will be more free time for hobbies and interests, more time with friends and family, and less stress and anxiety. You'll notice more present-moment awareness, improved sleep, deeper connections with others, better focus and learning, and productivity.

TRY THIS

You can do many things to add more balance between technology and your work and life. It starts with being aware and making healthy choices.

Here are a few ideas:

- Keep your phone out of the bedroom and use an old-fashioned alarm clock.
- Turn off your technology an hour before bedtime.
- When you spend a lot of time using technology, get outdoors.
- Eliminate old or unused or time-wasting apps.
- Turn off all notifications when working or spending time with people.
- Delete all old social media accounts that you're not using or don't enjoy.

- Put your phone on "silent" when you need tech-free time.
- Walk every day, and don't bring your smartphone with you.
- Turn your technology off for an afternoon or part of a weekend when you don't have to work.
- Be aware and decide if you need to respond to notifications at all.
- Create a device-free zone in your home, like your bedroom.

While it may seem that technology is a negative factor in our lives, there are many positives to using these tools. It allows us instant access to a lot of information, makes us more productive, and lets us stay in contact with people all around the globe. In fact, during the pandemic, access to technology was our saving grace. While the world was in lockdown, we maintained contact with family and friends, and some of us kept our careers going by switching from offices to remote work from home. As with anything, technology is best when used in moderation and balanced with other interests in your life. It's a valuable tool, and when used well, it's a great benefit to your work and personal life.

DOING NOTHING

> "Sitting quietly, doing nothing, spring comes, and the grass grows by itself." —Zen Proverb —Tani Rose Kageyama

There is a way of living in Italy called *dolce far niente,* or "the sweetness of doing nothing." It is a philosophy permeated into Italian culture and in stark contrast with North American culture.

In North America, there is the concept that if we spend our spare time doing absolutely nothing, then we are considered lazy people. However, this is why *dolce far niente* needs to be added to our way of living because we have a challenge slowing down or not accounting for our time. We often feel the need to be productive at all times.

We've learned to grow up with a reward system, which started when we first attended elementary school, and we got rewarded when we completed assignments and projects. This concept continued through high school and into our work lives.

This constant feeling of having to "be busy" takes its toll on our mental and physical state. We often start our day with a list of to-dos, which continues all day long. And we begin the next day the same way. It can feel a bit like *Groundhog Day,* where the main character wakes up, and each day is the same.

I've had moments when I feel like I'm having déjà vu when I question if I've done the same actions in the same order. Everything feels like a time loop. We need to calm down, relax, take a moment for ourselves, and even practice doing nothing during these exhausting days.

A movie sums up the Italian concept of the sweetness of doing nothing, and it's called *Eat, Pray, Love* (2010). The main character talks about her disappointment in herself because she's spent three weeks in Rome learning Italian and eating. Her Italian friends mention she doesn't know how to enjoy herself. She needs to learn *dolce far niente* and do nothing like the Italians, who say they are masters of it.

It may seem like a luxury to take time and do nothing, but it's essential to your physical and mental health. You need moments to rest and recharge if you're busy most of the time. Your "do-nothing moments" can be found in doing what you love or having a glass of wine outdoors at the end of a workday. The choice is yours.

You don't have to wait for the carefree days of warm summers to take a do-nothing moment or have a non-scheduled day. Build some time into your schedule by not overbooking your day.

Since I create and facilitate webinars and workshops, write, coach, and need to stay positive and energetic for clients, I practice embracing the Italian concept of doing nothing by taking time to spend in nature. Nature is my way to de-stress, and in the spring and summer, I stretch out in my canvas hammock, shaded under a cherry and apple tree. I can easily spend an hour resting, drinking a glass of wine, reading, and listening to the sounds of birds. This downtime has been the key to improving my mental health and happiness—it is more important than you realize.

TRY THIS

TIME: For this escape, dedicate an afternoon to a whole day for this adventure. Your time is not to be used to complete tasks or projects—this is relaxing, thinking, creative thought, or "spacing out" to "just be."

SUPPLIES: You won't need supplies to enjoy relaxing and just doing nothing; that is the beauty of practicing this mini-vacation.

When you finally have a moment or a day to do nothing, revel in it and enjoy every moment. Let your mood and interests dictate what you want to do, and don't be afraid of getting bored.

You might take a walk, read a novel, start writing your long-planned book, rearrange furniture, sleep in, play an instrument, exercise, or sit and daydream. There is magic in unplanned moments. Sometimes, the best ideas or answers to unsolved challenges bubble up when we least expect them to. When you finally have a moment or a day to do nothing, revel in it and enjoy every moment.

THE MOMENT

"A moment's thinking is an hour in words." —Thomas Hood

Did you ever wish you could stop time? Perhaps you were a parent, and your children reached a fun and magical time, and you wanted to freeze those moments. Or, you took the trip of a lifetime, and the experience was so incredible you wished the adventure would last.

I remember asking a group of participants in a workshop if they had superpowers, what would they be? Someone in the audience mentioned controlling time to make the fun times last and the challenging times pass quickly.

As we age, we ponder time, and our experiences and memories may flood back—moments when we were children with our entire lives ahead of us. Birthdays, in particular, have a way of making us consider time as we can easily measure its passing. If you live in a world region with four seasons, you may feel the passing of time as yet another season comes and goes.

We've all heard the saying, "Time flies when you're having fun." And it seems to stand still when we're not enjoying the moment. Yet, time never changes: seconds are seconds, minutes are minutes. What changes is our perception of time?

Do you remember hot summers that seemed to last forever when you were a child? Did time seem to move more slowly than it does now that you're an adult?

Why is that?

There are many reasons; the first one has to do with the novelty of life when we are young.

Scientific American published a relevant article, *Why Does Time Seem to Speed Up with Age?* The theory goes like this: *"Our brain encodes new experiences, but not familiar ones, into memory, and our retrospective judgment of time is based on how many new memories we create over a certain period. In other words, the more new memories we build on a weekend getaway, the longer that trip will seem in hindsight.*

This phenomenon, which Hammond has dubbed the holiday paradox, seems to present one of the best clues as to why, in retrospect, time seems to pass more quickly the older we get. From childhood to early adulthood, we have many fresh experiences and learn countless new skills. As adults, though, our lives become more routine, and we experience fewer unfamiliar moments. As a result, our early years tend to be relatively overrepresented in our autobiographical memory and, on reflection, seem to have lasted longer. Of course, this means we can also slow time down later in life. We can alter our perceptions by keeping our brain active, continually learning skills and ideas, and exploring new places." (1)

Another reason time seems to speed up is that we are not living in the moment.

Adulthood puts new demands on us as we have to work to survive and may have demanding jobs, children, family issues, health, and other challenges jockeying for our attention. We may also feel the need to keep going and not slow down.

For decades, society focused on speed, productivity, and busyness, in a whirlwind of never-ending commitments. The speed at which we operated in our lives made it challenging to slow down and notice special moments right in front of us. At least this was before the pandemic.

The pandemic put the globe on a long, temporary pause, causing industries like airlines, cruise ships, sports, and live events to stop. Around the world, countries went into "lockdown." People had to slow down, whether they wanted to or not; this experience opened up the idea that people needed to live in the moment.

It's not easy to "live in the moment," especially if the moment is unpleasant. These are not the moments you want to focus on. You want to pay attention to something that gives you "joy" and live in that moment. For example, if you find happiness while your dog curls up beside you on your couch, look for more moments like this and then savor these times.

What things give you joy, and how can you incorporate these into your special moments?

TRY THIS

TIME: For this exercise, take at least 20 minutes.

METHOD: To live in the moment, remove your watch or hide your smartphone so you can't pay attention to time. Take a walk, read a book, exercise, or engage in something enjoyable. Notice how many times your mind wanders from that activity to the past or present. Focus on keeping your mind on what's currently happening.

Paying attention to the moment may be a challenge for you if you're used to filling your mind with past or future thoughts. Keep looking for opportunities to practice this exercise.

When you speak to people, try to quiet your inner dialogue and actively listen to them. People are always impressed when they experience a person who is listening to them. It makes them feel valued and respected and may help to improve that relationship. You may summarize what they said or ask them, "Tell me more!" People appreciate those who listen because many of us are too distracted to take the time to be in the moment and truly listen.

An effective way to bring your mind to the "present" is to try this little exercise to help you relax. Start this exercise by slowing down your breath and then asking yourself these five grounding questions:

What are FIVE things you see?

What are FOUR things you can touch?

What are THREE things you hear?

What are TWO things you smell?

What is ONE thing you taste?

By asking yourself questions that involve your senses, you bring your wandering mind into focus.

TIMELESS GETAWAYS

> "All we have to decide is what to do with the time that is given us." —J.R.R. Tolkien

There is one thing no amount of money in the world can buy, and that is time; you may be able to pay people to do chores and tasks for you, but that is all. We get 24 hours in a day. Time with your family, friends, pets, hobbies, and passions—you can't duplicate these fleeting moments.

As we get older, we understand that time is finite, and we are running out of it. Every moment counts. Unlike money or objects, you can't get spent time back.

Often, its importance hits us hardest when we lose a loved one. Someone we spend time with today may be gone tomorrow; we need to treasure our moments with important people.

Helping and serving others is a great way to spend your time; you never know what impact your time with someone makes. Strong relationships happen over time.

We waste our precious moments watching mindless videos, doom-scrolling through news feeds and social media, focusing on anger and negative emotions. While we can't always manage our feelings and moods at every moment, we need to focus on better ways to spend our most precious resource—time.

Creating a "timeless getaway" can add more balance to your day if you have a job that involves heavy scheduling. For example, I use a calendar and have my entire workday structured and timed as I conduct numerous webinars and meet virtually with clients. Every once in a while, I find myself so time-starved that I miss lunch, and running the washroom is even a challenge. These are the days that getting away from structured time is critical.

A timeless getaway means just that: We take a break without looking at a clock. If you decide on a timeless vacation, this means no "peeking" at your cell phone, computer screen, clock in your home, or building. You want to avoid keeping track of every moment in your day.

TRY THIS

TIME: For this escape, you will want to have at least 30 minutes or longer.

Decide how much time you wish to dedicate to a timeless escape. Are you seeking 30 minutes, an hour, an afternoon, or most of the day? This mini-vacation will depend on your obligations, responsibilities, and your state of mind.

This mini-vacation is best when you're not working or need to attend a meeting or event. If you wear a wristwatch or use your phone to keep track of your day, you need to take off your watch and put your cell phone away for a while.

If you're new to a timeless escape, start with a shorter break as you may feel uncomfortable not being aware of what time it is in your day. Taking a respite of 30 minutes or an hour is good, and you might make it a "game" to figure out what the exact time is without any devices.

METHOD: Getting outdoors in nature without a cell phone or watch is a great way to take a break from your day's schedule. When you're engaged and enjoying yourself outdoors, you may lose track of time, so be sure you escape when you don't have to be doing anything specific.

So, enjoy your "timeless getaway"...

VISUALIZE VACATIONS

> "Visualize what you want to do before you do it. Visualization is so powerful that when you know what you want, you will get it." —Audrey Flack

Do you remember visualizing careers when you were little? Perhaps you thought about being an astronaut, scientist, artist, actor or actress, writer, professor, Olympic athlete, superhero, or inventor. You imagined what it would be like to do that job; you closed your eyes and imagined the sights, sounds, and feelings. Your imagination was powerful, and you felt transported to that time and place.

I remember being an eight-year-old and playing in my grandparents' neighborhood as I often stayed with them on weekends. I lived in the countryside, and there weren't any children my age in the area. My grandparents lived in town, and their house was on a busy cul-de-sac where many young families resided. I made many friends in this area, and we'd play for hours, often going from morning till dark. Our parents weren't too concerned with us as they knew all the children in the neighborhood.

When we played, we'd pretend we were superheroes and run around with makeshift capes, swords made of sticks, and overflowing imagination. It was a fun and free time in our young lives, but it didn't last; it slowly became replaced by more anxious times—those of pre-teens and their newfound worries. By the time we reached this point, we weren't playing superheroes or using our imagination as much; we attempted to "be realistic and act like adults."

In adulthood, we spend a large portion of our time acquiring skills and abilities, obtaining training, and gaining employment experience. We're also meeting new people, forming friendships, and creating families. It may feel like there isn't enough time in our day to think about being creative—we need to complete tasks and "do it now!"

Adding a tool such as visualization to our lives may be a "game-changer" as it may help us relax by taking our minds away from the stresses of life and helping us achieve our goals. We may also use visualization to solve challenges or improve relationships and careers.

Visualization refers to the concept of creating images to communicate a message. When you imagine what it feels like to take that long-awaited vacation, you may visualize what you'll be doing on vacation. You might envision being at a beautiful beach and surfing, kayaking, paddle-boarding, or dipping your toes in the ocean and feeling the cool water touch your skin. When you see a picture in your mind, you're visualizing.

Athletes use this tool all the time; they visualize the outcome of an event in vivid detail. For example, a sprinter might imagine the track, starting blocks, where other runners are, the audience, the sights, sounds, and running every single step from the moment the gun signaled the start of the race until the moment they crossed the finish line.

This tool is effective when practiced correctly—the subconscious mind can't tell the difference between reality and your imagination. When the athlete paints a picture in their mind, this stimulates the brain, similar to physically doing the actual action. The more the athlete runs the scenario through their mind, the more successful they are as they're priming themselves for success.

In an article in www.*SportsPsychologyToday.com, The Power of*

Visualization, author Matt Neason mentions,"*One of the most powerful effects of good visualization is that it programs the subconscious brain. You want to think of the subconscious brain as a self-guiding missile. When a self-guiding missile is fired, it starts moving toward its programmed target. As it moves toward its target, it assesses its coordinates in relation to the target and makes mini adjustments to correct its path. Our subconscious brain works in the same way. It identifies our coordinates and naturally moves us toward our target."* (2)

The challenge we encounter is that we tend to unconsciously program our brains with adverse outcomes and run less than successful scenarios through our minds and later wonder why we didn't achieve the desired result. Your mind is similar to a GPS in your vehicle; you won't reach your desired destination if you type in an inaccurate address.

If you're new to visualization, it will take a while to get comfortable with it; practice creates more success. As well as practicing regularly, you want to plan how you will visualize; being haphazard in how you do it won't be effective. You also want to put positive feelings into what you envision, as feelings are the fuel to inspire you.

When you decide on a goal, visualize the event, activity, or desired outcome. Think positive thoughts and really "feel" how it would be to achieve the plan. Run the whole event through your mind, taking time to imagine what you see, hear, smell, taste, and feel.

For example, years ago, I wanted to take my family to Hawaii, and money was very tight as we were operating a retail store and didn't have much money. I visualized we were in Oahu on Waikiki Beach. I was dipping my warm toes in the water and sand, looking at my family relaxing on the beach, gazing over at Diamond Head Mountain, smelling the faint aroma of sea salt, and hearing birds in the distance. That image represented my goal of saving enough money to take my family to this location.

It took over two years of saving a few thousand dollars, and one day, I was at a coffee shop and ran into a friend who ran a travel agency. I mentioned I had a little money saved and wanted to surprise my family with a one-week all-paid trip to Oahu. I secured a great deal for flights and the hotel and paid cash to get an even better deal. On Christmas Day, I had a surprise scavenger hunt, and my family found a certificate mentioning a trip to Oahu in February. They were in shock for a while as it had to sink in that this happened.

When I dipped my feet in the sand at Waikiki Beach, it was an amazingly similar experience to what I'd imagined in my mind.

TRY THIS

TIME: For this escape, take at least 10 minutes.

METHOD: If you're new to visualization, start slow and imagine a place you'd like to visit or an event you'd like to attend. Imagine who you'd be with, what you'd be doing, how the place would appear. Let your mind wander.

Choose something that makes you happy. Something enjoyable could be an event or goal you want to have. It could be just a practice session of something that seems like a "pipe dream" to you. It doesn't matter too much when you're just starting to practice this technique. But, as you begin to do this more and more, add in actual events or goals you wish to achieve.

Remember to get emotionally connected to the event or goal because your feelings will fuel your energy while you achieve it.

Happy escaping!

MINI-VACATIONS

"A vacation is what you take when you can no longer take what you've been taking." —Earl Wilson

I had the worst sleep; it didn't help that I ate nachos late at night, and my heartburn was literally "off the charts." I couldn't get comfortable, and my mind just kept "racing" as I'd also made the mistake of checking the news before bed. This habit of checking the news before bed has happened more times than I care to admit—I'm not a great sleeper, I "toss and turn," and my mind goes into "overdrive" at 3:00 am every time I do that.

When I finally have to get up for work, I feel exhausted, unfocused, and miserable. When I think this way, I know it's essential to build a "mini-vacation" into my workday, which may happen during lunch or after work.

During the spring of 2020, I was working from home. I thought about planting a garden, so, in early April, I planted a vegetable garden that included: carrots, peas, beans, tomatoes, and a few varieties of lettuce. By July, the vegetable garden was ready, and during my lunch hour, I'd make a fresh salad and sit in my hammock. I tied the hammock to my cherry and apple tree. Sitting under the trees in my hammock, eating fresh vegetables, and feeling a cool breeze on a hot day was the ultimate quick mini-vacation during my lunch. The bonus—my dog enjoyed relaxing under the trees with me.

Being outdoors was vital because I spent my working hours "tied to desk" in a dark, basement office. This simple escape was what I needed to boost my physical and mental energy to be productive in the afternoon.

A quick mini-vacation is an activity you enjoy that "energizes" you and can be performed quickly. It may take five minutes, or you may extend it to an afternoon. It doesn't matter how long it takes if you're able to fit it into your day. Depending on how much time you have, you'll want to tailor your mini-vacation; you may take a short walk with your dog, ride a bike, go for a hike, meditate, read, or exercise.

When you begin a mini-vacation, be sure to "silence" your cell phone. The point of this mini-vacation is to "unplug" from digital devices, to give your body and mind time to decompress and truly relax without the demands of the world intruding into your space.

Find a place where you relax for at least a few minutes without interruptions. You might choose a nearby park, your car, your office with the door closed, or a kitchen table. Do whatever it is that quickly relaxes you. Start with deep breathing to "ground you" during your mini-escape; deep breathing increases oxygen to your brain and promptly promotes a state of calmness. It also helps you focus on the present moment as you may be "not present" until you practice this exercise. Breathing has a way of bringing us "back to the moment."

TRY THIS

TIME: For this mini-vacation, you must dedicate at least 30 minutes to the activity.

METHOD: Find a quiet place and start your mini-vacation. Begin by breathing in through your nose for a count of five and exhale through your mouth for a count of seven. This simple act slows down your breathing, and your brain follows this pattern. You will notice you feel calmer and in control of your thoughts.

Next, use your senses to bring you to the present moment. Notice the aromas around you, listen to the sounds, and look around at your surroundings. Pay attention to your body temperature. Are you warm or cold? What is your body feeling at this moment?

Make your mini-vacation more interesting by using pure aromatherapy oils and breathing in the aroma. Or you may squeeze a stress ball, eat a piece of chocolate, or listen to relaxing music. Adding many sensory activities to your mini-vacation will enable you to relax and let go of worrying thoughts.

If you find it challenging to make time for this escape or it's not easy to actually "relax," remember that this process takes practice. Don't give up. It will take time to train your mind and body to relax, and if you do this every day, you will start to see positive changes. Happy escaping!

FUN FREE ASSOCIATION

> "My humor is channeling everything through my brain. For example, when I talk about something, it's how Richard Lewis feels about it. I'm a storyteller. I do a lot of free association." —Richard Lewis

You need to write a crucial report for your work, and as you sit in your chair, your pen sits idle, and the hands of time march ahead. Your mind is stressed and blank, and you're unable to type anything on your computer. You've reached the wall, the block, the uncreative moment.

Years ago, when I worked in marketing and advertising, I had constant deadlines. I loved creating new and exciting ad layouts and suddenly found that I couldn't think of anything original and cutting-edge for my account, a large Ford dealership. I had two hours to create an effective ad campaign for their new trucks and pitch it to my client. I frantically viewed images, wrote down phrases and words but felt stuck.

Desperate, I grabbed a notepad and started using a process called free association.

This term was coined by Sigmund Freud, who lived between 1856 and 1939 and was an Austrian neurologist and founder of psychoanalysis. Freud used free association to help patients unlock unconscious feelings and thoughts ignored or repressed. Using this technique, a patient would mention a word and think of everything related to the word and talk without editing thoughts and feelings. There would be no intervention or censorship, and this free way of thinking often unlocked information for Freud to help his patients.

Since Freud, free association has come a long way and is used to generate ideas for products or services. This technique works well when you brainstorm with other people. You choose one topic and start talking without censoring your ideas and thoughts. If you have someone who can record what you say on a smartphone or other device, this is useful to listen to later. You may write key ideas down on paper or in a journal. Try to avoid a computer as there is more activity in the brain when you purposely write things down on paper with a pencil or pen.

I asked my colleagues if I could get their input on my new truck campaign, and we sat at our desks, yelling out the first ideas that came to mind. They said the first things they thought of: heavy, built tough, dependable, rock-solid, powerful, kick-ass, and the list goes on. Eventually, I pieced together a great campaign with the help of my co-workers, and the client was impressed with the outcome.

Whether you brainstorm alone or with others, you'll discover this is an effective tool to unlock your creativity when you are stuck.

TRY THIS

TIME: Give yourself 10 or 20 minutes to use the free association technique when you have a challenge and need to generate new ideas.

METHOD: Write your challenge or concern at the top of a piece of paper or in the middle (if that works better for you), and then yell out ideas and quickly record them. Write down all words or phrases that pop into your mind, and do not second-guess yourself or start to edit. Record everything. There will be time to be critical later. You do not want to stop the "flow" in the middle of the process.

If you prefer to create a brainstorming web, write the topic in the middle of the paper, put a circle around it, and write down every related or unrelated thought or subject on paper. You may have ideas radiate out from the center if you like to think this way; this is a very creative way to brainstorm.

Great writers use a similar concept. They start writing without editing and getting critical, and they record all their thoughts until they feel complete. Later, they edit and create a more concise form of writing.

COLOR BY CRAYON

> "Color is a power which directly influences the soul."
> —Wassily Kandinsky

Do you remember coloring when you were a child? Did you use crayons or pencil crayons? Time seemed to stand still while you doodled and experimented. Sometimes you ended up with a beautiful masterpiece, and you may have scribbled "outside the lines."

When I was five years old, my mother had a part-time job as a mail sorter at a post office. One day, she had to take me to work with her as she didn't have a caregiver to watch over me. I was excited to see her workplace.

She led me to a small lunchroom and mentioned I had to stay in the room and behave as she had to complete her work. I remember being frustrated until she said she would give me art supplies. She left the room, and after a couple of minutes, she returned with a coloring book and a big box of crayons. I instantly felt happy.

I never considered the importance of coloring until around 2015, when I noticed many adult coloring books in the market. They were everywhere. Their popularity grew as people talked about color and posted their finished projects online.

There are many reasons the coloring-book craze became mainstream, and much of this was because adults needed a way to decompress from stress and responsibilities. Many people discovered they felt more relaxed and creative after losing themselves in the activity of coloring.

In an article by Dr. Nikki Martinez, Psy.D. LCPC, Contributor to *www.huffpost.com, 7 Reasons Adult Coloring Books Are Great for Your Mental, Emotional and Intellectual Health,* it was mentioned: *"Coloring also brings us back to a simpler time. An activity that can invoke the easier and happier times of childhood. A time when we did not have as many responsibilities and could do something because we wanted to, for the pure joy of it. To be able to tap into this time and these emotions is very cathartic and enjoyable. It can take you out of your present stresses and worries for even a few hours at a time, which can have an exceptionally recuperative effect."* (3)

Research shows that the physical act of coloring may be similar to meditation as people slow down and focus on objects right in front of them; this may benefit people who struggle with learning to meditate. Coloring may lower stress and anxiety and help you achieve mindfulness.

Children are naturally mindful and "live in the moment," paying attention to their current environment as many things seem new and exciting to their young minds. They're not concerned with being productive. They want to learn and try new things. Coloring is a childhood activity that isn't about being productive; it's more about being creative and playing with the pencil crayons or pens as they move across the paper, seeing the colors fill the lines (or not), and seeing a pattern or scene evolve into a colorful masterpiece.

Many intellectual benefits to coloring include problem-solving, organization, focus, concentration, and more. When we play with color, we use both sides of our brain because we consider color choices, the balance of color, and applying it. While we're coloring, we focus on the task, which minimizes stress. Coloring is a quick, fun, and great escape that you can do for a few minutes or longer.

Coloring books come in all shapes and subjects, with geometric patterns, inspirational quotes, detailed mandalas, nature scenes, scenes from around the world, animals, swear words, doodles, and may even double as a calendar or a journal. If you don't want to color in a book, color an individual drawing. Download a few images or create an original illustration and add color.

TRY THIS

TIME: For this escape, take at least 15 minutes.

METHOD: Find a quiet, relaxing place to do this activity. Make sure you have the materials available. You might have coloring books, individual drawings, and crayons, pencil crayons, and watercolors—any material you enjoy using.

Next, turn off your cell phone, get comfortable, and choose a page to color. Breathe in deeply and let your mind slow down as you grab a color and start to create.

Coloring books may seem like a passing interest, but these books are so much more. They are a respite from your busy day. You can use them during a break at your desk, while watching television, or during a rainy day—the moments to take a break are endless.

COLORFUL ESCAPES

"I am a believer that color affects people's moods."
—Lilly Pulitzer

I was lucky enough to sail with my grandparents in the Pacific Northwest when I was a child. We would often sail for a few days, sleeping on the boat and experiencing the sights and sounds of the ocean, visiting small islands, and watching the sunsets and sunrises. I will never forget the beautiful colors of the sky—breathtaking shades of yellow, gold, orange, pink, and red.

Nature showcases some of the most intense and beautiful colors, many of which show up in the spring with the burst of new flowers, changing sunrises and sunsets, and more. Color is all around and impacts us, yet we rarely think of its importance.

In some cultures, some colors have a different meaning, but certain shades have a universal message.

For example, warm colors are also known as the "red area of the spectrum," which may include yellow, orange, and red, and these colors may invoke emotions that range from comfort and warmth to anger.

"Blue-spectrum colors" are "cool" colors and may include: green, blue, and purple. These colors may be considered "calm" but may also inspire feelings of "sadness."

Although black isn't on the color wheel because it's not a color, it's considered the absorption of all colors. Sometimes it's seen as "elegant and sophisticated" or associated with "power." Other times, it may symbolize death, sadness, anger, and aggression.

According to a study about black, professional football players and hockey players who wore black uniforms were more aggressive and received more penalties. The findings indicated possible biased judgments from referees and overall aggressiveness in players.

There are many color meanings and extensive psychology behind the use of colors. For example, red represents love, energy, and strength. Orange represents success, confidence, and sociability, and yellow represents creativity, cheer, and warmth. Green symbolizes nature, healing, freshness, and blue is trust, peace, and loyalty. Pink represents compassion, sincerity, and sweetness, while purple is royalty, devotion, and spirituality. Brown is dependable, rugged, and trustworthy, and white is simple, clean, and innocent.

Color touches every aspect of our lives, from workspaces to living areas, clothing, and more. Who hasn't felt "red with anger," "green with envy," or "blue?" We often use color to describe how we think and use it in marketing and advertising to influence our buying decisions.

For example, studies show that specific colors may increase a person's heart rate. Colors such as: yellow, orange, and red have often been the backdrop of design for fast-food restaurants. These colors subconsciously make us speed up our actions, so the time we order food, eat, and leave the restaurant increases. Thus, eating establishments can have a quicker "turnover" of diners in their businesses, equalling more profits.

Color affects how you feel about your environment. Are you happy with the colors of paint in your home? Do you like the furniture colors and accents? Do you feel like something needs to change?

Changing colors is not too challenging if you're not happy with your space. You may paint a wall, buy new pillows or a throw blanket and add artwork, fresh flowers, and more. Many things add great color to your environment.

As well as your environment, you'll want to consider your wardrobe colors. For example, are you a person who wears many dark colors? Maybe a color change might inspire you.

I remember the power of color when I bought a red wool blazer with a blue undertone. I used to wear this blazer when I worked in advertising sales, and one day, I approached a Toyota dealership to sell a full-page newspaper advertisement. I was wearing the red jacket and didn't even realize that the salespeople were also wearing red jackets—the signature jacket of Toyota. I found my personality had to be more outgoing to compete with the colored blazer. As a result, I always had success when I wore this red jacket to sell ads to this dealership.

On the days I wore a black blazer, I didn't seem to have as much luck with selling advertising. I noticed high sales when I wore the blazer these days, so I started wearing it more frequently.

It doesn't take much to add color to your life, and when you add the "right" color, it makes a positive difference in your life.

TRY THIS

TIME: For this escape, take at least 15 minutes.

METHOD: Start by focusing on your work and home environment and studying the colors in your space. Have a notebook and write down what works and your changes.

Don't have money or time to make changes to your home or office? Adding fresh flowers, a new piece of artwork, new pillows, a tablecloth, a throw blanket, and other small accessories will make a massive difference in creating new color in your space.

As well as studying your home and workspace, also consider the colors in your wardrobe. What colors work for you? What clothing do you need to eliminate? Even if you love black and don't want to give up this shade, consider adding colorful accessories to dress up your look.

Enjoy your colorful escape!

PUZZLING PUZZLES

> "The world is a puzzle with a piece missing." — Ormily Gumfudgin

Did you ever play with puzzles when you were a child? Do you enjoy puzzles now as an adult?

Puzzles are a problem to solve that challenges one's creativity and resourcefulness. They entertain while offering a concrete solution. Consider jigsaw puzzles, crossword puzzles, Sudoku, Tetris, and others. What makes them appealing is how we "lose ourselves" to solve the challenge.

There are many types of puzzles, including cryptic puzzles, math puzzles, logic puzzles, mechanical puzzles, trivia puzzles, word puzzles, and riddles.

Cryptic puzzles consist of a crossword puzzle, and each clue acts as a word puzzle. These are popular in Canada, the United States, the United Kingdom, Ireland, Australia, several Commonwealth countries, India, South Africa, and Malta.

Math puzzles are algebraic puzzles that involve using algebra to reach a solution. Arithmetic puzzles involve general mathematics and calculus, and combinatorial puzzles use combinations assembled several different ways, but only a few offer a solution. One of the most popular math puzzles is Sudoku. It falls under combinatorics and varies in complexity and solvability.

Logic puzzles consist of many shapes and sizes, and in each puzzle, you have a series of categories, the equivalent number of options in classes, and each option used once. The goal is to decide the linked options based on the shown clues.

Mechanical puzzles are designed using wood, metal, or plastic and are mechanically interlinked pieces, and the solution to solve them is to manipulate part or the whole of the object. The most popular and well-known puzzle was the Rubik's Cube, invented in 1974 and popularized during the early 1980s.

Like many children, I got my hands on a Rubik's Cube and was determined to solve the challenge of taking the mixed-up color sides and manipulating them to create solid-colored ones. I never did solve this challenge. Out of frustration, I peeled off some of the colored stickers and placed the solid colors on each side to create the illusion of solving the puzzle.

Trivia puzzles are in demand. Look at the number of people who obsess with completing crossword puzzles. These involve different types of trivia, and once the reader figures out the answer, they write it in and then look to complete the puzzle.

Word puzzles are another example, and crosswords also fit into this category. These puzzles require a strong knowledge of the language, and they may be mathematical.

As well as other brain puzzles and teasers, there is a simple form of a puzzle called riddles. I enjoy solving riddles; the more I practice, the better I get each time. Riddles get your mind to "be creative and think outside the box." I will often have a riddle at the beginning of a PowerPoint webinar presentation to get participants to think while waiting for the webinar's start. I often find riddles that can't be easily solved by typing into "Google."

Last is the jigsaw puzzle, which dates back to the 1760s, with European mapmakers pasting world maps onto wood before cutting them into smaller pieces. Jigsaw puzzles have evolved a lot since then as they are no longer just depicting maps. They may range from hundreds to thousands of parts and from simple to complete to almost impossible images with minimal variation in color and design. For example, a jigsaw puzzle might depict the photo of a desert with mostly sand and very few other details.

TRY THIS

TIME: You want to have at least 30 minutes for this escape.

METHOD: For your next escape, decide what type of puzzle most appeals to you, as you won't be motivated if you're disinterested.

A great time to do this type of escape is when the weather outdoors is terrible, and you aren't motivated to travel or visit anyone, and chores are the last thing on your mind.

Take at least an hour and lose yourself in the puzzle(s). Can you solve it? Do you care? If you're doing a jigsaw puzzle, you may dedicate a space to build it, and once complete, you may glue the image to a board and hang the work. Some people enjoy doing this.

Whatever you decide, enjoy the process. Everybody deserves to have a puzzled escape.

MINI MASTERPIECE

> "Art! What a concept! It saved my life! A place where you can do as you please!" —William Wiley

My earliest memories of the concept of art began when I was three years old, and my mother caught me staring at a textured curtain for several minutes. Years later, she told me she had been concerned that something was wrong with me because I just sat still and stared at the curtain.

I remember this textured '70s-inspired colored wall curtain. I distinctly recall staring at it because it had many shapes and textures. My imagination flowed, and I could visualize animals and other objects in the curtains. This moment was the start of my unique way of seeing the world; I would notice patterns and shapes that others would not see.

I eventually became involved in the arts and experimented with many forms of creative expression.

I became obsessed with colors, textures, and design, and I spent hours drawing in notebooks, creating and illustrating stories, sewing, and doing arts and crafts as a child. Art was my life.

While attending high school, I sang and acted in theater and painted and designed elaborate sets for performances. As well, I hand-painted signs for school and community events.

In grade 12, I participated in an exhibition of my artwork, which got presented to three judges for my chance to win the BC Provincial Scholarship. I impressed the judges and ended up winning this scholarship and several bursaries, paying for my first year of university; I studied Visual Art and Social Sciences and eventually graduated with a degree in Visual Art.

After graduation, I worked in an art framing shop. A year later, I worked in advertising sales and designed advertisements for newspapers, and my art career grew.

All this changed once I had two children and had to work full-time to "make ends meet." My work was exhausting, and juggling two small children left minimal time and energy for art. I tried to create art on the weekends but took my sons to sports events, ran errands, and spent precious time with them. I stopped doing art.

Twenty years later, I started to delve into art again; I had a flair for photography and managed to capture a photograph of a bumblebee immersed in a flower. This piece was stunning and inspired me to create photo canvases of my photography and use oil paints to add to the final image. I didn't realize how much I missed being creative.

Art is relevant to many of us because it represents who we are as humans. From the very beginning, we painted and craved to tell stories. Our first art appeared on caves as far back as 40,000 years ago; the work may have had religious or symbolic meaning.

Art tells a detailed story about our history and cultural perspective, and it's a language understood by humans around the world. We're visual creatures, and a picture is "worth a thousand words."

Without art, our world would be stark. Imagine the inside of your home with no artwork or design—your furniture, rugs, curtains, bedding, towels, the art on the walls without color or artistic flair. It would not be pleasant. What about your clothing? What if there was no color or design?

Art is not only significant in the world but also relevant to you. Whether you are artistic or not, adding art activities into your day may be the best escape you may enjoy. For example, when you take out a journal and draw, your brain slows down, and you may alleviate anxiety as you are lost in a meditative, relaxed moment and focused on the task of drawing. Creating art also opens up your mind to problem-solving, future planning, processing emotions, lowering stress, and much more.

In their article, *Feeling Artsy? Here's How Making Art Helps Your Brain*, writer Malaka Gharib mentions: *"Studies show that despite those fears, "engaging in any sort of visual expression results in the reward pathway in the brain being activated," says Kaimal. "Which means that you feel good and it's perceived as a pleasurable experience."*

She and a team of researchers discovered this in a 2017 paper published in the journal The Arts in Psychotherapy. They measured blood flow to the brain's reward center, the medial prefrontal cortex, in 26 participants as they completed three art activities: coloring in a mandala, doodling, and drawing freely on a blank sheet of paper. And indeed—the researchers found an increase in blood flow to this part of the brain when the participants were making art." (4)

Creating art does need not be overwhelming; you may get a coloring book and color a mandala or doodle in a journal, play with watercolors, or take photographs.

Be sure to avoid the habit of comparing your art skills to others;

art is a very subjective discipline, and you need to focus on the act of creation. You can create great art without understanding the technical know-how. Just have fun.

Some things to get you started include abstract painting, doing a still life, exploring mixed media, taking photographs of a subject of interest, doodling or drawing cartoons, painting or drawing, creating a self-portrait, or taking a class.

If you already consider yourself an artist, push yourself and learn new art disciplines, try new techniques, buy new supplies, try things, and don't worry about the outcome. It's good to try and experiment and make mistakes to learn. Also, it's not just about the finished product. It's about immersing yourself in the activity, slowing down, focusing, and having a great escape.

Creating art is deeply personal and is a form of communication that isn't just for the elite. Art is for everyone.

TRY THIS

TIME: You need 30 minutes of uninterrupted time for your art escape.

METHOD: Make sure you also have a great stash of art supplies and a great space to work. You don't have to have a studio to create. You could have a spare room, garage, or the corner of a living room.

Decide what you would like to do for your art escape. Do you want to draw, paint, or carve? Once you decide, get your supplies ready, block off your space and time to create, and lose yourself in art. Remember, don't worry about creating masterpieces. You want your focus to be on the act of being spontaneous and enjoying the feeling.

PLAY-DOH PLEASURES

> "We don't stop playing because we grow old, we grow old because we stop playing." —George Bernard Shaw

What was invented in 1956 and smells like vanilla, cherry, salt, and flour? If you guessed Play-Doh, you would be correct. This wildly popular modeling clay for children happened by accident.

In 1912, Kutol, a Cincinnati company, was the world's largest soft compound manufacturer that helped remove soot from wallpaper. For a few decades, the company thrived, but as home decors changed and wallpaper was not in demand as much, and indoor heating switched to gas, electricity, and cleaner oil, the consumer demand for the product plummeted.

Joseph McVicker, a company owner, did everything to turn the company when his sister-in-law Kay Zufall had an idea. She had been reading the newspaper, and there was an article about how the soft nontoxic wallpaper cleaning compound got used as modeling material for children. Since Kay had a background in working with nursery school children, she tried the substance with the young children and discovered they loved to mold it into many different shapes. Zufall had the idea to call it Play-Doh, and she told McVicker, and the rest is history.

In an online article, *The Accidental Invention of Play-Doh*, published by the Smithsonian Magazine, writer David Kindy states, *"Of course, today Play-Doh Modeling Compound is a playtime phenomenon. Now owned by Hasbro, this accidental invention has grown into a worldwide franchise that is as much a rite of passage for kids as it is an opportunity to be creative and have fun. According to Fortune magazine, Play-Doh has sold more than 3 billion cans since its debut as a child's toy in 1956—eclipsing its previous existence as a wallpaper cleaner by light years. That's more than 700 million pounds of the salty stuff. 'Urban legend has it that if you took all of the Play-Doh compound created since 1956 and put it through the Play-Doh Fun Factory playset, you could make a snake that would wrap around the world 300 times,' writes Hasbro on the Play-Doh site. The dough was inducted into the National Toy Hall of Fame at the Strong in 1998."* (5)

In 2018, after many years, Hasbro finally obtained a trademark for their famous proprietary aroma.

Who does not remember opening a can of Play-Doh and taking a smell of the substance? Too young to know better, some of us may have even licked the modeling compound.

However, our treasured moment occurred when we got to knead, roll out, cut out, and create various animals and objects. Our imaginations came alive with the options. And, we found ourselves in a slightly relaxed, meditative, creative state as we generated our clay art masterpieces.

It may seem silly and childish to play with Play-Doh, but research indicates how this simple action can minimize stress and help us be more focused, and you do not need to have small children to enjoy the process.

When you smell Play-Doh, it may help you relax, get focused, and calm down if you had fond memories of playing with the substance as a child. The act of smelling triggers memories in the limbic part of the brain, and this is why scents often seem to transport you back in time to earlier moments.

For example, when I smell the scent of Old Spice aftershave cologne, my memories instantly transport me to a time when I was five years old and standing in the bathroom with my father, gazing up at him while he shaved.

The tactile feeling of Play-Doh is comforting, and as the compound heats up, it is easier to manipulate; squeezing the dough acts as a stress ball, and we may feel a sense of stress release. We often tense up in the hands, so kneading, rolling, and playing with the material may help us relax.

If we do not associate ourselves with being gifted drawers, we may feel more comfortable creating shapes from a solid surface; some of us have more talents in this area.

We can improve our brain function, boost creativity, stimulate our sense of sight, smell and touch, and add a social component by doing this activity with others. If we have small children, this is a creative time to spend with them, and we can enjoy it, too.

TRY THIS

TIME: For your mini-vacation, make sure to dedicate 30 minutes to this activity.

The next time you are in a gift, card, or dollar store and see tins of Play-Doh, buy a few in different colors. Keep some of these compounds at your desk at work and home.

METHOD: When you have a few minutes and your mind and fingers are tense, crack open a container of Play-Doh, take a whiff of the scent, pull out the substance, knead it, pull it, roll it out, and start creating. You only need a minimum of 10 minutes to notice yourself relaxing. If you have a few minutes more, challenge yourself to create an object, an animal, or a new creation. Have fun!

CRAFTY ESCAPES

> "Crafting is putting ideas into action and then holding them together with an inexpensive adhesive." —Amy Sedaris

Do you have any arts or crafts that you practice? Did you enjoy being crafty as a child?

As young children, we often engaged in numerous crafts at school and home, but this engagement often started to slow down when we grew up.

I remember spending hours with my artistic and crafty mother making art cards, drawing, painting, sewing, and creating new things. When I was pursuing these activities, hours seemed like minutes, and I had so much enjoyment and minimal stress and anxiety.

One of my favorite crafts was creating a homemade quilt. I spent weeks collecting an assortment of fabrics to sew a beautiful quilt that I later placed on my bed when I was a teenager. I remember being proud of this accomplishment.

Some people enjoy arts and crafts to relax and decompress, be creative, and solve new challenges, while others do arts and crafts and sell them professionally online and at craft events.

Arts and crafts play a role in society as they are often passed down from generation to generation and tell a story about history. As well, arts and crafts instill values.

These activities are essential for children, adults, and seniors and help on many levels. Children learn to focus, solve challenges, and achieve a final result, boosting self-esteem. Adults find arts and crafts bolster positive feelings, creativity, and minimize stress and anxiety. Older adults enjoy fun activities that enhance brain productivity, especially important as cognitive decline occurs with age. Older adults may also have health issues, and arts and crafts can help them socialize with others and keep busy.

If you already have arts and crafts you enjoy, see if you can dedicate more time to play and engage in these activities; it's great for your mind and body. Think again if you feel like you don't have an artistic or crafty bone in your body. There are many crafts you may enjoy.

You can buy individual materials for your chosen craft activities or simplify the process with craft kits that have assembled materials to get you quickly started creating crafts. Custom craft kits may include: paint by numbers, felt creation, knitting, crocheting, cross-stitch, soya candles, tie-dye, stamps, hand lettering, card making, jewelry making, macramé, acrylic paint pouring, watercolor painting, embroidery, pottery kits, and much more.

Crafts can be categorized into projects to enhance your garden or home, or they might be items such as clothing, jewelry, and other products. There are so many directions where you can focus your energy and talents. The list is endless.

Here is a small list of a few arts and crafts to get you started, and while you may want to do these as a hobby, if you get good, they may lead to side hustles or even a full-time business:

- Signs with inspirational sayings
- Wreaths
- Mason jar lights
- Dog lover items
- Wedding decorations
- Cards: photo, hand-painted, etc.
- T-shirts, sweatshirts, hats
- Wooden signs: greetings, sports teams
- Specialized gift baskets with homemade jams, jellies, cards, soaps, etc.

- Homemade soaps
- Bath bombs
- Beaded earrings
- Ceramic pottery: mugs, plates, etc.
- Knitting, crocheting, etc.
- Decorated tote bags
- Macramé plant holders
- Sewing and designing clothing
- Pillow making
- Resin arts and crafts
- Eco-friendly items: upcycled materials
- Tie-dyed t-shirts
- Stylish tote bags
- Homemade cosmetics
- Doormats

TRY THIS

TIME: For this escape, you need at least 30 minutes and uninterrupted time to engage in your activity.

Decide ahead if you will be working on an arts and crafts activity you know a lot about or if you will begin a brand-new project, learning new skills.

If the activity is brand new to you, be patient as you will make mistakes, learn, and may need to restart the project. Getting comfortable and learning new skills and techniques takes time and practice but can be fun.

METHOD: Before you start to work on your project, ensure you have the equipment and tools to work on the arts or crafts activity.

There is nothing more frustrating than noticing that the paints have dried up or the paper you would use for the cards is non-existent.

Once you're ready to go, lose yourself in the activity and ignore your digital devices. Enjoy the escape!

CHAPTER 2

Mental Relaxation

It is easy to feel anxious and stressed in today's world. Just watching the news, responding to every notification on our digital devices, or our health, finances, work, family obligations can make us feel unbalanced and miserable.

Stress and anxiety often start in our minds, so if we can learn to calm down, relax, and take a mental holiday, we can minimize some of the effects of our daily lives on our brains.

Just a few simple escapes are all it takes.

DIGITAL DIETING

> "Technology is a useful servant but a dangerous master." —Christian Lous Lange

In this connected world, we often find ourselves staring at blue screens and mindlessly swiping through real and fake news, friend updates, and surfing the Internet as time quickly passes. Digital stress and addiction are real issues. Marketers are aware of our weaknesses and use these habits to coax us to scroll down to check out the latest news and articles. Online addiction is so strong there's a lot of information about its effects on our relationships, work, and physical and mental health.

I have not escaped online screen addiction. One night, I wanted to research this book, but I checked my friend and family's updates on social media instead of working. I quickly slid down the slippery slope of online addiction, and two hours of social media perusing occurred. By the time I realized my actions, it was too late at night to work on my book.

I watched too much news and quickly felt depressed and stressed. To add fuel to the fire, I kept watching more and more news feeds and reading every negative article online. I was addicted to the chaos and wanted to know everything. The problem is that the news is negative and very repetitive, and when you realize this, you can drastically cut down on it without missing the key pieces you need to know.

Not long ago, people spoke about going on a "digital detox," which consisted of giving up digital devices and going "cold turkey" for a set time. Personally, it's not that easy to give up your technology for a day or a weekend. It's also not realistic; we've taught people when we are available and if we suddenly don't answer an email, instant message, or phone call, people may get upset or panic. Not to mention, we may feel frustrated and stressed because of digital withdrawal.

Instead of a total digital detox, try a digital diet. With a few simple rules, you'll still be "connected" without feeling the overwhelm of being available 24/7. When you set a few rules and create time boundaries, you'll discover you're more productive and less stressed.

Years ago, I heard a great story about Timothy Ferris, author, entrepreneur, podcaster, and early-stage tech start-up investor. He wrote several books, including my favorite, *"The 4-Hour Workweek."*

I remember hearing him talk on an online show. He described a nutrition health company he was running years before his book-writing days. He conducted business globally and had to get up to speak with business leaders in other countries. He'd habitually view his emails over 200 times a day, and the whole process would be overwhelming.

One day he reacted by scheduling a six-week trip to the United Kingdom. He needed to get away—he couldn't do it anymore.

Once there, he had an epiphany! What if he only checked his emails once a week and designed an autoresponder to let customers and others know when he would be available? This experiment proved to be life- and business-changing. He discovered his business was over 30 percent more productive because he wasn't spending his precious hours reading emails every other minute. Instead, he was engaged in the productive pursuits that built his business.

His discoveries led to simpler studying methods, and he started teaching these concepts at university. Students asked Ferris to write a book about his knowledge, and he wrote his bestseller, "*The 4-Hour Workweek.*" Ferris believed that one could outsource many business activities and be more productive.

TRY THIS

TIME: For this escape, take 20 minutes and start by setting up your digital dieting program.

METHOD: Begin by minimizing your notifications. Check your device settings and shut off phone notifications you don't immediately need.

Next, choose no-device times. Instead of the digital diet, you might decide when you look at your digital devices.

For example, many people say they take the first 30 minutes in the morning to drink coffee or tea, exercise, meditate, write in a journal, plan their day or week, and they don't check their digital devices first thing in the morning.

When you look at your device first thing in the morning, you invite the world into your life. You may see negative news at the start of the day. Why start your day out hearing negative news? There's power in grabbing those first few minutes for you. Research shows you will suffer less depression and anxiety and have a more positive frame of mind when you choose things that energize you in the morning.

Speaker and author Mel Robbins swears that not having your phone or digital devices in your bedroom allows you to belong to the first part of your day. The temptation to check your phone is less likely when you have to walk to the living room or kitchen instead of grabbing it off your bedside table. When you avoid looking at your phone first thing in the morning, you have those first moments of sanity and calm to yourself—except if you have children that wake up early, then your time is spent with them instead of emails, social media, the news, and more.

As well as giving yourself a buffer from distractions in the morning, you need to unplug from technology at least an hour or two before bedtime. Research shows blue light from digital devices interferes with your circadian rhythm (body clock). It disrupts your sleep, and light suppresses the secretion of melatonin, a hormone responsible for the sleep-wake cycle.

Finally, choose specific times during the day to view your social media. If you are at work, only check during your breaks and lunchtime. Employers often have challenges with employees checking their screens, so make sure you moderate your use. If you love to post overly personal information about yourself, do yourself and everyone a favor and stop this.

DISAPPEARING ACT

> "On the keyboard of life, always have one finger on the escape key." —Anonymous

Have you ever yearned to temporarily disappear? To escape the demands of work, family, and other obligations and run away? While most of us wouldn't pack our bags and leave, we have most likely indulged in a disappearing fantasy, and some of us may have even packed our bags.

I felt this way a few years back when I was balancing family and work. One of my children was struggling mentally, my mother was diagnosed with Alzheimer's but still living alone and a danger to herself, and I was commuting to a stressful job and a brand-new career field for me.

I reached my breaking point on one particular day, and I felt it. I was doing some research with my brother to find someone to watch my mother in her home until we could get her into an assisted living care home. I phoned to find caregivers during my lunch hour, dealing with issues at home and clients needing suitable employment. I strived to be the best I could be in all directions, and I didn't even know who I was anymore. I fantasied about renting a hotel for a few days and just sleeping, eating, and watching TV—somewhere I could focus on myself for a brief moment.

If you are part of the "sandwich generation," caregiver to children and parents, this may be a busy and stressful time in your life for you. Pausing for a moment during your day can make a world of difference to your state of mind.

Ever notice how problems in life seem monstrous and unfixable at night and when you wake up in the morning, they feel more solvable?

Think about short-term and long-term solutions if you have dreams of running away from endless responsibilities. See if you can make realistic plans to take some weight off your shoulders. Are there people in your life that can help you? Are there obligations you can drop? What can you do to simplify things a bit?

In the meantime, find a simple way to disappear for a little while. It may not be simple to disappear when you are at your workplace, but you can take a mini-vacation during your breaks. You may take a walk outdoors to get fresh air or find a quiet coffee shop and grab a tea or coffee.

Another way to have an escape is to go outdoors and explore. You might have a plan and drive somewhere, or leave your home and go for a walk without a plan.

TRY THIS

TIME: You will need at least 15 minutes to think of ways you can disappear from your life for a short while.

METHOD: From your workplace to your home or beyond, consider places you can go to and find peace and relaxation.

On your next escape, indulge in a disappearing act where you're unavailable for contact for a while. To make it successful, set your smartphone to silent and don't look at your phone while you are on your mini-vacation.

If you disappear correctly, you'll emerge feeling calm, relaxed, and ready to tackle your daily challenges.

A BREATHER

> "Being aware of your breath forces you into the present moment—the key to all inner transformation.

> Whenever you are conscious of the breath, you are present. You may also notice that you cannot think and be aware of your breathing. Conscious breathing stops your mind." —Eckhart Tolle

Have you ever experienced shortness of breath, asthma, bronchitis, or pneumonia or been injured, and the pain was so intense that you held your breath? You probably didn't give much thought to your breath until you experienced one of these situations. Suddenly, you became intensely aware of the importance of breathing.

Our bodies are beautiful biological machines capable of regulating numerous body processes; this includes breathing, which is automatic and controlled subconsciously.

Proper breathing is critical for our bodies; we're a nation of shallow breathers and often don't practice deep breathing or get enough cardiovascular exercise. Deep breathing allows more oxygen into the blood, thus into the body and brain. It also helps us deal better with stress in our lives.

In an article in *Scientific American, "Proper Breathing Brings Better Health,"* author Christophe André mentions, *"As newborns, we enter the world by inhaling. In leaving, we exhale. (In fact, in many languages, the word 'exhale' is synonymous with 'dying.') Breathing is so central to life that it is no wonder humankind long ago noted its value not only to survival but to the functioning of the body and mind and began controlling it to improve well-being."* (6)

When I researched breathing and techniques, there were strategies for anxiety, labor, singing, swimming, running, lifting weights, engaging in yoga, and more. Breath is life.

At age 20, I discovered the importance of breath when I contracted a severe respiratory virus while attending university. I had a history of respiratory allergies and bronchitis but figured that this so-called "cold" would go away because I was young, so I didn't care for myself. I stayed up late and partied with friends, ignoring the warning signs of a deep cough that lingered for weeks.

My cough evolved into pneumonia and exercise-induced asthma, and one day while working at an art gallery, I had to be rushed to the hospital because I couldn't say more than three words in a row. For a few hours, I found myself connected to a ventilator in the hospital.

This experience was a big "wake-up call." From that moment on, when I got a cold or the flu, I went to bed earlier, paid attention to the signs, and didn't take my health for granted.

One of the best gifts we can give ourselves is the gift of deep breathing. Having more oxygen in our body positively affects our heart, brain, digestion, and immune system, and deep breathing exercises immediately affect blood pressure and anxiety levels in the brain.

When you research different breathing exercises, you see many forms available to practice. You only need minimal time to do these exercises—take a few minutes to perform.

You might begin with five minutes a day and then increase your time. You may start with practicing the activity once a day, perhaps when you first wake up in the morning, and then as the days progress, add more times to practice.

TRY THIS

TIME: For this mini-vacation, you can take as little as 10 minutes or increase your time.

METHOD: When you have a few minutes, try any of these exercises to get started:

Belly Breathing

Find a quiet room and lie down in a comfortable position

Place a hand on your belly and the other hand over your heart

Breathe deeply through your nose and feel your stomach push out your hand

Breathe out like you would if you whistled

Practice breathing like this 5 to 10 times

Pay attention to your body and mind after you complete the exercise

The 4-7-8 Breath (My Favorite)

Begin by putting a hand on your belly and one hand over your heart

Take a deep breath from your stomach, counting to 4 while breathing in

Hold your breath, counting to 7

Breathe out and then count to 8 and focus on eliminating air from your lungs

Repeat this exercise 5 or 6 times until you feel relaxed

These are two beneficial breathing exercises. If you're interested in more techniques, do a quick online search, and you'll find one or two things you can try. Practice them in the morning, during breaks, when you feel stress or tension, and see how you feel after performing them.

Happy escaping!

MARVELOUS MEDITATION

> "Meditation can help us embrace our worries, our fear, our anger, and that is very healing. We let our own natural capacity of healing do the work." —Thich Nhat Hanh

After a day of back-to-back video conferencing meetings, constant smartphone notifications, and a barrage of emails, you feel overwhelmed, tired, and unenergetic.

Many people have expressed their concern and stress in dealing with technology and mentioned taking a "brain break" from their hyper-connected and fast-paced days. One great way to create a break from technology is to meditate.

If you've tried meditating in the past and gave up or don't have the patience to sit down and practice, there are simple strategies to help you be more engaged with meditation.

Closing your eyes and meditating is not the only form of practicing mindfulness. You can do at least three things to find quiet moments of meditation throughout your busy day, and if you consistently practice them, you'll have similar benefits. These include a hobby you enjoy, focusing on detail in your present moment, and having a positive trigger to bring your mind and attention to the present.

When you engage in a hobby and focus on the task at hand, this is a form of meditation. Hobbies such as cooking, running, walking in the woods, and spending time in nature, adult coloring books, gardening, painting and woodworking, and other interests may help you meditate. What doesn't count as meditation is sitting and passively watching videos or television. It is hobbies that focus your mind on specific activities that create relaxing moments. A great option for practicing meditation is to laser focus on a detail in your present moment.

For example, bring your attention to the present moment and notice something like your hot cup of tea. Pick up the cup and feel how warm the ceramic mug is in your hands. Place your nose near the cup and breathe in the aroma of the tea. Pay attention to your first sip of tea. Is the tea sweet, spicy? What do you notice about the taste? When you take a moment to pay attention to the present moment, mindfulness meditation is a form of mindfulness.

Another way to be mindful without sitting and meditating is to build a positive trigger into your day that reminds you to pay attention to the present moment. You might notice when you slouch, you straighten up your body, or when you feel stressed, you breathe deeply. You might put little notes in work areas that tell you to "stay in the moment." It doesn't matter your trigger as long as it's a gentle reminder to bring your mind back to the present.

By practicing these three ideas, you're meditating and once you get comfortable with these activities, try meditation again. If you're not patient and find sitting still a challenge for you, use a form of guided meditation to help you relax; guided meditation may use music in the background and have someone talking you through a series of relaxing exercises. This form of meditation is a great way to start this practice.

Meditation is a healthy way to calm down an overstimulated mind, and it has proven scientific benefits. It's the process of getting your mind focused and redirecting your thoughts. It may help you focus on the present moment, increase your self-awareness, manage stress and situations, increase your patience, creativity, and imagination.

An online article at www.*askthescientists.com, Change Your Mind: Meditation Benefits for the Brain,* states: *"Studies have shown it only takes eight weeks to change the shape of your brain, including an increase of gray matter volume. Gray matter is found in your central nervous system and makes up most of your brain's neuronal cell bodies. This tissue type is essential in areas responsible for muscle control, sensory perception, emotion, memory, decision-making, and self-control."* (7)

Meditation benefits include positive changes to your brain cells as they reorganize and create new pathways with this practice. The gray matter in your brain gets altered, improving connections between your brain neurons and many other functions.

Practicing regular meditation may help impact the level of critical brain chemicals, neurotransmitters that regulate specific hormones in the body. As well, this practice helps to control anxiety and increase positivity. If you have trouble focusing, it helps to lengthen your attention span, may help with memory loss, pain management, and sleep.

Meditation dates as far back as 5000 BC and has ties to religion from China and Egypt, with roots in Hinduism and other forms of religion; meditation is a significant part of Buddhism. Meditation is not inherently religious, but some use it in a religious context. In its simplest form, meditation is a skill.

Although it's been around for thousands of years, meditation didn't become popular in the west until later in the 1700s, and it grew slowly. Today, many people are aware of meditation and may practice it regularly. There are many forms of meditation, including mantra, transcendental, progressive relaxation, movement, focused, spiritual, loving-kindness, and mindfulness meditation. The kind of meditation you practice will depend on you.

If you are new or haven't practiced meditation, it's never too late to start. You don't need much time or props to start; you can begin with five minutes and work up to more time if you desire.

You don't have to remain completely still while meditating; you can meditate while walking your dog, doing chores, or sitting outdoors. And you don't have to clear your mind and stop thinking to practice meditation; you can pay attention to the things around you, including your thoughts. You may find it a challenge to still your mind when you first start meditation, as your brain will try to be busy and distracted. With time and practice, the process will get easier for you.

If you haven't practiced meditation or given up on the idea due to the frustration of sitting still, you will want to try again. The simplest type of meditation is starting and setting a time for approximately five minutes. Find a quiet, undisturbed place to sit, and don't put too many expectations on yourself. Your mind will be busy and distracted, even restless for those first few times you try to meditate.

You may close your eyes or focus your gaze on an object in your view while you pay attention to your breathing and let your mind work. It isn't good or bad meditating; focus on your breath and be aware of your mind, and then when you're distracted, bring your focus back to your breath. If you persevere, your periods between distraction and awareness will grow.

The best first step is to be disciplined and regularly commit to doing this practice. Choose the time you allot—10 or 15 minutes is a good starting point. Make sure you find a quiet, undisturbed place and a time that works well for you; it might be when you first wake up in the morning, during your lunch hour, or after dinner. The time and place are up to you.

When you meditate, you want to be comfortable, so wear whatever feels relaxed and loose. It's sometimes nice to have relaxed-fitting clothing suitable for meditation: sweatpants, yoga pants, and t-shirts.

When you sit for your practice, it may be easier to be in an upright chair that helps with correct posture, whether inside or outside. You want to sit up with a nice straight back and neck and have your chin tucked in while you rest your hands on your knees or lap.

Decide why you want to meditate. Is it to be more focused, less stressed? Knowing your goal will help you create your session and help you feel like you have accomplished the task.

You can focus on scanning your body, starting at the top of your head and moving downward from head to toes to get you started. As you pay attention to each body part, notice where you feel tension or relaxed. Focus on the area for 15 seconds and if your thoughts interfere, bring your attention back to that area of your body.

You may become sleepy, and this is perfectly normal when you begin a mediation practice because the brain gets confused if you are "not doing something." Over time, your mind will discern the difference between relaxing and a focused relaxation action.

TRY THIS

TIME: For your mini-vacation, take at least 10 minutes to practice this activity.

If you are new to meditating or given up on the practice a long time ago, you may wish to consider starting it again as the benefits outweigh the cons.

METHOD: Choose a quiet place inside or outside and a comfortable place to sit, wear comfortable clothing, and dedicate 10 minutes to practice. Consider guided meditation If you're frustrated and don't like sitting still due to your "monkey mind" acting up. You may listen to it with earphones, and you'll hear a voice talking, which is a good distraction.

I enjoy meditating by eating chocolate and savoring the entire experience. I'm obsessed with chocolate, so this is an easy way to enjoy meditating. This exercise is all about connecting with your senses and "being in the moment."

If you use chocolate for your escape, choose a type of quality chocolate you don't usually purchase. The chocolate might be sweet, bitter, organic, fair trade—the point is to buy chocolate you haven't tasted before.

Next, when you have a moment, break off a piece of chocolate and notice the sensation of warmth from your tongue as the chocolate melts and flows down your throat. Is the chocolate sweet, salty, bitter? Can you smell the chocolate? What are you feeling? Pay attention to your sense of sight, sound, smell, touch, and taste. If you do this right, it will be a great escape!

MINDFULNESS MAGIC

> "The thing about meditation is: you become more and more you." —David Lynch

Your life is busy. You may rush through your tasks, lose connection to the present moment, and feel anxiety and stress after watching the news and dealing with your challenges. You may feel like you are not "present" for your day. If this is you, you may need to find a way to be more mindful in your day.

Experiencing a lot of stress may cause us to get caught in a pattern of spinning thoughts, mulling over past events or possible future situations. This is where mindfulness may help us.

Mindfulness refers to a mental state when you focus on the present moment and slow down your racing thoughts, which helps calm your mind and body. There are many variations to mindfulness, but it usually involves breathing and awareness of your mind and body. It's a simple practice that doesn't require much preparation or props (candles, mantras) and only needs five minutes and a comfortable place to sit.

Everywhere I go, the word "mindful" or "mindfulness" seems to pop up again and again. Why? Because we're not mindful. We are lost in our technology while ignoring the people right in front of us, not paying attention when others are talking—we're the most distracted generation in history. So many distractions keep us from important things like connecting with people in person, working on new goals, and making a positive difference in the world.

I have to be honest and say I'm guilty of being distracted. At times, I'd be scrolling on my phone while someone talked to me; usually, it was when they kept talking for a long time, and my attention could no longer stay focused. I suffer from attention deficit disorder and have always struggled not to daydream at inappropriate moments, but it's not an excuse for "tuning out" when people talk to me. I'm working on this bad habit I have. Most days, I succeed, but when I haven't slept well, feel stressed, or overwhelmed, being mindful becomes a bit of a challenge.

Mindfulness mediation is a great tool that helps me stay "present" and focused, but I need to practice it regularly.

Mindfulness meditation is a practice that has its roots in Buddhism. It has quickly gained popularity in society due to the overwhelm people experienced. It's a form of meditation and involves calming down, focusing your attention on the present moment, accepting it, and avoiding judgment. When you practice mindfulness meditation, you pay attention to the present and notice times when your mind wanders and then come back to your breath. You can use breathing techniques, mental imagery, muscle and body relaxation, and awareness of your body and mind.

Scientists have studied this practice and discovered mindfulness meditation to be a key component in stress reduction and overall happiness. Mindfulness techniques relieve stress, lower blood pressure, improve sleep, reduce chronic pain, and alleviate gastrointestinal challenges.

The next time you feel like your mind is spinning out of control and not focusing on the "present moment," look to using mindfulness meditation to "center" yourself.

TRY THIS

TIME: Mindfulness meditation can be simple to practice, and you can do it in as little as 10 minutes a day. Some people practice it every day, several times a day, or every few days. The choice is yours, but once you try it, you may be addicted to it.

METHOD: You can do a few things to make it simple. It helps to use a program to get started if you're new to this practice. You also want to set aside regular meditation time—perhaps 15 to 30 minutes. You'll also want a comfortable place to practice.

To recap, follow these tips:

1. Quiet Area: Find a comfortable, quiet space. Start by sitting in a chair or lying on the floor with your back straight but not stiff.

2. Present Thoughts: Work on putting aside all thoughts of the past and future. Focus on the present moment, your breathing, and what you feel and smell.

3. Breath: Notice your breath and focus on the air moving in and out of your body when you breathe. See your belly rise and fall and the air entering your nostrils and leaving your mouth. Be sure to pay close attention to each breath.

4. Observe Thoughts: When you feel overwhelmed or stressed, observe your mind and return to your breathing. It takes practice, but the more you do it, the quicker you'll be to improve.

5. Ending Your Meditation: Once you have practiced, sit for a few minutes and become aware of your surroundings. Stand up gradually as you may feel dizzy or lightheaded.

How to Incorporate Mindfulness into Your World:

As well as mindfulness meditation, daily life gives you a chance to add meditation elements to your routine.

For example, you can practice mentally slowing down and being in the "present" by putting away dishes, brushing your teeth, exercising, brushing your dog, walking in a park, or gardening.

MONOTASKING MAGIC

> "The simple act of being interrupted is one of the biggest barriers to productivity… What looks like multitasking is really switching back and forth between multiple tasks, which reduces productivity and increases mistakes by up to 50 percent." —Susan Cain

Do you pride yourself on being a great "multitasker?" Do you feel like you can juggle multiple things at once and get everything done well and on time?

Many of us believe we achieve more by doing a lot all at once. If you've ever searched for employment and viewed job postings online, you've probably noticed many of the employer's job requirements include "must be able to multitask."

The world has promoted this working model of multitasking—wearing the badge of busyness. That is wrong.

It doesn't take millions of dollars and a multitude of scientists to show us that this model for our lives is ineffective; we feel it every single day we juggle multiple challenges at once. Our anxiety levels climb, our attention is fragmented, we question our memory, and feel exhausted.

In an article by Amy Vetter, on *www.inc.com, Science Says Monotasking – Not Multitasking – Is the Secret to Getting Things Done. Here are 8 Ways to Do It*, Vetter mentions what scientists have proven.

"Many studies have shed light on the downside of multitasking--trying to juggle multiple tasks at one time. One often-cited study from Stanford University found that people who multitask are more easily distracted, less productive, score lower on tests for recalling information, and make more errors. The reason is quite simple: the brain is not designed to work on multiple initiatives at one time. So, instead of multitasking, you should focus on monotasking—where you focus on only one initiative at a time. This approach not only cuts down on silly mental errors, but can help unleash your creativity and production since you can funnel more attention and energy to the task at hand." (8)

Scientists often refer to task-switching when the brain changes from one activity to another. The process is not as seamless as we think; we lose focus and attention while trading our focus from one task to another, reducing our productivity and ability to focus.

There is a lot of research about the benefits of monotasking—-doing one activity at a time and focusing on the task in detail. According to science, monotasking reduces mental stress and helps you focus on the activity with more energy; your attention is not fragmented, and you remember the information. You become more efficient with the task and accomplish more than multitasking.

When you monotask, you focus on the activity you need to accomplish, becoming more self-disciplined; distractions derail your progress. It improves your attention span, and it may also improve your communication.

You can use this monotasking concept when you plan your days.

Focus on three top priorities you wish to complete for the day and when you do the task, focus on that one task until it's complete.

Using a calendar system to record your priorities is the key to making this work. I currently use an online calendar and "block off" specific times to create webinar content, review material, make phone calls, work with clients, and so on.

When I want to achieve a lot during those "blocked-off moments," I place my smartphone in another room and keep it on "silent." I won't look at it until I've worked for a set amount of time, and by doing this, I'm able to work with minimal interruptions and achieve more.

Monotasking is a good option when you want to minimize stress, increase your memory and energy, and "deep dive" into a project. Consider creating a "20-minute rule" to focus for at least 20 minutes before switching to another task; this is especially helpful if you're not enjoying the activity. By choosing only 20 minutes, your mind will be able to focus for at least this amount of time before daydreaming or frustration hits.

While monotasking makes sense, multitasking isn't always a negative. There are exceptions when you may successfully do two things at once.

For example, folding laundry (lower brain activity) while watching videos (higher brain function) may work well. The challenge is when you attempt to engage in two higher brain activities simultaneously, for example talking to someone and reading the Internet. Two higher brain activities take more brain bandwidth, and inevitably both activities will suffer because they each require more focus.

TRY THIS

TIME: For this mini-vacation, take at least 20 minutes to enjoy the activity.

METHOD: Consider a project you need to complete and think about how to "monotask it." You can set yourself up for success by minimizing distractions such as people and technology. Next, prioritize the order in which you will work on the project and work in time batches.

For example, if you need to complete a report, research in 20-minute increments, write down your thoughts, and spend 20 minutes editing your project. By batching the tasks, you will be more focused and productive.

You may use this monotasking formula for work activities—this is also a fun concept to use when you wish to be creative.

Artists or musicians often escape the hectic pace of life using monotasking and working on drawing, painting, singing, or playing an instrument without multitasking.

When you lose yourself in something creative, your mind has a chance to pay attention to one thing, calm down, and focus. Often, you may "lose track of time" because you find yourself "in the flow." You'll find you're more "in the flow" when you monotask, especially if you combine your love of activity with your skill in it.

A powerful time management system I use to monotask is the Pomodoro Technique. How it works is you use the time you have and break your day into 25-minute increments separated by short five-minute breaks. You focus on a task, and if you've done four pomodoros, you can take a break from 15 to 20 minutes.

Francesco Cirillo developed the system in the 1980s to help him focus on university work. He noticed a tomato-shaped kitchen timer and decided to create this method to help him study and focus on boring or monotonous activities. Pomodoro means tomato in Italian.

The next time you feel overwhelmed, consider switching from multitasking to monotasking.

GREAT GRATITUDE

> "Gratitude is the highest of all human emotions. The more you express gratitude for what you have, the more likely you will have even more to express gratitude for." —Zig Ziglar

Are you feeling stressed, overwhelmed, and seeking more from your life? Do you feel like something is missing? Contrary to what you may believe, seeking things outside yourself may be the last thing you need. Instead, giving thanks and gratitude may change your life in positive ways.

Psychology research indicates that people practicing gratitude enjoy greater happiness; they feel optimistic, improve their health and relationships, and better deal with adversities in life. People express and feel gratitude in many ways and apply it to their past, present, and future thoughts. Gratitude helps people appreciate life and what they have instead of striving for new things to feel successful or happier. The focus goes from what they lack to what they have, and although it may be a challenge to practice this way of thinking at first, this mental state will grow stronger with use.

In an article by Catherine Robertson, *How Gratitude Can Change Your Life,* Robertson mentions Robert Emmons, Professor of Psychology at the University of California and author of *Thanks! How The New Science of Gratitude Can Make You Happier,* who has been researching gratitude for over eight years and states, *"Without gratitude, life can be lonely, depressing and impoverished. Gratitude enriches human life. It elevates, energizes, inspires, and transforms, and those who practice it will experience significant improvements in several areas of life including relationships, academics, energy level and even dealing with tragedy and crisis."* (9)

Gratitude has the power to transform frustration to peace, dissatisfaction to contentment, criticism to appreciation, and defeatism to resilience.

As well, gratitude will improve your physical life, mental health, and psychological well-being. You will be less stressed and sleep better, be a better leader, have more energy to work on your goals, and you will attract more positive people in your life.

While this may seem easy, you may be experiencing significant challenges or general life annoyances and may not feel like you have anything to be grateful for in your life. What are you to do?

While you will have days that challenge you, you want to practice gratitude as even tough days have life lessons. Your gratitude thoughts may be as simple as, "Today I'm grateful I have a job," or "Today I am grateful I have a roof over my head and food in my fridge and to have my health."

Be kind to yourself; it's not about positive-thinking your way from horrific events, or creating long gratitude lists. You want to direct your thoughts away from what's not working to what is working and still acknowledge the hard reality you may be experiencing. Gratitude brings you to the present moment and focuses on the positive.

To make this work in your life, you'll need to practice every day. To make this work for you, dedicate a paper journal to this exercise and keep that journal where you'll pick it up and write in it.

Contrary to the popular notion that it takes 21 days to create a habit, it takes longer. Recent research from the College of London indicated 66 days for a practice to become habitual, but some people need longer to create a permanent habit. So, be kind to yourself as you make some changes and know you may have better days than others to engage in this habit.

TRY THIS

TIME: For this escape, you need at least 10 minutes in the morning, during the day, or at night to feel the positive effects.

METHOD: A great way to start with this exercise is to buy or use a current gratitude journal. Start small by writing down three to five things you were grateful for in your day. You may wish to write it down before you go to bed, as your mind may focus on positive thoughts before you hit the pillow.

When you write down events in your gratitude journal, these don't need to be huge—you may be happy you had a good day at work, grateful your back didn't act up, and happy you had time to reconnect with a friend at lunch.

Other ways to create more gratitude in your life include: thanking someone in person or writing a letter and delivering in person or the mail, meditating, praying, and counting your blessings.

JOURNAL JOY

> "Writing in a journal reminds you of your goals and of your learning in life. It offers a place where you can hold a deliberate, thoughtful conversation with yourself." —Robin Sharma

In grade six, I won a spelling contest and was awarded a yellow journal with a lock and key. That journal was like a friend; I used it to record my feelings and frustrations as a pre-teen, and it was my safety net, therapist, and a great escape.

Whether you use one journal that tracks many subjects or several journals for each item, the choice is as individual as you. There are no rules when it comes to journaling.

Many famous people made their best discoveries and contributions using a journal. Albert Einstein and Leonardo da Vinci recorded theories and ideas in the books they carried with them. What if they never recorded their thoughts?

I bought a journal with a dot grid pattern (bullet journal) and used it for my business. I added my yearly plan, websites I wanted to review, courses I wanted to write, and new ideas for this book.

In recent years, I've noticed a growing trend toward journaling; there are numerous articles on the benefits of this practice.

In an article, *The Health Benefits of Journaling,* written by Maud Purcell for *Psych Central (psychcentral.com),* Purcell mentioned: *"Scientific evidence supports that journaling provides other unexpected benefits. The act of writing accesses your left brain, which is analytical and rational. While your left brain is occupied, your right brain is free to create, intuit and feel. In sum, writing removes mental blocks and allows you to use all of your brainpower to better understand yourself, others, and the world around you."* (10)

With the proliferation of screens and time online, our eyes tire, and many of us enjoy writing on paper with a pen; taking time away from screens is what we need to minimize stress, eye strain and trigger newfound creativity.

Bullet journaling became popular because people could quickly bullet-point ideas, challenges, whatever they desired in a quick format instead of writing long pages of notes in a journal.

Other benefits of journaling include recording life memories, tracking patterns, manifesting goals and dreams, clearing emotions, and planning.

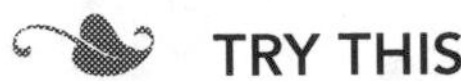

TRY THIS

TIME: If you don't own a journal, take at least 30 minutes to go on a field trip and make it a fun escape to find a blank book you like. Choose an attractive book that is not too beautiful, or you may be too intimidated to write. The journal should feel good to the touch and be easy to write in so you can quickly and easily record information.

METHOD: Once you have your journal, take at least 10 minutes and write every day or every other day. Many people like to keep a journal near their bed, and they may record challenges in their book before they go to sleep or wake up in the morning.

Your journal doesn't need to read like a book or a diary; it may be an eclectic mix of things.

For example, I have a bullet-grid journal to record ideas, websites, dreams, and more. This journal allows me to write, draw, or design things easily. I don't feel constricted with a blank or lined journal, and the bullet grids help me be more creative with my thoughts.

If you are unsure about writing in a journal, use it for design ideas, fitness logs, meal planning, daily to-do lists, doodling and drawing, story-writing, scrapbooking, and travel plans. You can also use a journal for party planning, bucket lists, accomplishments, recipes, song and book lists, memories, diary writing, holiday shopping lists, important dates, self-care ideas, goals, and dreams.

If your mind comes up with great ideas while running errands, carry a pen and pocket journal and stow it in your purse or knapsack for when inspiration hits.

POSITIVE AFFIRMATIONS

> "Our greatest weapon against stress is our ability to choose one thought over another." —William James

Do you remember working on a large project but being stopped by the negative voices in your head? Maybe you started with an optimistic mindset, but challenges and roadblocks along the way triggered self-doubt, anxiety, and pessimism.

We often begin things with enthusiasm and think, "I can handle this project… I'm capable." But after significant issues with the project, we may quickly change our thoughts.

I know about self-doubt as I'm a visual artist and haven't created art for a few years. I wrote, coached, and raised a family, and I didn't create artwork during this time. One day, I started an oil-painting scene of Greece. I hadn't painted in oils in years, and I felt "in over my head" on this project. I immediately felt my energy diminish, leaving the painting unfinished in my basement.

Time passed, and I decided to purchase a popular book by Julia Cameron called *The Artist's Way*. The book was inspirational and filled with practical exercises to remove negativity and creative blocks. Best of all, the book contained positive affirmations that reflected the life of an artist; this greatly inspired me, and I recorded some of these affirmations and placed them where I could see them every day.

Borrow an affirmation escape from Eastern meditation practices when you need a break from stress and negativity. An affirmation is a phrase in the present tense that helps you feel positive and energized, and they work on a deep level in our subconscious mind.

When you choose an affirmation, be clear about your intentions because your mind will map your suggestions.

If you say, "I am strong," this is effective, but if you mention, "I will be strong," there is doubt. When will you be strong? It is crucial to say your affirmation in the present tense and stick to "I am" phrases or choose other positive affirmations to repeat at night and first thing in the morning. You may even write down affirmations and leave them by a mirror, desk, or area that you see frequently.

TRY THIS

TIME: For this escape, take 15 or 20 minutes and search for quotes and affirmations that "speak to you." They can be found in books, online, or you may find something in your home library. If you enjoy wearing t-shirts, you may find a few positive affirmation t-shirts and wear these.

METHOD: Once you find an affirmation that "speaks to you," print it out and place it where you see it every day. You might put it by your computer or on a wall. The choice is yours.

Never underestimate the power of words; words have sparked and ended wars, won over the hearts of lovers, and inspired many people. Choose your words wisely.

CELEBRATE "WINS"

> "Life is too short not to celebrate nice moments!" —
> Jurgen Klopp

Have you ever worked on a goal or specific project for so long that once you accomplished it, you felt "deflated" or the completion of the task felt "anti-climatic?" There's often a "high" when we pursue a goal and believe that feeling will grow once we complete it. Sometimes we feel relief or euphoria (depending on many circumstances), and sometimes we feel exhausted and disappointed.

If this happens to you, you may not be taking the necessary time to "pause" and "celebrate your wins." We live in a society that focuses on accomplishments and moving forward, and we don't take time to process what's just occurred—our thinking focuses "on the next thing."

The problem with this way of responding is that you haven't acknowledged your win, and you don't feel complete. Sometimes, the accomplishment may be simple, such as speed-reading through 500 emails, cold-calling a prospect when we feel anxious, and performing well in a job interview. The small victories often go unnoticed; you may only notice the big wins and your mistakes, and this leaves you feeling drained, stressed, and apathetic.

You must pay attention to your small victories as these successes give you joy, increase your happiness, and motivate you to accomplish more. When you complete a project and receive good news after a long period of stress, you need to find ways to celebrate your accomplishment. It motivates you to move forward with other projects and experiences when you do. A small win is an activity you have done successfully that you may not have been sure you would complete; it doesn't have to be world-changing, but it should add to your confidence, make you feel happier, and inspire you to set new goals.

For example, if you work from home and experience a challenging week and still manage to complete a report for work, you need to celebrate this victory. Choose something you enjoy, and be sure to reward yourself. You might take a long walk at lunch, buy a specialty coffee, or read a new novel. Treat yourself to something you enjoy.

Here are some tips for celebrating your wins:

Pay attention and live in the present. Pay attention to your actions and struggles throughout your day, and notice when you achieve something you were unsure you could accomplish. When you live in the moment instead of the past or future, you will feel more content and notice more positive things in your life. When you accomplish something large or small, give yourself credit and add a treat to your day.

Be happy and excited. We often try to downplay our wins. You need to stop doing that and get excited, and with it, boost your happiness and motivation.

Record your small wins. Another thing to do is keep a work journal and record your large and small "wins" in the book. You may use your accomplishments in a future resume if you apply for work. If you stay in your current position, having the book may be helpful if you decide to ask for a promotion, as you'll be able to recite your accomplishments easily.

Tell others about your wins. When you accomplish something that makes you feel good, tell someone you know, like, and trust; this will increase the bond with that person, as you are reaching out and sharing something positive. Who doesn't like hearing about small wins during a busy and stressed day? It is one thing to use social media to showcase your accomplishments and another thing to reach out to a good friend and let them know about your wins. There's more power in that feedback from online strangers.

When you notice your daily accomplishments and celebrate them, you'll feel motivated and happy and want to do more. In life, it's the small things that add up and create your amazing life.

TRY THIS

TIME: For this escape, take 10 minutes to think about what you have accomplished in your day.

METHOD: Did you blast through 500 emails efficiently and quickly? Did you complete a small report before a deadline? Did you make those five cold calls? Whatever you accomplished, be sure to pay attention and then give yourself a treat to celebrate.

Your treat will be as individual as you are. For example, if you're a coffee-lover, you may visit your favorite coffee shop and order a specialty coffee. If you've been putting off a small purchase, you might buy the item you wanted. If you love to be outdoors, you might go for a hike, check out a new mountain biking trail, go on a picnic, or walk your dog. The list is endless.

Celebrating the small wins adds fun to your life because when you feel like you are moving forward, you're more motivated when things become challenging.

ARTFUL ANTIQUITY

> "Give me insight into today, and you may have the antique and future worlds." —Ralph Waldo Emerson

Have you ever thought about time travel? Do you wish you could go back in time and revisit special memories with past family members or jump ahead in the future and choose the winning numbers for a lottery ticket?

Our fascination with time has been around for centuries but may date back as far as the ancient Greeks, who believed in an underworld where you could meet your ancestors once you traveled the River Styx to Hades. Styx was the gateway that formed the boundary between the Underworld, Hades, and Earth, and once someone crossed that boundary, they could reunite with their ancestors, which was like time travel.

The concept of time travel garnered a lot of interest after 1895, when writer, H.G. Wells, wrote a science fiction novella called *The Time Machine*. Wells coined the words time machine, referring to devices and vehicles traveling backward or forward through time.

My fascination with time and the "old days" stemmed from having the opportunity to spend time with my grandparents when I was a child. My grandfather, Gunder, was born in 1897 and lived for over 95 years. I used to sit with him and ask him about his childhood, and I always learned things about him and the era he lived. He lived to witness the first airplane, World War I, women's suffrage, the Prohibition, The Great Depression, the invention of the atom bomb, War War II, the Cold War, c, the Vietnam War, the advancement of science and medicine, the first man on the moon, and the advancement of computers and technology. I always wondered what it would be like to travel back in time to experience my grandfather's life.

While we might not have time machines, we may create the feeling of traveling back in time by visiting an antique shop. As soon as you step foot into the store, the smells, sights, and sounds may transport you to another era.

There's something magical and nostalgic about setting foot in a store like this.

I remember visiting an antique store with my sister-in-law, a highly talented interior decorator. We spent the afternoon wandering through a store filled to the brim with furniture, statues, pictures, jewelry, dishes, books, vinyl records, vintage clothing, and numerous unique and unusual trinkets.

It didn't take long to get lost in this escape. I found so many treasures, and my focus was on old advertisements from the 1940s and 1950s. I found elegant, detailed, and funny advertisements showing cars, clothing, and other products, and studying them made me feel like I'd traveled back in time.

I found an advertisement from 1958 that featured a Bel Air Impala convertible, the star in Chevrolet's 1958 lineup. I loved the look of the ad because the retro green convertible was beautiful, and situated beside it was a lady wearing a red, flowing dress.

While perusing the antique store with my sister-in-law, I located a cherry chest with elaborate designs carved into it, lined in cedar, and the original key and lock. I decided to purchase it. Every time I look at the chest, I think of the great visit with my sister-in-law, the adventure of walking through the antique store, and finally coming home with a piece of history.

TRY THIS

TIME: You will want to take an afternoon or longer to enjoy the activity for this escape.

METHOD: List shops you would like to visit and then take an afternoon or day to visit them. Bring a friend or family member who enjoys antiques or history, to make the trip more enjoyable.

Decide whether you're seeking something specific or are going into the shops with an "open mind" to see what may stand out for you. This escape is more fun when you don't have anything you're specifically seeking because you can finally focus on what is right in front of you.

Take time to look closely at the objects in front of you; you will notice many details if you pay attention. Books, photographs, advertisements, and artwork are fun to study, and you feel like you a traveling back in time when you focus on these items.

For this trip, make your adventure an experience by having breakfast or lunch before or after antique shopping. Take your time and lose yourself in antiquity.

NINE NEW LIVES

"A cat has nine lives." —Traditional Proverb

Do you ever wonder what your life would've been like if you'd chosen a different path? When we reach a certain age or experience a life-altering event, we wonder if we've made wise decisions, and we may begin to second-guess our choices.

I often wonder what would've happened if I had pursued one of my dreams of being a university professor in Visual Arts. I obtained a Bachelor of Fine Arts Degree with a minor in Social Sciences, but I didn't get more education. I gave up on my dream of teaching art in university and veered down another path. Sometimes I wonder.

Movies are often an inspiration for ideas, and a few years ago, I found a movie, *Mr. Destiny*, which addressed the concept of a life not lived.

In the movie, Larry (played by James Belushi) is celebrating his 35th birthday, and he's feeling a little "blue" about the normalness of his life. On his way home from work, his car breaks down in front of a bar, and he curses and complains as he enters the establishment. The bar is empty except for a mysterious bartender (played by Michael Caine), who approaches Larry and asks him what's wrong with his life. Larry mentioned he disliked his small house, annoying job, and bad luck he experienced years ago. He complained about how he missed hitting a championship baseball in high school and how his life would have been better if he had hit the winning ball.

Mr. Destiny's bartender mixes up a mysterious drink that Larry gladly drinks. Shortly after his drink, Larry's life unfolds, showing an alternate life where he hits the softball to win the championship. In this reality, Larry is the town hero and the CEO of his current company and marries the boss's wife. His current wife works under him and is unaware of who he is; she has no concept of really knowing him. His new life includes phony friends, a high-maintenance wife, and a lot of stress. Everything has changed but has not gone in the way that he anticipated.

A series of crazy events happen, and he is forced to run from the law and ends up in the cavern where Mr. Destiny first appeared. Desperate, Larry grabs a drink from the bartender and gets transported back to his current life where he is an employee, and his life is simple. He wonders if he left the bar and had a different life or if the bartender was God. No one knows.

In the book, *It's Only Too Late if You Don't Start Now,* Barbara Sher wrote a beautiful passage about people who had more than one dream or goal or people who dreamed of dropping everything to follow abandoned dreams. She mentioned that if you desire to be a writer and an accountant, you may dedicate two years to writing and the next two years to learn about accounting. You may be a full-time or part-time accountant and writer on the side.

I was a store owner, mother, writer, speaker, artist, and career and life coach. As my children have gotten older, my life has become more simplified, but I still juggle multiple roles and think about "what might have been" and "what is to come." There are still many more "lives" I want to pursue, and while I won't be quitting my current profession and running away, I'll be adding hobbies and passions to my life.

TRY THIS

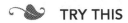

TIME: For this escape, start by taking at least 30 minutes of uninterrupted time, grabbing a journal, and quickly writing down nine paths you have not pursued in your life. These may be small interests and hobbies or career paths.

METHOD: If you find this a challenge, find old photographs of you when you were a child. Sometimes photography triggers memories of past ideas and passions. If you had a diary and still own it, read through the pages and pull out ideas.

You may have dreamed of being a writer, doctor, veterinarian, pilot, firefighter, actor, dancer, or scientist. While your career may have taken you in a different direction, you may be able to pull ideas out of what you loved as a child.

For example, if being an Olympic athlete was a dream, but this didn't happen in your life, study what it was that you loved about this idea. Did you want to succeed at something and be in the frontline? Did you want to set a big goal and achieve it? Maybe you could strive for a goal others don't commonly pursue, or perhaps you need to challenge your body physically and want to start a training program. Look for parts of the dream that you could complete.

The nine lives adventure should inspire you, get your mind and body working, and challenge you to make positive changes in your life. See what you can do to add another life to your current life.

Have fun!

CHAPTER 3

Rejuvenating Rituals

Do you remember family traditions and rituals when you were growing up? Practices are integral to our families, friendships, work, and personal lives. They help us create identities as well as build ties to our community and country. We use rituals to pass our beliefs and wisdom to the next generations. All societies across the globe practice rituals, and some of them involve our daily activities.

The consideration when participating in rituals is how we choose to participate. We want to be "fully present" and not focused on our digital devices; this is a time to be present and connect with our family and friends.

Whether we find ourselves making homemade blueberry pancakes for our family or telling a cherished bedtime story, we want to do so mindfully and joyfully and engage in new experiences.

FAMILY TRADITIONS AND RITUALS

"Exercise, Prayer, and Meditation are examples of calming rituals. They have been shown to induce

> a Happier Mood and provide a Positive Pathway through life's daily frustrations." —Chuck Norris

The definition of a ritual is "any act done regularly without much thought and is a set of words or actions performed the same way, often as part of a religious ceremony." Rituals may be a sequence of activities using words, objects and performed in a special place in a specific order.

For example, enjoying a coffee every morning at the same time before you start your work may be considered a special ritual you use to "ease into your workday."

Rituals date back thousands of years, and this is apparent when we study ancient Egyptians; theirs was a culture steeped in traditions that involved eating, drinking, bathing, hunting, and burying the dead. Rituals also give our life meaning as they help us celebrate and honor our lives. Predictability, stability, and imagination bring a sense of calmness to an otherwise chaotic existence.

My husband, children, and I had a ritual for finding the perfect Christmas tree. We'd drive out a large tree farm in the country and let our two sons wander through the tree fields until they found the best tree for our home. Once we found the tree, we'd saw it down, place it in our truck, and proceed home to decorate while savoring hot chocolate and cookies and watching the "classic" movie, *National Lampoon's Christmas Vacation*. We kept the funny movie on while decorating the tree and connected as a family. If we missed one of those things on our list, the ritual would never feel quite right.

Another family ritual was to make homemade whole-wheat pancakes with blueberries and bananas added to the recipe. My sons helped me make the pancakes. We poured the tiniest ones and called them "the world's smallest pancakes."

As you look at your life, you'll notice you have rituals you celebrate with family and friends. These may be larger and involve the community, workplace, or household.

Rituals are critical to your mental health and happiness when faced with life challenges.

I always start my day by grinding quality coffee beans, boiling water, and pouring the water over the ground beans in my French press. I also have a fruit smoothie with plant-based protein, which keeps me energized for the morning. It's a small ritual but gives me a sense of control at the start of the day.

A ritual may be performed once and still be powerful and effective—the feelings, thoughts, behavior, and actions will determine how you practice it. For example, if you broke up with your partner and wrote a letter, you might create a ritual and burn the letter as a one-time act and feel the effects of saying goodbye to the relationship.

Little rituals also play a role in our lives. These may include: the way we "roll" out of bed, how we brush our teeth, shower, and dress, and have breakfast. If we change the order or miss some of these rituals, we may feel unorganized and uncomfortable. Don't believe me? Think about a time you slept in too late on a workday, woke up in a panic, and rushed through your morning to get to work. Chances are the whole day felt "off."

Some may see exercising as a ritual; they may perform mini-rituals within the exercise: walk at lunchtime each day, go to the same park or beach, wear the same exercise clothes. Doing this gives them a sense of control and minimizes stress and anxiety.

The concept of the ritual isn't about practicality. It's about creating a sense of control, calming nerves and anxiety, bringing together people, creating a sense of community, and having fun!

TRY THIS

TIME: For this mini-vacation, you want to dedicate at least 10 minutes or longer to enjoy this activity.

METHOD: Rituals may consist of waking up earlier and engaging in a regular activity that is energizing, such as expressing gratitude for your day, listening to uplifting music, or taking a walk.

Give yourself the gift of 15, 20, or 30 minutes to exercise, meditate, stretch, walk, or do what makes you happy before you begin your day. Having this buffer of time is critical when you are a caregiver, parent, have a demanding job, or have lots of life challenges; when you have your own time, you'll feel less resentful when you need to give your time and energy to others.

Thinking of three things you are grateful for or writing them in a gratitude journal every day can be very energizing. Doing this helps to focus on the big and small things that are positive in your life. Research shows if you practice this every day for 30 days or more, positive changes occur in your brain.

Upbeat music may boost your mindset in the morning. If you have an alarm clock (not a phone) in your room, choose one that lets you wake up to relaxing and uplifting music. Alarms are never a great way to wake up. Who loves waking up to the shrill *beep... beep... beep* sound?

Never underestimate walks and the power they give you. It works on your body, mind, and spirit in many ways as it may offer you fresh air and exercise, a change of scenery, respite from digital devices, an "escape" from work or family, and time to think without constant interruptions. When you spend time outdoors, it helps you clear your mind and destress. You may decide to go on your own or invite family or friends and meet somewhere beautiful such as a beach, park, or other places. If you have time, try to get out for a walk every day, even if only a few minutes. If the weather is not favorable, bundle up and stay warm and dry, or if it is warm weather, take a walk in the early morning before the temperatures climb. Enjoy.

FAMILY REUNION

> "In every conceivable manner, the family is a link to our past, bridge to our future." —Alex Haley

Have you ever attended a family reunion? What do you recall? Do you remember your uncle's laugh, hearing great stories from your grandparents, enjoying playing funny games, eating many varieties of food at the barbeque, and the games you played outdoors?

A family reunion is an opportunity for families to meet, reconnect, and strengthen relationships. The event may occur at the same time each year. It could be a statutory holiday or a specific date that works well for many family members, or the reunion might be every few years and planned around the most popular times for people to attend. A family reunion may include close family members and even friends outside the family, and the size of the event may vary from a few members to hundreds. Family reunions include meals, games, outdoor events, and passing down stories and history to the younger generations.

Family reunions carry much significance. As well as building familial bonds, this time allows you to find out more about others, gives you time to experience an environment away from home—unless you are hosting the event at your place—and you have moments to sit back and relax. Young children have a chance to learn about family history, and older members get to reconnect.

If you find that you are in charge of organizing a reunion and this is new for you, consider crucial things. Planning well in advance will make the event more successful, so give yourself at least a year as people need to decide what dates work best, book their work holidays and plan for transportation. If possible, give your family members options for location and dates and create a poll to determine the best availability for them to attend.

When planning a reunion, decide on a budget and what each family may pay to be involved. Check to ensure that the figures work well for all families.

You should send out informal notices in advance to notify families of the event; this allows families to consider work and vacation times, scheduling, budgets, and more. If you send a formal invitation, send that out a couple of months before the event.

Planning a reunion does not fall on one person, so get volunteers to help in the areas of communications, reservations, food, travel and lodging, and entertainment.

As you plan, you may want to consider off-peak travel times to keep costs low and transportation less stressful. Check for group rates for travel and hotels; flights, hotels, campsites, and restaurants sometimes offer group rates if you ask.

In terms of locations, reunions may occur at a park, community center, campsite, restaurant, summer cabin, a family member's home, or your place.

To have fun at your reunion, create a themed t-shirt that each family member can wear when they attend. Having a specially-made t-shirt helps create fun photos and great memories. Reunions can take on many themes, such as a Hawaiian Luau, Beach Party, Mexican Fiesta, and more.

Reunions are more successful when various activities suit ages from young to old and all skill levels. Activities that add value include having family members bring and take photos to add to a photography book at the event. You might even hire a professional photographer or a talented family member to take a group photo of all members. The reunion might consist of a barbeque or a potluck where every member brings their favorite dish or secret family recipe. Events may include water and land sports, card and board games, musical contests, arts and crafts, family traditions, and traveling at the family reunion. Other activities include storytelling, scavenger hunts, family talent shows, and more. The events will depend on your guest's ages and stages in life, the time of year, and where you are holding the reunion. My best advice? Offer lots of choices for activities for your guests.

You want to have a way to record the family reunion—a video or photographs—and then keep in touch with family members and send them mementos after the occasion. Creating a fun reunion will give the gift of great memories to family members for years to come.

TRY THIS

TIME: For this escape, you will need a day or longer to enjoy this activity.

METHOD: See if your immediate or extended family plans any reunions in the next year or two. If they are, ensure that you take the time to study your schedule and book time off to attend the event. Reunions are precious moments, and you may walk away with memories that last you a lifetime. Life is unpredictable, and we may not realize it at the time, but the precious moments we spent with an uncle, grandparent, or cousin might be the last moments we have with them.

If your family does not have any reunions planned, take the initiative and plan something. It does not need to be an overnight or day-long event; it could be an afternoon meeting at a park or restaurant. You might include food or not—the choice is yours. The most important thing would be to reconnect with those you have not seen for a while. That is the most significant part of the reunion.

MUSEUM TRIPS

> "A visit to a museum is a search for beauty, truth, and meaning in our lives. Go to museums as often as you can." —Maira Kalman

Have you ever visited local museums in your town or city? Stepping into a museum may feel like traveling back in time and witnessing another era.

I remember visiting the Royal BC Museum in Victoria, BC, with my grandparents when I was young. That visit impacted me, and I remember the area of the museum dedicated to the twentieth century that featured cobblestone roads and storefronts representing each decade. I sat in the Majestic Theatre, featuring Charlie Chaplin's black and white movie he wrote, produced, and directed in 1925 called, *The Gold Rush*. Sitting in the darkened, tiny theater watching this old film transported me back in time.

Walking on cobblestone roads, viewing old storefronts, and hearing the sound of horse hooves clicking on the road made me feel like I was living during that time. There was even the scent of cinnamon apple spice wafting through the air.

I never forgot those memories, and I had the opportunity to revisit the Royal BC Museum and see exhibits such as Leonardo da Vinci, King Tutankhamun, and more.

Museums have helped preserve stories and history about our communities, society, cultures, and nation. Without them, we'd lose our stories and history as time progressed.

Museums educate and engage the community and inspire us with ideas, items, and periods. Museums are great for researching an era, object, culture, and more. They make us learn more as we have a chance to delve into the past to study specimens and artifacts. They also allow societies to collect and safeguard pieces of history for future generations.

There are many types of museums located all over the world. They may come under the category of historical or general museums such as The Museum of Qin Terracotta Warriors and Horses, The Egyptian Museum, Auschwitz-Birkenau State Museum, Smithsonian National Museum of American History, The Royal Ontario Museum, The National Museum of Anthropology, Tokyo National Museum, and numerous world-famous historical places.

Other types of museums include art museums such as The Louvre, Van Gogh Museum, Victoria and Albert Museum, Picasso Museum, The Metropolitan Museum of Art, Uffizi Gallery, State Hermitage Museum, Tate Modern, Museo Nacional Del Prado, Art Institute of Chicago, and The National Gallery among others.

Some museums were former residences, and then there were the specialty, cultural, religious, and outdoor museums. As well as preserving history and imparting knowledge and learning to people, museums also generate jobs, positively impacting tourism as many visitors stop at a museum of interest while traveling.

TRY THIS

TIME: You will want to spend an afternoon or day with this activity for your mini-vacation.

Will you be visiting a museum in your town or city or traveling out of town?

You might make a "day of it" and travel to another city and take in the sights and sounds as well as make a museum visit.

There are so many options when planning, and this will depend on the time you have, the type of museum that interests you, and whether you want to travel far or be closer to home.

Whatever you do, enjoy your museum trip.

MUSICAL MOMENTS

> "Music gives a soul to the universe, wings to the mind, flight to the imagination, and life to everything."
> —Plato

It's a Friday afternoon and the end of a long, stressful week, and as you're driving toward your home, you hear a song on the radio, a song that transports you back in time when you were a teenager. You remember where you were when you first listened to the music. Suddenly, the stress of the last few days seems to dissipate.

Music can move you to tears, making you break out in song. It may symbolize war and love and every emotion in between. Music plays a crucial role in setting the mood and creating the scene, and the right music makes the movie a success.

Music is fundamental to humans, and throughout history, we've sung or hummed, clapped, or danced. Music is a universal language, and we don't even need to know lyrics—we can get immersed in the beat and rhythm of a song. Before we are born, we know the difference between music and noise, repetition and rhythm, tunes and tones, and this may have started with the first beats we heard—the beating of our mother's heart.

Many cultures believe music can heal, and research has shown that stroke victims heal faster when exposed to it. People with Alzheimer's disease may remember more after hearing tunes from when their research shows that playing or listening to music boosts our physical and mental health. It may lower stress, help you sleep better, reduce depression, strengthen your learning and memory, and make you happier.

As a teenager, I walked a distance to catch a school bus in the morning, and to ease boredom, I sang out loud. I loved music and eventually joined a choir group, was involved in talent shows, and thought I might sing for a profession.

I dreamed of being a singer when I was younger but suffered from severe allergies. I didn't think singing would be a career I could sustain, so I pursued my other dream—visual art.

I never gave up my love of music and used it to feel better. I remember being frustrated by several events at my first job after university, and while I was driving home, I heard a song by Tom Petty called, *I Won't Back Down.* Besides the beat of the music, the lyrics spoke to me, particularly the line, *"No, I'll stand my ground, Won't be turned around, And I'll keep this world from draggin' me down, Gonna stand my ground, And I won't back down."* These lines helped me when I was going through challenges at work.

Are there songs that resonate with you? Pay attention to the music that "moves you" and add it to your daily life.

If listening to music isn't enough, play an instrument. If you have minimal experience playing an instrument, challenge yourself to learn to play something. You might teach yourself, hire a music teacher or quickly go online and learn from a video; whatever you do, you'll be amazed by how your mind slows down as you focus on learning the instrument. It's hard to be stressed out (except for the frustration of learning a new instrument) when focusing on the learning process.

Playing an instrument offers many benefits like the possibility of creating and playing your music, playing in a band, or providing entertainment at a party or event. There are numerous benefits for your brain when you play instruments.

Research shows that playing an instrument is more beneficial to your brain than sitting back and listening to music.

In an article by Sally Sapega, *Playing an Instrument: Better for Your Brain Than Just Listening,* on Penn Medicine News, she mentions, *"Playing an instrument may be one of the best ways to help keep the brain healthy. 'It engages every major part of the central nervous system,' said John Dani, Ph.D., chair of Neuroscience at Penn's Perelman School of Medicine, tapping into both the right and left sides of the brain."* (11)

If you learned to play an instrument when you were a child, there are life-long benefits to your brain health. However, you can still improve the health of your brain even if you learn to play an instrument when you are older.

The benefits to learning to play an instrument include: learning to be more patient, persistent, and disciplined as you need to put time aside to practice regularly to see results. Other positive reasons to play include: helping with creativity, benefits to many brain areas, time management, improved memory, confidence-building, social activity, and helping with reflexes and brain development. In other words, gray matter in the brain grows with instrument practice.

Finally, playing an instrument decreases stress because you are in the moment as you practice playing music. There is no time to worry about other things in your life when attempting to learn a new note or music progression.

TRY THIS

TIME: For this escape, you want at least 30 minutes or longer.

METHOD: Pay attention to the music in your life. How can you add more music to your days? How about listening to music you never listen to? What can you learn from new genres?

Consider when you may listen to music. Is it while you work on a hobby while driving in your vehicle or taking a walk? How might music enrich your life?

When you're feeling down or sluggish, quickly change your mood by turning on some music. Upbeat music may make you feel more excited and optimistic about life. You may even be motivated to get up and dance or do a full cardio workout.

If you're feeling stressed, you might listen to slower tempo music to help calm your mind and relax tense muscles. Slower tempos help soothe the mind and might be effective for stress management and relaxation.

Are you a musician? Pick up your instrument and practice, play, and have fun.

Are you new to the idea of playing music? If you want to learn to play a new instrument, do research, talk to others, take lessons, practice, make mistakes, and have fun. The key is to lose yourself in the moment of making music.

One of the most powerful ways to quickly change your mood is listening to or making music. The next time you're feeling stressed or overwhelmed, consider a musical escape.

LIVE EVENTS

> "A live concert to me is exciting because of all the electricity that is generated in the crowd and on the stage. It's my favorite part of the business, live concerts." —Elvis Presley

Take a moment, close your eyes, and think back to a time when you attended one of your favorite live musical performances. What do you remember about that event? What band was playing? Where was the event, and who did you take to the musical performance?

There's something magical about attending a live performance of our favorite musical artists and bands. Traveling to the event with family or friends, taking in the sights, watching the performers, and hearing the music permeate the airwaves is truly an experience and a great escape.

I remember being excited because I heard the popular band, U2, was scheduled to play in Vancouver, BC, in October 2009. It was exciting to know the band was coming, and I quickly went online with the idea of securing three tickets to attend. Tickets sold out within two minutes. I was disappointed until I noticed an auction section on the website. After a close bidding war with another online participant, I scored the tickets and paid two hundred dollars per ticket. It was worth it.

The concert was something I will never forget. The opening band was the Black Eyed Peas, setting the tone for U2. They were phenomenal. U2 was wrapping up their 360° Tour in Vancouver, producing a memorable concert. I had front-row seats with my family, and near the beginning of the show, the singer, Bono, was standing less than five feet away from me; this memory stays with me as a fond memory of a live event.

An article in The *Washington Post* called, *Large events can be cesspools of germs. Here's why we ache for them, anyway,* writer Galadriel Watson, states: *"And the effects of such gatherings can linger. Nick Hopkins, a professor of social psychology at the University of Dundee in Scotland, did a study that looked at a Hindu festival in northern India. Even a month after the event, participants reported feeling more content than similar people who hadn't attended the festival."* (12)

Live events may include more than musical concerts such as sporting events, live theater, rallies, marches, markets, retreats, fairs.

Our preference for live events may have to do with the fact that we still carry the biological urge to spend time with others doing activities.

We desire to be "part of something larger," and this was because as we evolved as a species, we needed each other to stay safe from other animals. We needed to be part of a tribe because our lives could be in danger and become prey. We've carried this thinking into the present day and experience primitive feelings of seeking to be part of a larger group.

The pandemic was a challenge for many of us because we had to self-isolate, and live events got canceled and replaced by virtual ones. While we were happy to have the technology to engage in some events online, it was not the same as listening to live music with others in person.

When things started to open up in our towns and cities, we clamored to book and attend events; we no longer took live activities for granted. We had a taste of losing our freedom and options for living our lives, and we felt the insatiable need to experience events in person.

We feel a strong urge to attend live events, and we enjoy sharing a common passion with like-minded people, and we thrive on new adventures. Without experiencing live events, our days might be a bore.

TRY THIS

TIME: For this escape, you want at least two hours or longer to enjoy this activity.

METHOD: Consider a live concert experience you'd like to attend and research to find out when it's happening, and arrange to book your tickets for the event. If it's out of town, you may need to arrange and book accommodations.

Decide who will be attending with you as having the right people there with you adds to the adventure; you'll have someone to share the experience with and stories to tell when it ends.

If you're attending an event out of town, be sure to get a hotel in advance to avoid overbooking.

SOUND ESCAPES

> "The sound of water says what I think." —Zhuang Zhou

Do you often awake to an alarm clock ringing? As annoying as this may be, being able to hear the alarm is a miracle in itself. When you hear your clock ringing, more is happening than you realize. The energy of the clock sound flows through the air, arriving seconds later in your ears before being interpreted by your brain. The whole process is so complex and quick you seldom consider it.

Sound is essentially energy produced from things when they vibrate and the physical process of sound creation. A psychological process occurs when the soundwaves get converted into sensations we understand as speech, singing, music, and noise.

Sound is vital for interacting with others, sharing information, navigation, communication, localization, medical ultrasounds, warning animals and humans of impending dangers, and so much more.

When you pay attention to the complexities of sound, you realize how fortunate you are if you have good hearing. It's not something to take for granted.

For example, as you are reading this book, stop for a quick moment and pay attention to the sounds in your environment. What do you hear? Do you hear the sound of vehicles, birds singing, a plane in the air, the sound of your neighbor talking outside your window?

Unless you're wearing quality noise-canceling headphones, you will likely get to listen to many noises—soft and loud. If you pay attention, you'd be amazed at how many sounds you encounter in a day. City living can be particularly challenging as you may hear air traffic, construction-site noise, traffic, animals, music from nightclubs, and other noise.

Some sounds may cause noise pollution if they exceed 65 decibels (dB). Loud sounds may cause people to feel agitated, experience headaches and other issues. It may cause anxiety, fatigue, and depression and keep you from having a deep sleep.

If you live in a noisy environment, pay attention to the daily sounds.

Sound is more than noise. Sound is music. Sound is healing. If you've ever had the opportunity to hear Tibetan singing bowls, there's almost a feeling of "calm" that comes over you. Tibetan singing bowls have been utilized for centuries and produce low frequencies that relax the nervous system and heal.

There has been much research on the healing power of sound bathing. Research psychologist Tamara Goldsby, from the University of California San Diego, studied the effects of Tibetan singing bowls on human health. The impact of sound and healing is discussed in an article by Anna Sharratt in *The Globe and Mail, The healing power of sound: Studies show how sound baths can improve not only mood but also physical symptoms such as chronic pain.* The article states: *"Years later, Goldsby decided to study the impact of sound bowls on human health. Her 2016 study published in the Journal of Evidence-Based Complementary and Alternative Medicine found that people attending singing-bowl meditations or sound baths reported a reduction in pain symptoms as well as less anxiety, tension, anger and feelings of sadness."* (12)

Tibetan singing bowls are an excellent way to add the practice of "sound bathing" to your life. You may purchase a small or large bowl—the choice is yours.

I enjoy using sound bathing and listening to binaural beats. Binaural beats are an auditory illusion when you listen to two slightly different tones in each ear. The frequency differences create the illusion of an additional sound, also known as a rhythmic beat. You may find that focusing on the sounds causes you to calm down, relax, and feel less stress. For an even more beneficial effect, add guided meditation.

For years, I suffered from insomnia and would toss and turn for hours, so I downloaded binaural beats with meditation and music in the background to help with falling asleep. It worked so well; I used it for months until I could get my sleep regulated and didn't need to rely on this method to fall asleep.

If you can fit in a few minutes, you can play a Tibetan singing bowl, gongs, bells, or crystal bowls.

The first time I heard a crystal bowl played, it literally "blew me away." I had just finished a five-needle biopsy to see if I had cancer (a large tumor in my spine and shoulder). Twenty minutes after this painful procedure, I was with friends in their apartment and didn't mention I had this procedure; I just wanted to spend time with them and enjoy their company. After an hour, my friend retrieved a twelve-inch white crystal singing bowl from her bedroom. She placed it on a wooden table and then hit the bowl with a wooden mallet. The sound ("e note") resonated and started building and building. I could not believe my ears. This experience was unlike anythin I had experienced.

Whether you decide to do a sound bath or go out in nature and listen to the sounds of birds, you will discover that if you pay attention to sound, you may learn to use it to benefit you.

TRY THIS

TIME: Take at least 10 minutes for this activity.

METHOD: If you listen for bird sounds, sit still and listen to the first bird noise. Then, listen for other sounds. Do you hear different types of birds?

If you enjoy music, listen to it while you work, at lunchtime, or after work. Do you hear music when you take a walk outside? Are there outdoor bands? Do you play an instrument? Perhaps you could end your day by practicing it.

If you can visit a park with flowing water, take a moment to sit and listen to the sound of flowing water. Research shows that listening for a few minutes helps you calm down, breathe slowly, relax, and de-stress. If it's a slightly breezy day, take a walk outdoors and listen to the sounds of the breeze as it moves across trees and other things. If you have time to go for a hike or nature walk, take the time to do so. You will hear so many relaxing sounds such as flowing water, birds, bees, squirrels, and other creatures making natural noises that allow you to slow down and relax.

If the weather's not great and you have a Tibetan or crystal singing bowl, make sure to take time to make those bowls sing and sit back and listen to the sounds.

DANCE BUSTING

> "Find fitness with fun dancing. It is fun and makes you forget about the dreaded exercise." —Paula Abdul

After a particularly stressful day, I turned on music in my home and started to dance. I'd been taking a few minutes every other day to learn new hip-hop moves, and I would listen to music and practice a few new "moves." I enjoyed the challenge of learning dance steps and trying them out without an audience. After at least 20 minutes of dancing, my mood improved.

I've never "loved" doing cardio workouts unless they involved great music and cool new moves I could learn. Since I'm not a talented dancer, I enjoyed learning dance moves and routines to practice and use when I was out in public.

Dancing is a great option if you desire an energizing and fun activity that boosts your energy. It helps you get in shape by improving your strength, muscle tone, and endurance. The plus? You have an opportunity to create social connections as you meet new people and build your network.

From a physical standpoint, dancing may offer the following benefits: increased endurance and muscular strength, aerobic fitness, weight management, reduced risk of osteoporosis and improved bone strength, better agility and flexibility, improved coordination, special awareness and balance, greater self-confidence, and psychological wellbeing and social skills. Finally, it helps to improve your mental health.

For example, dancing often involves a social aspect as you mingle with others on a dance floor, creating a feeling of interconnectedness. You may meet new people or catch up with old friends, which helps improve your mood and lower your stress and anxiety or depression.

Dancing offers many positive benefits to the brain; this includes a feel-good hormone, serotonin, developing brand new neural networks in regions that affect long-term memory, spatial recognition, and executive function.

According to an article by *Harvard Medical School* titled *Dancing and the Brain*, *"While some imaging studies have shown which regions of the brain are activated by dance, others have explored how the physical and expressive elements of dance alter brain function. For example, much of the research on the benefits of the physical activity associated with dance links with those gained from physical exercise benefits that range from memory improvement to strengthened neuronal connections."* (13)

There are many benefits to dance, an activity that supposedly dates back to at least the times of the Egyptians. Some research has proposed that dance showed up in cultures before written language. Dance has always been important as an expression in culture to symbolize significant events in a community or family. For example, dance has been used for weddings, births, celebrating changing seasons, food festivals, and more. And, traditional dance may have imparted religious traditions and cultural morals. Dance often brought people together in a customary space.

Dance is a versatile activity that you can do alone, with a partner, or in a group. You'll find venues for dancing at schools, community events, clubs, and your home and community halls. Dance can be social, competitive, recreational, and physically challenging, as anyone can be involved. While you may not need equipment to dance, some types of dancing may require you to buy items such as a costume and shoes.

Dance also involves many styles including, ballroom dancing, ballet, belly dancing, hip-hop, jazz, salsa, square dancing, and tap dancing.

When you're considering a style of dance to enjoy, decide if you want to move fast or slow, with a partner or to be on your own, if you desire private lessons or to learn on your own. Also, consider if you're working on improving your coordination, flexibility, and fitness.

There are many types of dance and routines you can do, so make sure you have fun and learn something new and exciting.

Before you begin a new dance program, ensure your health is good to do this. See your medical professional for a check-up if you're unsure or have a health condition.

Start by wearing layered clothing that you can remove as you warm up your body. Also, ensure you have the proper footwear to protect your feet. Do proper stretches to warm up your muscles before you dance, and drink plenty of water before and after you dance.

After dancing, make sure you cool down adequately by stretching out your muscles.

TRY THIS

TIME: For this escape, you want to take at least 20 minutes to feel the effects of this activity.

METHOD: You may take five minutes to "bust a move" at home or increase the time and boost your energy reserves and blast stress.

If you're thinking of dancing outside of your home, this can add to the fun if you attend a wedding, special event, or club. The music, people, and atmosphere can add to the experience.

If you want to learn new dance moves, you can watch videos or take public or private dance lessons. Learning a new dance routine is very beneficial to your brain, body, and social life as you can showcase your new skills at the next great event.

Happy dance escaping!

GREAT HOBBIES

> "When a habit begins to cost money, it's called a hobby." —Jewish Proverb

Did you have any hobbies when you were a child? What about now?

Many of us are so busy in our lives that our hobbies have often taken a back seat to our daily tasks and responsibilities.

There are many reasons why hobbies are important in our lives. When we make time for something fun to do with our leisure time, we learn new skills, increase our self-confidence, learn from our mistakes, become more patient, reduce boredom, and minimize stress.

People have turned to numerous hobbies to help cope with feelings of loss of control, stress, boredom, lack of free time, and more. They started gardening, reading, baking, brewing wine and beer, drawing and painting, crocheting and knitting, building furniture, fixing cars and motorcycles, renovating houses, and pursuing arts and crafts.

These activities were a more productive way to spend time and energy instead of doom-scrolling through negative news feeds and social media. Whether it's the world or life events that have caused stress, the best remedy is hobbies.

Hobbies are great for helping you relax, calm down, and get lost in the flow of the activity. You may make new social connections as you share your interest in a hobby with someone else. You are more interesting if you have something other than work or family to discuss.

Besides gaining skills, passing the time, and minimizing stress, when you engage in hobbies, this may also lead to a great side-hustle business that brings in extra revenue or even an opportunity to change careers.

Here are some hobbies to inspire you, and they may even lead to a 'side hustle' or business:

- Writing and blogging
- Refinishing furniture
- Catering or baking
- Making music
- Playing the stock market
- Proofreading and editing
- Writing a book or e-books
- Public speaking

- Coding
- Designing websites
- Online content creation
- Driver
- Graphic design
- Handyperson services
- Landscaper
- T-shirt designing
- Starting a YouTube channel
- Decorating or home staging
- Dog walking
- Social media marketing
- Buying and selling real estate
- Flipping real estate properties
- Creating videos/editing videos
- Consultant services
- Life coaching services
- Computer technician
- Music teacher
- Art teacher
- Fitness instructor
- Financial planning
- Tutoring students
- Writing music
- Animation
- Woodworking
- Exercising
- Hiking and outdoor activities
- Gardening
- Knitting and crocheting
- Weight lifting

- Motocross
- Biking
- Kayaking, paddle-boarding, sailing
- Wine tours
- Dancing
- Volunteering
- Pottery
- Road trips
- Drawing, painting, photography
- Learning a new sport
- Golf or mini-golf
- Jewelry making
- Learning/playing musical instruments
- Board games
- Sculpting
- Podcasting
- Inventing
- Storytelling
- Creating videos or online courses and tutorials
- Camping
- Swimming
- Airsoft or paintballing
- Drone flying
- Trail running
- Traveling
- Backpacking
- Horseback riding
- Skiing or snowboarding
- Mountain biking
- Rock or sea glass collecting
- RV traveling

- Whale watching
- Art collecting
- Acting and theater
- Investing
- Scrapbooking—paper or digital
- Stargazing
- Quilting or wall art

There are thousands of hobbies and interests, and you may find your challenge is narrowing down your list.

TRY THIS

TIME: For this mini-vacation, you want to have at least 60 minutes to engage in this activity.

METHOD: If you're not using leisure time to enjoy a hobby, now is the time. Decide on whether you wish to pursue an old passion or try something new.

Next, ensure you allow sufficient time to pursue your hobby free of distractions. It's advisable to allocate at least an hour as most hobbies will need this amount of time to ease into the activity and feel like you are making some progress in the task. Be sure you don't put too much pressure on yourself, though—this should be fun and stress-free.

BOLD BOOKS

> "Just the knowledge that a good book is awaiting one at the end of a long day makes that day happier." —
> Kathleen Norris

Do you remember the first moments when reading started to make sense to you, and you felt comfortable and confident reading a story? Suddenly, the world seemed to open up to you. If you were lucky, you explored new worlds with books such as *The Lord of the Rings* and others.

An intriguing book is hard to stop reading because, unlike television or movies, a well-written book invites you into the character's world, and you see into a protagonist or antagonist's way of thinking. A movie usually doesn't have the time to delve into as much detail as a book; directing, acting, the budget, and other factors significantly limit the movie.

A book may be as elaborate and detailed as your imagination, providing it is well written.

For example, when you read a horror novel, your mind may conjure specific frightful feelings; the same story made into a movie may display blood and gore and lose the psychological interpretations.

While many people read books on screens, a growing number of others love the tactile sensation of holding a paper book; they enjoy the visual break from digital screens and have experienced the effects of screen fatigue. Reading on paper is easier for human eyes.

While I have nothing against portable reading devices, reading a book is a nice break. It is more convenient to have a paper book when you travel to a park or beach; you need not worry about charging the digital device, damage from the sun, or someone stealing it. If I take a fictional book to the beach and lose it, I might be annoyed if I didn't finish the story, but that would be nothing compared to losing a digital device.

TRY THIS

TIME: You will want at least 30 minutes to enjoy this activity.

METHOD: If you don't have any books at home you wish to read, visit a new or used bookstore in person, not online.

While you might choose an online digital book, avoid this for this exercise. You want to find a book that you can read without worrying about a dying battery; you also want to give your eyes a screen-time break.

If you don't want to buy a book, visit your local library. If it's been years since you stepped into a library, make this a real escape.

COFFEE OR TEA FOR ONE

> "If this is coffee, bring me some tea; if this is tea, bring me some coffee." —Abraham Lincoln

Years ago, I worked as an advertising executive and balanced full-time work with two young children. Fatigue was a constant for me as my job was busy, stressful, deadline-driven, and physically taxing as I'd often be getting in and out of my car, driving all over town, and seeing multiple clients. I never slept well at night because one of my children would wake up in the middle of the night. I drank three or four cups of coffee every day at work to cope.

I made a ritual out of my time when I drank my coffee. I'd take my cup of java and create a mini 'time out' either in the parking lot or at a local park in between clients. This coffee break was sanity for me.

Caffeine propped up my low energy reserves until I started having health challenges and heart palpitations. I'd feel good during the day, but my heart would beat out of sync when I relaxed. I dismissed this as stress, but a pattern of heart palpitations scared me enough to see my doctor. I was referred to a local hospital to perform an electrocardiogram on my heart. After the study, doctors stated my heart was healthy, and there was nothing wrong. I had subsequent tests and discovered I was sensitive to caffeine. Medical recommendations were for me to eliminate caffeine from my diet.

I was miserable for a while but knew it was important to follow medical advice, so I switched to caffeine-free coffee. I knew there was a minimal amount of caffeine in decaffeinated coffee; it was a safe alternative to caffeinated coffee.

Along this journey, I discovered many healthy tea alternatives and cut back on drinking coffee. I filled my cupboards with many tea varieties: chamomile, spearmint, lemon, green tea, and others. I had the good fortune of having spearmint growing in my garden, so I would grab fresh sprigs and brew up a spearmint tea, especially helpful when I had an upset stomach.

Whether you drink coffee or tea, know the health benefits of the drink you have. One thing to consider is you want to moderate your coffee or tea drinking as too much may create health issues. If you are making dietary changes, you may consult your medical health practitioner to ensure a healthy lifestyle.

Harvard Health Publishing published an article, *Tea: A cup of good health?* In the article, it was mentioned, *"As with tea, antioxidant and anti-inflammatory substances called polyphenols may account for coffee's purported health benefits."* (14)

Once you know what you enjoy and what's healthy for you, stock up on your favorites and keep those cupboards filled. You never know when you can engage in a coffee or tea break.

Creating a little ritual around your coffee or tea break energizes you and adds normalcy to a busy day.

Have a happy coffee or tea escape.

TRY THIS

TIME: For this escape, take 15 to 20 minutes of quiet time.

METHOD: During this time, brew coffee or tea, or pick one up at your favorite café.

Find a place to rest and relax away from the stress of the day. Engage all your senses in this escape.

Start by looking at the cup that is holding your drink. Is the cup a take-out one, or is it a porcelain mug given to you by someone special? Is there a message on the cup?

Next, breathe in the aroma of the drink. Does it have a sweet smell? How does it smell?

Next, pick up your cup and feel the warmth of the drink in your hand. If it's a cold day or you feel slightly "under the weather," feel the cup healing you. Imagine the energy in the cup is filling you up.

Then, bring your mouth to the cup and savor your first sip of the drink. Pay attention and keep your mind on the present moment. How does the drink taste? Are you drinking coffee or tea? Is it sweet, spicy, or slightly bitter? What are your taste buds sensing?

As you slowly savor your drink, keep your mind on the present. Where are you sitting, and how does your environment look? Try to keep your mind on what you see, hear, smell, taste, and feel around you. Focus on this present moment and feel a sense of safety and contentment. You're taking care of your needs for this present moment—focus on building up your energy reserves so you can power through the rest of your day.

Happy escaping!

CALMING CANDLELIGHT

> "When was the last time you spent a quiet moment just doing nothing—just sitting and looking at the sea, or watching the wind blowing the tree limbs, or waves rippling on a pond, a flickering candle or children playing in the park?" —Ralph Marston

Since the beginning of humanity, fire has played a crucial part in our history and evolution. Besides cooking food, keeping people warm, huddling and telling stories around the fire, and honoring our dead, it kept us safe from animals and danger and helped us bond.

This calm feeling often happens when we light a single candle. Something about the mesmerizing effects of the flickering flame causes us to change our pace; it may be that our eyes are bringing in low light, which creates a slightly sleepy feeling in our brain.

I've used candles to navigate in a dark house at times after unexpectedly losing power. One night, I ate sushi by candlelight, and that was a great experience; I focused on the meal instead of technology. I felt relaxed, and instead of choking down my food under artificial light and blue-light screens, I savored the flavor of the meal. There's a lot to be said about lighting candles and turning out your lights; this is especially effective when engaged in mindful meditation.

I remember reading an article about employees who worked in the technological sector; they would come home after a long day and create a peaceful environment by lighting candles in their homes.

To add to a relaxing ambiance, buy scented candles if you enjoy certain scents. One word of caution: Be sure to choose all-natural candles made from soy or beeswax and essential oils; you don't want to be breathing in artificial chemicals, especially if you suffer from allergies.

You can create your ritual by lighting candles while eating dinner, watching a movie, or at the end of a busy week. Consider all the ways you might incorporate candles into your home.

Safety is critical, so ensure the candle is stored away from drafts, furniture, and other items and that it's placed on a flame-proof surface and monitored. To make your candle last longer, experts recommend you burn it for one hour and then extinguish it as the candle will last longer by not burning down too far in the center.

TRY THIS

Take time and seek all-natural candles made of beeswax or soy and be sure you have enough to create a nice effect at home. As well as having these candles for times of relaxation, you may need to resort to candles for emergencies if you lose your power. Be sure to stock up on enough candles.

For this escape, take at least 15 minutes, light a candle and study the flame, letting your mind wander.

CHAPTER 4

Cozy Home Retreats

Home is where the heart is. It has always been significant to humans as it protected us from harsh environmental elements—it was a place to gather, a sanctuary, and a space to escape the intrusiveness and busyness of the world.

We get a sense of belonging and identity, and we are centered as we go out into the world.

A home may make us feel calm and focused, but we want to ensure it reflects our personality and makes us feel good to spend time in it.

HOME OASIS

> "Seek home for rest, for home is best." —Thomas Tusser

Our homes have always been crucial to our safety and sanity. Whether we live in an apartment, basement suite, or own a house, the feeling of being at home is universal. Our home represents our sanctuary, a place to rest, eat, relax, spend time with our family, friends, and make memories.

Over the years, the number of before-and-after home-decorating shows has grown exponentially. All the attention to our living space has caused a surge in home renovations, consuming of office equipment, video conferencing equipment, and more.

Whether your house is large and spacious or you reside in a bachelor apartment, you need a relaxing, comforting place to cushion you from the stressors of the day. When you're seeking a quick and relaxing mini-holiday, borrow these ideas to convert your home into a private oasis. Your house, apartment, suite, or home must be a place that promotes peace and relaxation so it can act as a "buffer" from the day-to-day stressors you'll encounter.

Believe it or not, one of the quickest ways to have an impact and create an oasis at home is by decluttering your space. If you've lived in your home for a while, you may have accumulated more items than you realize. People often aren't aware until they get ready to move. Then, they're overwhelmed by the possessions they own.

While researching this book, the concept of a minimalism-inspired approach to organizing stuff appealed to me.

A growing minimalist movement has been building as people review their possessions and look to simplify their lives. This shift has to do with the number of events and negative news we've witnessed in the last while. We lost a lot of our freedom and had to quarantine with our closest connections; this inspired us to consider what is most important in our lives.

Creating an oasis at home starts with surrounding yourself with things that you enjoy and love in your residence when it comes to creating an oasis. If we love the things we own, we'll take better care of them and keep them organized. While this is a good plan, sometimes we will own things that aren't exciting, but the items are necessary for our day-to-day lives.

Use your imagination when you lack the time or money to make substantial changes to your space.Just cleaning your home and decluttering excess papers and items may immediately make a huge difference to the feeling of a room. Your space should speak to your five senses by adding artwork, decorative drapes, woven cloths or throws, cozy pillows, throw rugs, glass pieces, fresh flowers, aromatherapy candles, flowers, calming music, and yummy snacks.

You need a personal retreat to escape but if your space is small and there isn't extra room, create this space in a large room. You can use a decorative screen to partition a corner of an area or hang blinds from a ceiling. Venetian or paper blinds are inexpensive and divide a room by adding interesting textures and color. A wall of plants may provide privacy as well.

TRY THIS

TIME: When you create a mini-vacation, consider how much time you wish to dedicate to designing your home oasis.

METHOD: You may gain ideas to design your oasis by visiting a home center and picking up "fun, relaxing" pieces to add to your décor or reading home-design magazines. Use your imagination.

When decluttering, take photos of your home before you begin the process. Start by decluttering your space and going through everything you own. Be sure to do this when you have the energy and time, as it will take a lot of your resources to conduct this project.

Start the tidying-up process by reviewing your clothes. We often find clothing organization the most challenging as we hold onto the clothes we wear, whether heavier or lighter. Many items will not spark joy; you may own them for convenience. If you own clothing that no longer fits or is damaged, donate it. Someone else will enjoy it.

If you have sentimental items, save these for the last of this project; this is often the most challenging part of tidying up. We don't want to throw out something someone has given us. These items are memories, and when we throw them away, we may feel like we are experiencing a "loss." You will want to take your time reviewing sentimental items.

A good rule is to consider is this: For everything you buy or bring into the house, eliminate something else. Considering this will keep stuff from accumulating quickly.

Then, the fun begins by adding items to make your home a relaxing oasis. One can set a tone for a calm and relaxing home by adding flowers, candles, lighting, and relaxing paint colors. Flowers add great "pops of color" and are soothing visually and aromatically. Adding white candles also gives a feeling of calm. Taking advantage of natural sunlight is healthy and recommended. Finally, the paint colors you choose will make a difference to the feel of the space. Tranquil blues, grays, and greens are relaxing, and bright colors are energizing and tend to work well as accents—pillows, throws, and artwork.

You may create a relaxing bedroom by removing clutter, straightening your bed, placing a soft area rug by your bed, fresh flowers and a candle on your nightstand, soft wall-shade colors, relaxing artwork, and calm lighting.

To create a relaxing living room, consider placing your furniture; you want a focal point and keep furniture grouped in a comfortable setting. If the placement doesn't feel right, move the furniture. Add more pillows to your couch, keep extra blankets nearby, have a lamp for nighttime reading, add fresh plants, hang family pictures, use area rugs, let natural light shine in, and keep clutter to a minimum.

One way to create a bathroom oasis is to add flowers and candles in the bathroom (if there's room). You can also buy an inexpensive bath pillow, replace old and ripped towels with new ones, hang art on the walls (waterproof art), replace your shower head with a massage style, and add a soft, machine-washable area rug near the tub.

Since the kitchen is generally the home's busiest area, keep it organized. Store similar items together, clean your pantry and cupboards, and remove clutter. Have a snack drawer and an area in your fridge for healthy snacks if you have children. Keep clutter-free workspaces, food prep areas, and kitchen tables. Add fresh fruit bowls and keep them on the table so hungry people have a quick, healthy snack to grab. Place plants or flowers on the kitchen table or nearby to add color and life to the area. If you enjoy using cookbooks, review and organize them.

You can do so many things to create a more relaxing space at home. Use your imagination, visit home centers, ask friends and family, and do your research but be sure to make it fun.

BEAUTIFUL ESCAPES

> "Have nothing in your house that you do not know to be useful or believe to be beautiful." —William Morris

Have you ever walked into a home or a business, and it felt calm, welcome, and spacious? Maybe it was the color of the walls, the artwork, the placement of furniture, or the flow of the space. Whatever it was, it grabbed your attention, and you may have walked away thinking of things you could do to improve your living spaces.

I'm convinced that we may feel stress because we work or live in dirty or disorganized spaces. If you don't believe me, remember a time when you were outside, and the beauty of an area had you awestruck.

The sunset, water, trees, rolling hills, and openness calmed you, and you felt free, relaxed, and energized. It's hard to replicate this feeling in cramped, dirty, and disorganized spaces.

Years ago, I worked in a small office where the air quality was poor, and the room was disorganized and cramped. I found it hard to concentrate and feel productive and knew there needed to be some changes made. I didn't have much money but moved the office furniture, added beautiful nature posters, plants, and placed colorful objects on my desk. These changes made me feel more inspired to work in the space.

It doesn't matter whether you rent or own a place. What matters is adding peace and beauty to your space. Start by eliminating clutter, using drawers to increase your storage space, and focusing on having a more open, inviting space. You may end up rearranging furniture to make your place feel spacious and less cramped.

You might add beautiful furniture, art, blankets, and lighting and arrange furniture to create a beautiful environment.

If your budget is tight, you may add beautiful things to your space by visiting farmers' markets, garage sales, second-hand stores, or even getting stuff from friends or family. The key is that it should add beauty to your space.

If you have a porch, deck, or space where there's an overhang, you can add a beautiful wind chime.

Another way to add beauty is to place candles around your house. It's nice to have the candle near the entry when guests arrive. A naturally scented candle in the bathroom is a good idea, and a beautiful candle adds to the area. The best candles consist of beeswax or soy; you want to avoid the cheap, aroma-scented candles because some of these candles may release toxins or chemicals that may trigger allergies and other issues.

Adding cozy blankets or throws to a living room or reading area adds color and interest and creates a comfortable and beautiful space. You can also add an accent pillow to a window seat, bed, or couch. You don't need to eliminate all your current cushions; you can add an accent pillow to create a focal point.

If you have laminate or wood floors, buying a colorful, beautiful throw rug and strategically placing it in the space can instantly create a great place. Adding an accent lamp to a reading space or living room is also a great way to add beauty to the area; try placing it near a chair, desk, or above a bed.

Lighting plays a large part in the mood, and it can easily be unwelcoming and sterile. Look around and see if you may be able to replace a floor piece or table lamp with something more beautiful. Also, consider the type of light bulbs you use; going for a warm tone may add richness to the look of the space. Shelved lighting and backlighting may be something to consider.

Buying or adding colorful curtains will instantly add beauty to an area; this is a great way to impact a place.

Changing a duvet cover or the blankets in your bedroom can give that space a quick update and quickly add beauty to the area.

If you have an old kitchen table or want to create color and beauty in the area, buy a new kitchen tablecloth or add a colorful runner to the table. Then, you might add some colorful bowls to the table to create a focal point. If your chairs are cloth-covered and looking "ratty," you might be able to reupholster them in a beautiful fabric or replace them with newer chairs.

String lights can add beauty and look appealing to a front porch, deck, patio, or backyard area. They don't cost a lot, and you can purchase white or colored lights to create special effects.

Bringing nature indoors is one of my favorite ways to add beauty to a space; plants that flower or are big, leafy tree-type plants can transform a simple space into an almost tropical area. For a full effect, you can have vintage bowls or jars filled with shells, rocks, seedpods, or anything interesting to display on a table, bookshelf, or windowsill.

Adding a bouquet to a room adds a pop of color to the place, creating beauty. You might decide to get a big bouquet of wildflowers and have that on your kitchen table or take the large arrangement and break it into smaller sections and place it in small vases throughout the house. This action will instantly cheer up a room, especially in the winter and when it's dark and rainy outdoors.

You can add beauty to your space and personalize the area by hanging your favorite photography. As well as photographs, you can hang unusual things on your walls such as ironwork, plates, framed fabric, or old maps—get creative!

If you have a beautiful front door, consider adding a colorful wreath that reflects the time of year. For example, you might hang a colorful summer wreath with dried summer flowers on your front door, and during the winter, you might have a cedar wreath with red holly.

For darker areas in your space, adding mirrors can make a difference as it bounces more light back at you and makes the room appear larger.

We often don't consider the smell of a place unless it's very unpleasant. To add to your space and create a beautiful environment, you may consider diffusing a blend of pure essential oils in a diffuser in your living space. You can create an essential oil blend that reflects the time of year and mood you wish to convey. Common oils used may include lavender, lemon, peppermint, and orange. Before you diffuse oils, do your research to understand the best ways to use the oils.

Adding a spectacular piece to your living area will enrich the space and add beauty. It might be a cabinet, chandelier, unique-styled couch, or chair; it doesn't matter as long as you love it.

There are so many things that add beauty to your living space, and the ideas don't need to be extravagant or cost a lot of money—you can use your imagination. If you're very artistic or enjoy doing crafts, you can research ideas and then make things from recycled materials or thrift-shop finds; there's no limit to the beauty you can add to your space.

TRY THIS

TIME: For this escape, take at least 20 minutes, grab a notebook, walk around your home, and record all the things that need to be changed and improved.

METHOD: You will start in one room and write down things you don't like about the space and what you might add to make it more beautiful. Next, you will choose the room that needs the most work to improve, and that area will be your focus.

For example, if you wanted to focus on your living-room space and couldn't afford to replace your old, stained couch, perhaps you could get it professionally cleaned and add a beautiful throw and a couple of accent pillows to it. If you wanted to do more in that space, you might add a beautiful floor lamp, change a picture on the wall, or add a diffuser.

When you make your space more beautiful, you'll feel more inspired to spend time in that room, so use your imagination and have fun with this escape.

HOME-OFFICE FENG SHUI

> "The most important thing to understand is that Feng Shui is really about the energy that's surrounding you in your personal space." —Lillian Too

For the last few years, the "work-from-home" phenomenon has been growing as more and more people have had access to technology to work remotely.

In March 2020, this push to work remotely was more of a shove as companies suddenly changed how they conducted business due to the novel coronavirus global pandemic.

Depending on the industry, some employees had to work from home. While many companies had employees return to the office several months later as the situation improved, some quit because they got used to the remote lifestyle. They enjoyed working in a home office.

Whether you have had a home office for a while or whether your office is new, you want to ensure your room helps you focus and be productive in the space. If you find it challenging to create a separate space for a home office, consider building visual separations between your home and workspace. You may have to be creative, but some ideas may include: a folding screen, bookcase, large and leafy plants, or a curtain.

Whether you have a dedicated work area or not, create more peace and tranquility by using the ancient principles of Feng Shui to increase your productivity and make your work environment more positive.

Feng Shui is a traditional practice and philosophy that originated in ancient China over 3,000 years ago and involves arranging, constructing, and creating a relaxing, flowing environment for work and life. Feng Shui also means "wind" and "water" and is associated with good health and fortune, and the practice helps optimize businesses and homes and brings abundance, peace, and harmony. It includes garden and field design, interior design and architecture, and urban planning and focuses on the placement of objects to complement the natural flow of Chi' (energy).

Feng Shui may help you create an office at home or the workplace that allows you to be focused and productive.

When you use Feng Shui principles, consider the position of your desk as it's the commanding position. Your desk should be placed to see the door but not directly in line with the door. If it isn't possible to position your desk this way, you may use a small convex mirror to help you see any door reflection; this is important as you won't feel relaxed if you are uncertain about who may enter your space. Your work desk should be rectangular, solid, and brown as this presents the earth element and allows for a positive working space. On your desk, having a small green plant adds life and promotes the idea of "growth." As well as a plant, it's a good idea to have your favorite ceramic mug that's solid and means a lot to you.

Make your workspace organized and clean to ensure you are not distracted when working.

The desk chair should offer stability and support, have a high back and be ergonomically correct to support your spine. If you're using your kitchen chair and noticing you're suffering from a sore back, you'll want to spend a little money to ensure you have a decent chair.

Color is crucial in your workspace and if you have a dedicated room, be sure to ensure the color doesn't distract. For example, cream or earth tones may create a calming atmosphere for some people.

Lighting is paramount to the workspace, especially if you offer live webinars or conduct video chats; you need a light that is not too bright or creates shadows on your face. Natural lighting is great, but you may need additional lighting for your workspace.

Artwork is also significant to your office space. You want to ensure it is positive, inspirational, simple, and not distracting; this is especially crucial if the artwork appears in a video background.

TRY THIS

TIME: Take at least 30 minutes to review an area in your workspace that is challenging for you.

METHOD: Perhaps you need better lighting, new artwork, or a coat of paint to spruce up the place. If your work chair is hurting your back, it may be worth it to "ditch" the kitchen chair and put aside money to get an ergonomically correct chair with lumbar support for your back.

Study your workspace and see where you need to focus your attention. Do you need to improve your lighting or move some lamps? Do you need to reposition your desk to see the door? Is there too much clutter in your office? These questions and others will help you focus and make positive changes to your office space.

When you are aware of the design elements that need improvement, take time to research and update your space. Treat the experience like an adventure and be open to new ideas to create a more fun and efficient work area.

DESK STRESS-BUSTERS

> "My own prescription for health is less paperwork and more running barefoot through the grass." —Leslie Grimutter

It's Wednesday, and the day feels like it should be Friday. After numerous hours tethered to your work desk, answering email after email, reading and correcting reports, you feel your stress levels rise.

Work stress takes a toll on your mental and physical health, so you want to be aware and take steps to combat its effects on you. While it's great to be able to walk, ride a bike, exercise, or do yoga, when stress hits, you're most likely at work and unable to engage in the long form of stress reduction. So, what can you do? Engage in desk stress-busters.

Visualize Your Holiday

When you're feeling stressed and not able to get away from your work desk for a long time, try the art of visualization. Think of the most relaxing place your mind can imagine—a forest, a beach, a hammock. You can trigger your mind by displaying a beach screensaver or your favorite outdoor place on your computer.

While sitting at your desk, close your eyes and engage your senses. Imagine the sights, smells, and sounds. Do you feel anything? Are you eating something that triggers memories of a place you love? The more senses you can engage, the better the escape.

Desk Breathing

If you spend a lot of time at your desk, chances are you may be sitting slouched, and your hips and lower back may be holding tension, which prevents your diaphragm from moving freely. Your diaphragm is responsible for close to 80% of breathing, and if it's not moving right, you won't receive as much oxygen as you need. Therefore, you may feel sluggish and tired if you sit for more than 30 minutes at your desk without moving.

Standing and moving around after 20 or 30 minutes helps to give you energy. You want to pay attention to your breath and perform deep breathing exercises to increase oxygen to your body and brain. There are many techniques, and you can even combine breathing with visualization. Just taking slow and deep belly breaths can immediately make you feel better as more oxygen enters your body.

Desk Exercises

There are numerous exercises you practice at your desk to relieve stress, tight, and sore muscles. Here are few popular ones I enjoy doing at my desk:

Arm Circles: Stand on the floor with your feet shoulder-width apart, and your arms extended straight out by your sides at shoulder height. Move your arms in small backward circles and do this 20 times before switching directions and repeating.

Wall Push-Ups: Stand a few steps away from your office wall and lean toward it, placing your palms on the wall. Lower yourself to the wall and keep tight abs and a straight line down your back. Push back from the wall until your arms are straight but not locked. Do this for 20 reps.

Calf Raises: You may stand behind your chair and use it for support. Raise your heels from the floor until you're standing on your toes, and then slowly lower yourself to the floor. Try three sets of twelve.

Lunges: Put one leg out in front of the other, ensuring your knee is aligned with your foot. Lower your knee of your back leg to the ground and do this ten times per leg.

Oblique Twists: This works well if you possess a swivel chair. Sit upright and with your feet just hovering above the floor. Hold the edge of your desk and use your body core to swivel your chair from side to side. Try this ten times.

Triceps Stretch: To relieve tension in your shoulder and triceps area, raise an arm and bend your elbow, so your hand reaches to touch your opposite shoulder blade. Next, use your other hand and grab your elbow, pulling it toward your head. Hold for 3–5 deep breaths and repeat.

Shoulder Stretch: While sitting or standing, clasp your hands together above your head with your palms facing upward. Next, push your arms up, stretching up to the ceiling. Hold for 3–5 deep breaths.

Shoulder Rolls: While sitting, raise both your shoulders upward and slowly roll them backward. Repeat the exercise by allowing your shoulders to move forward.

Neck Rolls: Sit and relax. Lean your head forward while slowly rolling your head in a circle to the side for 15 seconds. Then, repeat these actions on the other side.

TRY THIS

TIME: You only need 10 minutes to begin the activity for your mini-vacation.

METHOD: You should be taking a mini-break every 60 minutes if you are working at your desk. Medical professionals recommend you avoid sitting for long periods.

Depending on your available time, you may wish to do a series of exercises or choose one or two to practice throughout your work session. The choice is up to you. Practicing desk exercises every hour is a great mini-break when tension builds at work.

MOVIE MAGIC

> "You know what your problem is? It's that you haven't seen enough movies – all of life's riddles are answered in the movies." —Steve Martin

Since the beginning of time, storytelling has played a large part in human identity; we gathered around campfires and told stories, entertaining ourselves and giving insight into the human condition. Stories allowed us to get a glimpse into another person's life without having to experience the trials and tribulations of that existence.

Movies, a visual and auditory storytelling experience, are an effective way to relay moments in time. Consider movies that you never forgot—the movie that changed you as a child, the movies whose lines you quote. Even if you're not a massive fan, movies have likely inspired, scared, moved you, made you cry, question life, made you sing, laugh, or feel powerful emotions.

Films may reflect what's happening in society at the time and may be based on real-life events, loosely based on life, or fictional. Even with fictional movies, there are some elements of current life mixed in—the language, the sets, clothing, technology, and environment. When you watch a movie of a year like the 1960s, you'll see societal reflections and many elements of that current culture.

Films may depict a character suffering from the same challenges as you, and you feel like you are part of the story. For example, if you relate to the main character and encounter something difficult, you may feel like it happened to you. Sometimes, movies trigger a certain feeling when you watch them; this marks effective movie-making.

As a child, I remember watching a movie, *Jaws*, which scared me; open water suddenly seemed like a threat. After viewing this movie, I had nightmares about sharks, and I wasn't alone with this fear. There was a whole generation of worried swimmers.

Movies appeal to us for reasons like providing a distraction from real life, losing ourselves in someone else's life and learning new things, broadening our perspective, taking us to places we've never traveled, and so much more.

Sometimes we walk away from viewing a film and think about society and areas to improve, we feel inspired to try new things, we feel empathy for a character in trouble, and we may realize we have more power to make changes than we realize. Other times, movies are just true escapism and don't offer anything too significant but give us space and time to relax, laugh, and lose ourselves in another life story. Often, these movies are comedies, and after watching them, we feel as though we've had a mini-holiday.

Whether you're an avid movie watcher or not, there may be a time when you're not inspired to read, do homework or tasks, you're not tired, and you want to have a quick escape.

There's an abundance of movies available through streaming companies and theaters, so you should be able to watch movies that appeal to you. Even if you're not a huge movie fan and worry about spending up to two hours of your life watching a sub-par film, you should be able to select a movie worth watching. You may want to quickly read about the story and check reviews if you're uncertain.

TRY THIS

TIME: For this mini-vacation, you will want to have 90 to 120 minutes to enjoy your movie.

METHOD: Do a little research and write down movies you want to see. You might ask friends what they've seen and enjoyed, figure out what movie genres you gravitate to, and then do a quick online search for movies you haven't seen.

Next, turn off your phone, ensure you have at least two hours of uninterrupted time and then make yourself comfortable. You might watch a movie alone, but it's often more fun to watch something with others; choose something "light" like a comedy to make it fun.

Next, turn off all electronic devices, dim the room, get blankets, order food in or have snacks ready, and lose yourself in some magical movie moments.

The next time you're looking for a quick escape to another world, choose a movie.

FABULOUS FOOD

> "Food is our common ground, a universal experience."
> —James Beard

Do you have a favorite memory of smelling fresh bread, cookies, or a casserole when you came home from school as a child? Or, do you have fond memories of making dinner with a relative or parent in the kitchen? For many of us, food represents not just sustenance but precious moments spent with those we love, creating a meal for others. It may also be a focal point for a special event, ritual, celebration, or momentous occasion. In fact, at the center of many of our most precious moments spent with family and friends, food often plays an integral part. Since the beginning of time, humans have gathered around fires to cook food and socialize.

If you have fond memories of creating food, you may enjoy baking or cooking as a true escape. There are many benefits to baking and cooking; the first benefit is that a dish may have a smell that reminds you of spending time with your grandmother in the kitchen or trigger memories of a great vacation you experienced. The sense of smell is associated with the limbic part of your brain that holds memories, so when you smell a particular scent, you may feel transported back in time. You may also feel calm, relaxed, and happy.

When I was young, I spent hours in the kitchen with my Norwegian grandmother while she created her mouth-watering meals. She was a great cook as she used to run a boarding house in her past, and she also fed her family through challenging times. She worked in the kitchen, making *Lefse*, a traditional Norwegian flatbread (similar to crepes), *Kumla*, tender potato dumplings, and other traditional Norwegian dishes. These times in the kitchen with my grandmother were precious; we often laughed and joked and created these meals together.

My other grandmother was also a great cook, and I helped her bake cakes, cookies, and other mouth-watering meals. When she baked, she made an excess of treats and would freeze them; she always had goodies available when company arrived at her home.

When I felt uneasy or stressed as a child, I would reach for milk and cookies. While I love these comfort foods, I discovered I was allergic to the whey protein in milk, so I switched to non-dairy alternatives and baked healthy and delicious cookies and muffins to satisfy my sweet tooth and need for comfort.

If you went online in the last while, you witnessed an explosion of online videos showing professional cooks, bakers, and amateurs making meals and showcasing the results. Cooking and baking is a therapeutic way for people to reach out and connect through a universal human history with food.

An article by Danny Lewis, *Feeling Down? Scientists Say Cooking and Baking Could Help You Feel Better: A little creativity each day goes a long way,* for the *Smithsonian Magazine* mentions, *"This isn't the first time researchers have drawn a line connecting making food with positive feelings. In recent years, psychologists have started spending more time exploring cooking and baking as a therapeutic tool to help people dealing with things like depression and anxiety, Meager reports."* (15)

Baking or cooking in a kitchen is calming to an overactive or stressed-out brain because you focus on one task at a time, so your mind must focus on the present moment instead of past issues or future worries. You will have more success at paying attention when you know there is an intrinsic reward at the end of working.

There is a lot of satisfaction in following a recipe, engaging in ordered tasks, and seeing, smelling, and tasting the final result.

Some of us enjoy baking while others enjoy cooking, and there are definite differences between the two forms. Cooking involves preparing food with heat, while baking uses dry oven heat. The two forms have differences; cooking focuses on daily meals, and baking may include bread, cakes, and sweet treats. Cooking is an art that allows you to be creative and improvise and substitute ingredients and create new versions of a meal. Baking is like a precise science because measurements must be accurate, involving heat and chemical reactions, and substitutions are more challenging.

Even though I prefer the art of cooking because I can be more creative, less accurate, and substitute items when my pantry gets low, I still enjoy baking from time to time. Something is comforting about smelling a sweet treat baking in the oven and then having the opportunity to eat the final product.

TRY THIS

TIME: For this escape, you will need at least 60 minutes or longer as this is a fun, engaging escape that usually requires more time than other activities.

METHOD: When you are overwhelmed, tired, bored, or creative, food can be a wonderful escape. Whether you wish to follow a recipe, use a recipe and alter it, or create your invention, be sure you incorporate fun into the adventure. You may wear a chef hat or funny apron, encourage help in the kitchen and tell funny stories while preparing food—use your imagination.

You may have themes for the week. In one week, I had a Mexican and Hawaiian focus for food and created recipes from these two countries.

Another time when my children were young, we went to the grocery store and had what we called a "weird-food" week. We chose foods that were not common and then figured out how to make things with them. This exercise helped us get out of the food rut, where you may end up when you are uncertain what to make, and you end up creating the same type of food all the time.

Stock your cupboard or pantry with ingredients that make baking and cooking easier; it is frustrating when you decide to make something but are missing one thing for the recipe. You should be ready when inspiration hits if you do a little planning.

Have a happy and yummy escape!

SACRED GARDEN

> "More things grow in the garden than the gardener sows." —Spanish Proverb

When I was a child, I was lucky enough to spend some summers with my grandparents, who lived in the Pacific Northwest. We sailed, explored, and visited many beautiful places like the world-famous Butchart Gardens in Victoria, British Columbia.

The gardens are so awe-inspiring that people worldwide have

come to visit. Nestled in a valley in Victoria is a paradise with every type of beautiful plant and flower you could imagine. This mini-paradise consists of four gardens: the Sunken Garden, Rose, Italian, and Japanese Garden. Each garden is so gorgeous that you slow down and enjoy the view.

The story behind this famous site is a story in itself. Founder Robert Pim Butchart traveled to the West Coast of Canada during the late 1800s in search of rich limestone for his company. He owned a cement business and realized limestone would be the key to producing quality cement. By 1904, his family established their home near his factory at Tod Inlet on Vancouver Island.

Butchart quickly depleted the limestone in the quarry near his home. His wife was full of innovative ideas and disliked the large, muddy pit, so she arranged to have tons of topsoil hauled from nearby farms to this abandoned quarry to fill the giant hole. The pit eventually evolved into a gorgeous garden with exotic plants and garden ornaments from Butchart's world travels.

By the 1920s, Mrs. Butchart's gardening talents gave her much publicity, and thousands of people came to view the garden paradise.

If you ever visited this famous garden and felt intimidated by the thought of creating your own, do not worry. Viewing these gardens in person or virtually may inspire you to create your little oasis. Your garden may be large or small, filled with flowers or herbs and vegetables. No matter what type of garden you create, it has to bring you joy. Your idea of paradise may include potted plants on an apartment deck, planting and growing a garden, or maintaining an orchard on your property.

I did not have a traditional garden for many years; I planted wildflowers and had small herb gardens and enjoyed picking the wildflowers and putting them in vases in the house. I wanted to grow a vegetable garden, but my children had a giant trampoline in the best space for a garden, so I created small areas where I could plant herbs and wildflowers.

When my children grew and lost interest in the trampoline, we removed it, created three large planter boxes, and I planted tomatoes, peppers, beans, peas, carrots, lettuce, spinach, kale, and a variety of herbs.

I would pick fresh, red, and ripe tomatoes from the vine during the summer and have them for lunch. I would grab a few carrots, lettuce, peas and have a beautiful salad. I ate well and had the opportunity to be outdoors in the fresh air and sunshine, and this was therapeutic and relaxing after sitting in front of a computer for many hours.

We all need a sanctuary, and you can find it in any patch of land that brings you into proximity with nature—even if it's just your backyard. Just as you can decorate an interior space in a way that suits you and makes you feel happy, you may create a garden to feed and nourish your body and help your spiritual and emotional well-being.

TRY THIS

TIME: You will want to have 60 minutes or longer for this activity, depending on where you create your garden.

METHOD: The time varies for this escape as you need to plan your garden, get supplies, plant, and nurture your garden. A great space does not evolve overnight but over months and years.

Whether you have a mini-garden or a vast expanse, flower garden or vegetable garden, will depend on your needs.

There are many things you can do to create a sacred garden space. If your property allows this, you might add metal accents and outdoor furniture or add bird feeders, birdbaths, fountains, and other outdoor pieces.

Container gardening is a practical way to garden when you have small spaces or minimal time to fuss with a big garden.

For example, if you live in an apartment with a balcony but no backyard space, container gardening may be an option for you. You may plant strawberries, raspberries, flowers, or herbs. There is the versatility of moving the plants in the containers if necessary.

Your garden may be an extension of your home by creating quiet spaces with lots of plants, adding trellises, small trees, flowers and shrubs, trailing vines, and perennial beds. Adding a hammock, benches, tables, and chairs can bring the inside out.

Many people find digging in the dirt relaxing and the rewards of lush greenery, colorful flowers, and fresh and ready-to-pick food very appealing. If you are would like to use your green thumb more, this may be the time to create your sacred garden space.

FLORAL FINESSE

> "Flowers are like friends; they bring color to your world." —Unknown

After a long, cold, challenging winter, spring is a welcome time for many. What makes spring so inviting is that the cooler temperatures turn to warmer weather, birds start singing, and great bursts of color from flowers may be present, depending on where you live.

The significance of flowers is "far-reaching" and critical to the survival of birds, insects, animals, and humans. Some flowers are edible, while others provide medicine and are crucial to the reproduction of plants as their beauty entices pollinators. Without flowers that attract pollinators, the Earth's ecosystem would collapse as scientists estimate that over 80% of the flowering plants on the planet need pollinators to reproduce. And, since we grow a lot of our food, we need flowers.

Flowers are exquisite in their beauty, and while they serve an esthetic benefit to humans, the beauty of the flower is critical to the success of the plant being pollinated. The flower, a by-product, grows with detailed petals and UV colors to attract many pollinators. Sometimes, the flowers also have an enticing scent to attract pollinators; they advertise to insects, birds, and animals.

It's not just insects, birds, or animals attracted to flowers. Humans also enjoy flowers, and this interest may date back more than 5,000 years. According to science, humans enjoyed beautiful flowers and didn't eliminate them when they cleared land for fields and buildings. They kept the flowers and cultivated them, and the flowers evolved.

As well as the practicality of flowers for our planet's survival, their obvious beauty, and occasional sweet scents, humans used flowers to symbolize events and sentiments.

For example, beautiful flowers may be given in bouquets to new mothers in the hospital, used as a corsage for graduation, showcased abundantly in weddings, displayed at funerals, used as a backdrop when taking photographs, sent to friends, family, or a lover.

We have added meaning and symbolism to flowers in countries throughout Asia and Europe over many centuries. Flowers have come to symbolize almost any sentiment from loss, healing, hope, and love to good luck. The fascination with the "language of flowers" became popular in the 1800s when guidebooks to flowers appeared in many Victorian homes.

Common flowers included the carnation, chrysanthemum, daffodil, daisy, forget-me-not, gardenia, honeysuckle, lily-of-the-valley, rose, tulip, and violet. The carnation, for example, presented love and women and depending on the color, there was a specific meaning. A red carnation represented heartache, and white represented pure love or innocence, while pink represented the idea of always remembering someone. The red chrysanthemum means “I love you,” and the white chrysanthemum represents truth. The daffodil, a symbol of spring, represents regards and love. The dahlia symbolizes good taste when gifted as a single flower. The daisy symbolizes hope and innocence and reminds me of a sunny, happy face and the beginning of spring. The tiny little blue flowers of forget-me-not say, “Do not forget me.” The gardenia symbolizes secret love, and the honeysuckle represents bonds of love. The lilac symbolizes the joy of youth, while lily-of-the-valley symbolizes pure love and purity. The rose, the most popular flower, has many colors and meanings. It represents love, the dark crimson rose represents mourning, pink is sweetness or elegance, white is “worthy of you,” yellow is friendship, joy, or caring, and peach is modesty or sincerity. One of the first flowers to bloom in the springtime, tulips often represent regrowth or love. Violets represent modesty, faithfulness, and humility.

We’ve taken the flower and elevated its status to communicate sentiments and events in our lives, and this interest in flowers will continue to grow.

Flowers are critical for pollination, symbolism, the creation of medicines, crafts, dyes, beauty products, gardening companion planting, and decorating food.

The sight of a beautiful bouquet may help ease stress and anxiety.

Dr. Leonard Perry, Extension Professor of the University of Vermont, wrote an article, ”*Relieve Stress with Flowers,* in which he states: “… *’A study from Harvard University Medical School by Dr. Nancy Etcoff focused on the “home ecology” of flowers-- the effects of flowers in the home on personal well-being. With flowers in the home for less than a week, she found that participants felt more compassion toward others, had less worry and anxiety and felt less depressed. Just a few days of flowers* *at home made people more positive, and all these effects carried over into work as well."* (16)

When I moved into my home many years ago, I noticed my yard had ten huge rose bushes. One day, a single yellow and orange-tinged rose grew up past my living-room front window, so I went outside and cut the rose, gathered others, and arranged a gorgeous bouquet to place on my dining room table. Not only did the flowers cast colors in the room, but they also filled the space with a slight, sweet aroma.

You don't need many flowers to add color and beauty to your home; you may use a small vase and add a single rose, daisy, or another type of flower to create a mood. If you don't have a vase, use a bowl, jar, or basket, which will add more interest.

I never paid much attention to vases until I purchased a magazine called *Real Simple*. The spring issue cover featured a yellow backdrop; three tall and square, clear vases sat on a table. A single tulip was in each vase with two inches of water. The flowers leaned against the inside of the vase, and the effect was simple and elegant.

To make the most of any flowers you wish to showcase, be sure to have at least two vases: one with a large base for big bouquets and a small and narrow one for a single flower or a tiny bouquet.

When you have a large bouquet, you can keep it looking great for a long time by eliminating the dead or dying flowers, ensuring the flowers have clean water and plant food. Once most of the flowers die, and you have a small grouping, transfer the flowers to a smaller vase, and you will be able to enjoy that bouquet longer. Many people make the mistake of throwing out the whole bouquet when many flowers die, and they don't notice there may be quite a few flowers left.

TRY THIS

TIME: For this activity, you only need 10 minutes.

METHOD: If it is spring or summer and you have blooming flowers in your yard, take a few minutes and grab enough for a small or large bouquet. Ensure you have plant food, adequate water, and a great space to show the flowers.

You can create a substantial bouquet by keeping it simple. Think about color, symmetry, scale, balance, and be creative in what you hold the flowers in—a jar, pot, old perfume bottle will add contrast and interest. You can create a "masterpiece" like a florist by getting a shallow bowl, adhesive tape, scissors, wire, and two blocks of florist's "oasis" material (green, spongy-like substance to hold flowers). Soak the blocks in water and attach them into the bowl with tape.

Flowers with tall stems get placed in the center of the blocks, and the short, small flowers are near the edge of the bowl. Place moss on the edge of the container and attach with wire. You'll have a gorgeous arrangement if you get creative and "have fun."

If you don't have blooming flowers but wish to add a burst of color to your home or office, you may purchase flowers from a florist or buy them at a grocery or convenience store. You generally don't have to pay a lot for these flowers, and this may be all you need to "brighten up."

If you decide to purchase flowers at a florist's, but your budget is tight, you can do what I did to keep fresh flowers at my work desk during the winter months. After creating a bouquet, I asked florists for their "seconds," the leftover flowers they had. Often, you can spend a few dollars for a decent arrangement of flowers, and it can be so uplifting to see these sprigs of color on a dark, rainy day.

CONTRAST SHOWER ESCAPE

> "My best ideas come in the shower, where I'm showered with water, but also ideas." —Ryan Lilly

Years ago, I decided to take kayak lessons with a group of beginners, and we hit the beach in Ladysmith, BC, in March. It was cold, but we were adorned with our wetsuits to help stay warm. We went out into the harbor, paddling along behind our kayak teacher. We had to do a wet exit practice at one point—roll the kayak, go upside down, and pull the skirting up and away to escape and swim to the surface. I remember the piercing cold of the water as it entered my nostrils while I was upside down. I immediately rushed to get out of the water and swim to the surface.

It seemed like I was underwater for minutes, but it was much less time; the instructor was impressed by my time. (In truth: I was freaked out and wanted to get out of the water as fast as possible; I was not too fond of this exercise.) I remember being so cold I felt like I was experiencing hypothermia. I drove home and immediately hopped in a warm shower, and it felt great to sit under the heat of the water; I didn't make it too hot but just warm enough to make a difference.

Showering is also great after you've had an intense workout and feel sweaty and tired. Just hopping in that warm or cool shower can make you feel energized. Showering can also help you when you're feeling tired, stressed, anxious, or depressed. Hopping in a shower and experiencing hot, cold, or warm water cascading onto your skin can change your thoughts and quickly improve your mood.

Contrast showers are a great way to do this and so much more. If you've not heard of this term, it simply refers to alternating shower water between hot and cold for two to five minutes. For example, you might start with hot water for two minutes, change the temperature to a cold temperature for two minutes, and then end with a hot two-minute shower.

This technique improves blood flow and circulation and may help with inflammation in the body. Athletes already practice showering to help prevent muscle soreness by boosting blood flow and eliminating lactic acid and toxins that build when muscles get worked.

When you have a warm shower, your blood vessels open, your heart rate speeds up, and with a cold shower, your blood vessels constrict, and your heartbeat slows down. The contrast shower stimulates your circulation and may help with fatigue, muscle soreness, and calming your mind.

Many people don't enjoy cold showers except when they're stuck in a "heat wave" and need to cool down. If you're not a fan of a cold shower, try easing into the contrasting shower by allowing cool water to touch your toes (not the midsection near your heart) and do this for a couple of minutes. If you slowly start introducing cool water to your showers, you may find it easier to alternate between cold and hot showers. Be patient and give it time; it won't be something we're excited to do for many of us.

It's essential to check with your healthcare provider before doing this exercise, especially if you're unsure of your health—particularly your heart and blood pressure. Doing this exercise may cause heart arrhythmia in some people, so if you're uncertain if this is safe for you, stick to warm and cool showering and have the water touch your feet instead of your heart region, or have a warm shower.

As well as checking with a healthcare provider if you're unsure, consider the water temperature when you shower. You don't want the water too hot, or it will damage your skin; you also don't want to have a long shower as this will deplete your skin of its natural, protective oils.

TRY THIS

TIME: For this activity, you will need at least 10 minutes.

METHOD: If you feel comfortable practicing this escape and you've consulted your healthcare practitioner, get ready for a "game-changer."

Shower with warm water for two minutes, and then switch to cool water for this exercise. Don't set the water to go from hot to cold; increase the heat and cold slowly over weeks to make this transition easier for you.

Whenever you feel stressed, tired, sore, or sad, hop in the shower and have a contrasting shower. Enjoy!

GRATITUDE JOURNALING

> "The real gift of gratitude is that the more grateful you are, the more present you become." —Robert Holden

Do you have a gratitude journal, or have you heard of this concept? In the last few years, journaling has been gaining popularity because this type of journaling may impact your mental health and life perspective positively.

In an article, *Gratitude Journal: A Collection of 66 Templates, Ideas, and Apps for Your Diary*, found on www.positivepsychology.com, writer Courtney E. Ackerman, MA, states, *"As we recently wrote in a piece on the benefits of gratitude, performing simple daily acts of gratitude can have a big impact on your health and happiness.*

These effects are particularly evident in the practice of gratitude journaling. It only takes a few minutes a day, but it can give you a lasting mood boost that can take you from feeling 'okay' to feeling 'great' on a more regular basis." (17)

The concept of expressing gratitude may have profound effects on our life as we shift our focus from negative to positive thoughts, and if practiced over time, this may change the way we view the world.

There are numerous other benefits to having a gratitude journal, and they include: helping to lower stress levels, gain new perspectives on challenges or what's important, learn more about yourself, be more mindful, focus on the good things, and feel more accomplished. A gratitude journal differs from a diary as a diary consists of a recollection of events in your day. The gratitude journal focuses on the good things that have happened in your life.

This exercise is easy to begin as you need a piece of paper, notebook, or journal to record your thoughts. You want to focus on the positive things that have happened but if you feel inclined to write down the challenges you've faced, show how you are grateful for the lesson you learned.

I prefer to have a journal instead of a sheet of paper. That way, I can keep track of what I'm grateful for and then review the journal, adding to the positive impact. You may purchase a gratitude journal with images or keep it simple and visit a dollar store for a plain journal; it doesn't matter what type of journal your purchase as long as it works well for you.

If you're new to this exercise, this may be challenging when you first begin. The best way to tackle this is to start small. If you are experiencing a lot of stress in your life, and it's not easy to feel grateful, don't be hard on yourself—you may need to wait until you feel positive.

You can start this exercise slowly by simply thinking of three to five things you're grateful for in your life or the last week. Was there a challenge you tackled and solved? How did that make you feel?

You may also ask yourself some of the following questions to get inspired:

If you look at the past year, what are you grateful for?

Who are you thankful for in your life right now?

What abilities, skills, and experience do you possess that you're grateful to have?

Concerning your health, what are you grateful for?

What are you grateful to learn this week?

Instead of questions, you may use the following prompts to start writing:

I had fun this week when —

A good thing that happened to me this week or day was —

I am grateful for my family because —

I am pleased because I have a friendship with — and —

Something good that happened to me this week was —

Today, I accomplished —

A funny thing that happened was —

Someone I was thankful for this week or day was —

Whatever you're grateful for varies from person to person and may range from something as simple as hearing the sounds of birds singing to landing your "dream job." It doesn't matter what you're grateful for as long as it's something positive—that's the only prerequisite for writing in your journal.

Some people focus on gratitude toward friends or family, others may feel gratitude toward non-living and living things, or we may be grateful for opportunities, events, and experiences.

Here are a few other tips to help you maintain your journal:

- Try to do this exercise daily, and if you miss a day, start writing when you can

- Take at least 10 minutes and write in the morning or at night before you sleep
- Keep your journal beside your bed on a nightstand
- Write down as many items as you wish in the journal
- You can use bullet points to list the good things or write sentences, paragraphs, or pages
- List many types of things in your journal

There are many benefits to gratitude journaling. If you consider this exercise, you will find it makes a difference in your life, particularly when faced with stressful and challenging situations. The act of focusing on the positives and what you're learning can make a substantial difference in your life.

TRY THIS

TIME: For this mini-vacation, you need as little as 10 minutes.

METHOD: If you're new to this idea of gratitude journaling, start right by getting a journal that you will enjoy writing in. Don't make it too pretty, or you may be intimated and not use it.

Dedicate time every morning or night before bed to take 10 minutes or longer and record one or more positive things in your life. If you're feeling challenged, choose just one thing you're grateful for and write it down in a bullet point, a sentence, paragraph, or a page.

Over time, you may notice your mind focuses on more positive situations. It takes time, but you are essentially rewiring your mind to see positive outcomes.

DREAM BOXES

> "Life is a box of chocolates. You never know what you're going to get." —Forrest Gump

Years ago, I fantasized about writing a book. While pondering how I would achieve this, a friend told me to grab a large box and fill it with research and ideas for the book. I loved this idea.

Since dreams live in our minds and hearts, and we are a species that loves concrete objects, our dreams disappear unless we can see and act upon them. Having ideas does not help; we have thousands of thoughts every day, and it's easy to forget them.

Many people create vision boards to record their dreams. A vision board may help you focus and clarify your life goals and is often made on cardboard or paper and consists of photos, letters, quotes, handwriting, and anything two-dimensional.

If you love the concept of a vision board but want to take it a step further, try a three-dimensional approach and create a dream box. Your dream box should be large enough to hold papers, journals, photographs, and other items. You may decorate the outside of the box with photography, quotes, and words. It should be personal and portable and a visual interpretation of your dreams.

I bought a large, plastic Rubbermaid container and designated it my dream box. Having a box is a good idea as the contents are kept safe from bugs, water, and other elements. I filled the box with newspaper clippings, business cards, articles, scraps of papers, maps, wish collages, photographs, and small objects within a year. After a year, I had enough information to start writing my first book.

The wish box is similar to a "manifestation box." You set the intention and place things that resonate with this inside the box. The dream/manifestation box benefits include a vision with what you desire, more focus and creativity, and fun. The other pluses are that you could still create a vision board and store the board in the box, along with all the collected objects.

TRY THIS

TIME: For this escape, take 30 minutes or longer to find and create your dream box.

METHOD: Size and materials for your box will depend on you; choose strong materials if you plan on having the box for a long time.

Your box may be plain cardboard, plain wood, or plastic, and you can decorate it.

Designate a time to decorate the outside of your box if you wish. Next, buy a few journals and pens and put them in the box. These will come in handy when you have ideas; it's crucial to have a place to write things down when inspiration hits.

Some people have different boxes for various things in their lives. For example, if you are changing careers, get a decent-sized box and put this somewhere convenient. If you're visiting a career center and pick up brochures or business cards, put them in the box.

If you plan on traveling, create a travel box with brochures, maps—anything to inspire you to make this travel dream happen.

The point is to have fun and create a place to "house your dreams" so they will grow. By physically seeing papers, photos, and objects, you will see evidence that your dream builds day by day.

MAGICAL BOARD GAMES

> "Chess is everything: art, science, and sport." —
> Anatoly Karpov

Did you ever play board games with your family when you were a child? Do you remember beating a family member at *Monopoly, Clue, Scrabble, Trivial Pursuit, Pictionary, Sorry, Chutes & Ladders, Risk,* or *Mousetrap*?

For many of us, board games were a welcome break from school or chores, a great way to connect with friends and family and create some fun memories.

Research indicates that the history of board games dates back several thousand years; there have been board games excavated from ancient sites. The appeal of this gaming format has been around for a long time.

I remember spending many fun hours playing *Monopoly* with my friends and family—this was one of my favorite games. Over the years, I've bought a couple of modernized versions of this game, *Lord of the Rings Monopoly* and *Pirates of the Caribbean Monopoly*, as well as other popular board games.

Playing board games is a respite from screen time and is especially beneficial for young children. When you allow your children to play this game instead of video games and online screen time, this allows your children to practice essential problem-solving cognitive skills. It also creates a stronger connection with your children as you're all playing in the same room.

With the advent of video games and modern technology, one would think that sales of board games would slow down, but it has done the opposite. More people are interested in playing board games because online gaming has called attention to the fun in playing games;

this has opened up the board-game industry, and there are many more new board games.

By introducing board games to children, children may minimize their screen time. Board games are also a great activity for adults as they don't involve blue screens but create stronger connections with family and friends. Board games allow people to talk, think and strategize, share laughter and fun, thus promoting empathy, trust, and strong relationships. Many board games may encourage memory formation, help to speed up your responses, reduce stress, and help reduce risks for mental illnesses.

The *Health Fitness Revolution* article mentions, *"One of the side effects of playing board games is laughing. Laughing has been shown to increase endorphins, those are chemicals that bring up the feeling of happiness. Sharing laughter and fun can promote empathy, compassion, and trust with others."* (18)

I don't need an article or study to convince me that playing board games is beneficial. I need to think about the fun this activity produced when I played as a child or with my children.

TRY THIS

TIME: For this activity, make sure you dedicate 60 minutes or longer.

METHOD: If you don't have any board games or are bored by the ones you own, make a list of ones you'd like to have in your household. Once you purchase games, create your family game night or day and get busy playing.

Some people designate a weekday to game night, and some families do the activity on a rainy weekend—it doesn't matter what you do as long as you infuse some good old-fashioned board game fun into your life.

CHAPTER 5

Quick Escapes

When a lot is going on in your life, it is crucial to engage in a short, fun escape to re-energize yourself. If you do not have a lot of time in your day, why not engage in a quick getaway to have fun and help you relax?

A quick escape may include any activity that is five minutes to a few hours, depending on what it is. The primary consideration is that it easily fits into your busy day and allows you to feel better once you complete it.

Here are a few ideas to get you started.

RELIEF FROM ROUTINE

> "Habit and routine have the unbelievable power to waste and destroy." —Henry de Lubac

Do you have certain routines in your life? There are many benefits to routines; you stay on track, are organized and productive, have structure, and know what to expect with predictable times. Routines can be the key to feeling more secure.

You may have daily routines that include how you start your day, work, spend your free time, and more. These routines often help you save time because you don't have to think too deeply while getting dressed and making coffee. You also save mental energy and complete chores and activities more quickly.

While routine is critical and helps us feel safe as we know what to expect, just like anything, too much of it robs us of creativity, fun, and spontaneity. Sometimes we need the unexpected. Too much predictability in our day makes us move through "autopilot" in our life. For example, if we spend our time scrolling through social media on our phones, we may miss the sights and sounds around us.

If you're feeling bored or disconnected in your life, you may want to infuse more new things into your days. There's a reason why holidays have a magical feel; when we're on vacation, we have less routine in our days, and we experience more novel experiences. We remember more while on vacation because everything is new. When we spend our weekends at home, the hours may blend into each other, and then if we're back to work, we may wonder where our weekend had gone.

When you need to change things up a bit, consider changing your daily routine a little. You may start with your morning and keep it simple by waking up a bit earlier and adding something new to your day. If you typically wake up and start running around in the morning, you might use the earlier wake-up time to meditate, do yoga, take your dog for a walk, or read something inspirational.

If you have the same breakfast every day, you might switch up your breakfast and try something new.

Tiny changes are all it takes to add some novelty to your routine.

TRY THIS

TIME: This activity does not take much time as you can infuse a change in routine into your daily tasks.

METHOD: If you're wondering how to infuse new things into your day, here are a few ideas to get you started:

- Add humor to your day
- Dance, dance—put on some fun music and get your blood flowing
- Sing in the shower
- Do something silly in your day—draw a cartoon, make a funny face, call yourself a different name when you go to your virtual meeting, wear a funny hat, etc.
- Reach out to an old friend
- If you work away from home and drive to work, try a slightly different route coming home
- Eat something you wouldn't normally eat for dinner
- Have breakfast for dinner
- Wear different clothes you wouldn't wear—be bolder in your choice
- Change your surroundings—move a chair, add new pillows or a throw, add decorations, create a piece of art to place in a room
- If you exercise regularly, incorporate a new stretch into your routine
- Add music to your day, listen to new music
- Read a few pages of a book every day

There are many ways to add little things to your daily routine to switch things up. Have fun and be creative, and you'll feel less like you're reliving "Groundhog Day."

SPONTANEOUS DAY

> "To be creative and spontaneous, you have to live with imperfection." —John Abercrombie

When did you stop in to see your friend without warning them via text? Or get in your car and drive to town to wander and look at downtown stores?

Spontaneity gets lost in the chaos of our busy lives. We have scheduled days even when we're not at work. There may be a million errands we need to pack into a Saturday so that we can enjoy our one Sunday before heading back to work for the week.

Our calendars and apps keep us notified of plans, and instant-communication technology allows family and friends to reach out and plan events. While planning can help us be efficient and pack a lot into our days, it can also cause anxiety and stress if we feel that we have to check out digital devices every moment of our day. Sometimes, we need to step away from the highly regimented calendared days and have a day that we call a spontaneity day.

What is a spontaneity day? It is just that. You take a non-work day and avoid planning it out. Instead, you wake up when you do, eat what you want at the last minute, and take the day as it comes. You want to make the day more than just napping all afternoon, though.

This day should take you away from home and engage in something different.

What is the benefit of having a spontaneity day? When we allow our mind to pay attention to the present moment instead of running from one planned activity to another, this is beneficial to our mental and emotional health. When we allow ourselves to have an open schedule, we allow our minds a chance to relax and calm down. We may also be more creative.

If you think back to being a child, you may have had a routine, but there were also many daily moments where you had time to play, daydream, and be in the moment. Sometimes your family would tell you to get in the car and go somewhere with them, and you may have felt it was spontaneous, but you enjoyed the surprise.

Your spontaneity day might have a couple of things you need to complete, but then you want to leave the calendar open to be free to act on impulse. For example, you might be driving to get something from a store, and then you decide to stop off at a local ice-cream shop for a treat. You might walk to a park, eat ice cream, and then relax on a bench. While you're experiencing this, pay attention to the sights and sounds around you, really be in the present moment.

TRY THIS

TIME: For this idea, you want to enjoy being spontaneous, but if a day is a lot of time away from responsibilities, choose an afternoon.

METHOD: Choose a non-work day with minimal responsibilities planned for your spontaneity day. Then, complete the things that must get accomplished and leave most of your day open for fun.

You might randomly phone a friend and arrange to meet somewhere and see what happens after this point. Or, you might go for a walk in your neighborhood or drive to a new area and then have a walk. Perhaps you're craving a treat—you may move around until you see a store with enticing treats.

If you feel creative, pull out a sketchbook, paints, pencils, and pens and randomly draw an object in front of you. Don't worry if you do not feel like an artist—draw something anyway. You can always toss the drawing after.

To make this escape more effective, don't wear a watch or look at your smartphone; turn off notifications for a while and just get lost in the moment of spontaneity.

SIMPLE SEEING

> "If the sight of the blue sky fills you with joy, if a blade of grass springing up in the fields has power to move you, if the simple things of nature have a message that you understand, rejoice, for your soul is alive."
> —Eleonora Duse

How do you see the world? Do you wake up with a sense of awe and wonder, excitement and enthusiasm, or do you wake up anxious and contemplate how many things you must accomplish on your to-do list?

Adults view the world very differently from children. Children see the world as one big adventure and novelty, and they live in the moment because that's all they know. They pay attention to what's in front of them, and they watch and observe and notice everything from big to little things such as worms moving along on the ground, the wind on their face, running their hand over their dog's backside, relishing the flavor of vanilla ice cream and more.

If you find yourself stressed and overwhelmed, consider changing your perspective and viewing the world through the eyes of a child. If you're a parent with younger children, let them be your guide or teacher: sit down and draw with them, play an instrument, walk through a forest, sing, run, lie in the grass—be "in the moment" with them.

I remember working a long day at the office and then rushing to pick up my son at daycare before they closed. My nerves frayed, and I was hungry, stressed out, and tired, and growing more and more impatient as my son ran around the vehicle and then pointed at the ground.

"Mom… Look at this, look at this!" he squealed.

"We have to go. I have to make dinner… Get in the car!" I yelled.

"Mommy…Look! Does this worm have a family?" my son replied.

Suddenly, I stopped in my tracks, walked around the van, and crouched down near my son, sitting on a patch of grass. My elevated blood pressure started to drop; I needed to live in the moment and calm down. I took a few deep breaths and crouched low to the ground beside my son and an earthworm crawling along the ground near a large patch of grass. My son was so excited; this was his moment to study the world. I realized there are more critical things besides errands and work. For the remainder of the day, I paid more attention to my son and his comments and curiosities, and I started looking at my environment with the "eyes of a young, innocent child."

We lose our childlike innocence when going through the school system, live with our families, endure challenges, trauma, and experience the pressures of becoming an adult.

We can begin to recapture our childhood sense of wonder by changing how we visually perceive the world.

There are many ways we can view things, and it starts with our eyes and how we physically see the world. We gain more than 80% of our information through our eyesight, but it's not our eyes that see; our brain that interprets and "sees" the information we receive via the optic nerve.

The amount of visual information that our eyes and brain process is more than we can imagine; the amount of information we absorb would amaze us on any given day.

Imagine you're in a forest and surrounded by trees, and you see a lake in the distance and a cabin by that lake. You're looking at the view and processing and seeing everything appear three-dimensionally;

the trees have individual leaves, there's a reflection of the blue sky and sunlight reflecting off the lake, there's grass moving in a slight breeze, and your brain is recording this information. You may not consciously remember all the details, but your subconscious mind has recorded all this.

You can change your way of seeing by physically slowing down and breathing slowly. Stop what you're doing and stand or sit and look at what you see in front of you.

If you're outdoors, do you see the sun shining, clouds in the sky, a breeze moving leaves in trees, a ripple on a lake? What do you see? Now, crouch down or sit on a park bench and look at the ground. Do you see bugs crawling along the ground? What about stones, branches, or leaves? If you see a bug, what do you see? Do you recognize it?

To have fun, imagine you're a visitor from space, and you've recently landed on Earth and are conducting experiments and gathering data to bring back to your planet. You're studying human civilization and tasked with recording as much detail as you possibly can. This exercise may seem silly and out there, but the point is to get you seeing things in a way that you've long forgotten.

TRY THIS

TIME: For this activity, you need 10 minutes or longer.

METHOD: To begin this activity, you will be focusing on what you can physically see around you. Begin by breathing deeply and slowly and focus your eyes on your current environment.

For example, are you sitting in your office? Are you in front of your computer? What's on your desktop? Are there pictures hanging on the walls? Are there people in the office?

If you're outdoors, where are you? Are you in a park, hiking a trail, biking, walking along a street? What do you see around you, right in front of you and in the distance?

If you're sitting outdoors, what do you see around you? What time of the day is it? What season is it? If it's spring, are there flowers in bloom? Or if it's autumn, are yellow, orange, brown, and red leaves falling from trees?

Take this time to look at your environment around you—really soak in the details. Imagine that you're seeing things for the first time; you're studying the shapes, textures, colors of what you see.

You can take this escape and break it into a mini-break. For example, you might have a day where you go into a park or forest and study different kinds of leaves, or if you enjoy watching birds, you might take your camera and binoculars and visit an area that has a lot of birds. It doesn't matter what type of escape you do as long as you slow down, focus, and pay attention to the little things around you. Keep an open mind and focus on the physical forms of the objects you see in front of you.

ESCAPE TO NAP

> "Think what a better world it would be if we all, the whole world, had cookies and milk about three o'clock in the afternoon and then lay down on our blankets for a nap." —Barbara Jordan

I'm a terrible sleeper. There, I said it. I initially fall asleep quickly but wake up for that annoying trip to the washroom. Being a light sleeper keeps me from a decent sleep. I want a quick 20–30-minute nap, but napping isn't possible with working.

During the early days of the viral pandemic, my sleep deprivation amplified as my mind (like most people's) was overstimulated and stressed. During the day, I felt exhausted and wished I could take a short, recharging nap.

Many of us don't have the luxury of having a nap mid-day.

According to the *National Sleep Foundation,* over 80% of mammalian species sleep for short periods during the day. If you own a dog or a cat, you've probably witnessed their "all-out" napping and may have even experienced pangs of jealousy as you know you have to get back to your work without a nap. Many of us don't nap, but young children and the elderly often do, as do other cultures. It seems others have "figured it out."

There are so many benefits to having a short mid-day nap, including feeling more relaxed and alert, focusing for long periods, enhanced memory and performance, fewer mistakes and accidents. Many catastrophic disasters were caused by human error directly attributed to fatigue.

An article on *Entrepreneur, The How-To: Making Naps Work For You,* mentions, *"Taking 20-30-minute naps can restore alertness, enhance performance, and reduce mistakes and accidents. A study at NASA on sleepy military pilots and astronauts found that a 40-minute nap improved performance by 34% and alertness by 100%. Even companies like Google, Nike, Procter & Gamble, and Zappos are starting to support naps at the office."* (19)

In a day, our brain operates from hyper-aware to sleepy, semi-hypnotic, and other states in between. Having a nap buffer may help boost our focus, memory, and productivity, reduced fatigue, increase alertness, improve mood, and help us relax.

Not everyone can nap. I am one of these people; I can only have a nap if I'm suffering from an illness. And when I do rest, I need to be careful, as I tend to suffer from sleep inertia and wake up feeling disoriented if I sleep more than 20 minutes.

If you're not able to have a nap during the day, do this when you can. If you're a parent, find out if there's someone who could take your children to give you a break. Maybe you could take your close friend's children one weekend and then on another weekend, swap time so you could nap. What about a lazy Sunday?

TRY THIS

TIME: For this activity, you only want 20–30 minutes.

METHOD: Timing is crucial for this mini-vacation as anything longer than 20–30 minutes creates sleep inertia. You may go into a sleep cycle (sleep cycles tend to be 70–90 minutes) and later awake feeling sluggish and groggy. The ultimate nap time is approximately 15 minutes—just long enough to have a mini-break.

Be sure to avoid napping after 3:00 pm as this may interfere with your nighttime sleep. Certain factors such as your sleeping schedule, need for sleep, age, health, and medication use may determine your best time to sleep.

Create a calm, restful sleeping environment. Nap in a dark and quiet place with a low temperature and few distractions. If you live in the city and there is a lot of noise, use earplugs, a white-noise machine, or a fan to dampen the sounds. Make sure you set your alarm to avoid oversleeping.

When you awake from your nap, give yourself time to be present before continuing your activities.

Happy napping!

Lisa Rickwood

GUILTY PLEASURES

> "There is no such thing as a guilty pleasure." — Douglas Wilson

After an anxiety-driven day, you procrastinate and watch funny online animal videos, and before you know it, one hour has passed. You feel a slight pang of guilt as you know you should be making dinner, but the sheer joy of engaging in this small guilty pleasure lifts your stressed-out spirits.

The *Merriam-Webster Dictionary* defines guilty pleasures as "something pleasurable that induces a usually minor feeling of guilt." Guilty pleasures may include things such as watching a television program or a film, playing a video game, listening to a piece of music, eating calorie-ridden food, reading "trashy novels," and other "guilty" pleasures.

For example, people may say they don't enjoy reality television, but they secretly watch a series whenever they can despite knowing their friends find the series "fake."

Ironically, I was writing about the topic of guilty pleasures when I had a knock at my home door. Dressed in a Girl Guide outfit was a young girl of around ten years old. She was selling Girl Guide Cookies for a fundraiser. After giving her money for the cookies, I took the vanilla cookies and started eating them. Immediately my first thought was, *I shouldn't be eating all this sugar.* However, I quickly dismissed this and washed the cookies down with a glass of almond milk.

According to an article, *"Science of guilty pleasures: Study uncovers how feeling bad can boost your happiness,"* by *DailyMail.com* writer, Ellie Zolfagharifard, feeling bad may boost your happiness. She mentions, *"Professor Ravi Dhar from Yale University was inspired to investigate the emotion after watching a colleague eat a chocolate bar, and expressing both enjoying and distaste at the same time. 'For certain types of items, when you feel guilty, you may get more pleasure,' Dhar says. According to Yale Insights, the idea that guilt and pleasure are often tightly coupled in people's minds, so activating one of these concepts can draw out the other."* (20)

One of my guilty pleasures is eating top-quality chocolate; when I feel stressed at work, I ensure I have chocolate near my desk, so I can reach for it when anxiety hits. I usually choose dark chocolate, and then the guilty pleasure is only minimal.

My family knows of my chocolate addiction and often gives me mini care packages featuring chocolate.

TRY THIS

TIME: For this escape, take at least 10 minutes or longer and indulge in something small that gives you pleasure.

METHOD: To decide what makes you feel good, it might include watching animal videos on your smartphone, eating a sweet treat, retail therapy, or some other small indulgence. Think about your feelings while you are engaged in the activity—focus on feeling the pleasure of this escape.

Not sure what guilty pleasure to add to your list? Here are a few ideas:

- Ordering takeout
- Buying a treat for yourself
- Watching cat, dog, or animal videos
- Staying in your pajamas all day
- People-watching
- Eating a bag of chips all at once
- Going back to bed on a Sunday afternoon

- Drinking milk or juice directly from the carton
- Eating food in your bed
- Procrastinating with your chores
- Calling into work sick when you are not
- Binge-watching movies or TV shows but no Internet searching

PROGRESSIVE MUSCLE RELAXATION

> "For every moment of concentration, there is an equal moment of relaxation." —Derren Brown

After two hours of navigating through meetings and online conference calls, you feel your neck and shoulders tense up, and your anxiety levels start to climb. Your body is tense, and you know you need to eliminate this tension quickly.

One of the best ways to relieve tension from stress and lack of activity is to engage in progressive muscle relaxation. With this activity, you tense up muscles while breathing in and then relax them while breathing out. You focus on working on your muscle groups in a specific order. This method is one of the quickest and easiest relaxation exercises and very beneficial.

The technique works because you can't feel stress and anxiety when your body is relaxed. This process takes time to learn, so be patient and practice regularly.

Tensing and relaxing your muscles works to relax your body and mind.

When you practice this stress-busting technique, consider four stages in the process of progressive muscle relaxation. These are: being aware of the tension, tensing your muscles, releasing the tension, and relaxing.

Once you're aware you have tension in your mind and body, start this mini-escape by finding a quiet place where you can lie down and stretch out. Next, you want to focus on your breathing technique. Breathe in and tense your muscles (you choose the area of muscles to start) hard but not painful for 4 to 10 seconds. Then, breathe out and completely relax your muscles. After this, relax for a few seconds before you work more muscles. Pay attention to the difference between your tense and relaxed muscles. Finally, when you've practiced progressive muscle relaxation, count backward from 5 to 1 to bring yourself back to the present.

After you've practiced tensing and relaxing your muscles, you may notice if there's a tense muscle that may need more attention.

Begin at your feet and work up your head, or reverse the order for tensing and relaxing your muscles.

Here are the muscle regions and what you can do:

Hands — clench them into a fist, hold and release

Forearms and wrists — extend them and gently bend your hands back at your wrist

Upper arms and biceps — create a fist with your hands, bend your arms at your elbows and then flex your biceps

Shoulders — shrug them by raising them toward your ears

Back of neck — while lying down, press the back of your head onto the floor

Front of neck — gently try to move your chin to your chest

Chest — breathe deeply and hold for 5 to 10 seconds

Back — arch your back away from the floor in an upward movement

Stomach — pull it in and hold in a tight knot and hold

Buttocks and hips — press and hold your buttocks together tightly

Thighs — clench hard and hold

Lower legs — point toes toward your face and then away from your face

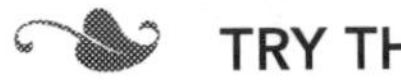 TRY THIS

TIME: For this activity, you need 10 minutes or longer.

METHOD: You can choose to start your muscle progression activity by starting with your head and working down to your toes, or you may wish to start with your feet and work up to your head. Your method will depend on how much time you have and how deep you want to go with these exercises.

When tense and stressed, this activity is a great way to release pent-up anxiety and tension and only takes a few minutes.

YOGA ESCAPES

> "I love yoga. I love the mindfulness of it, where not only are you exercising your body, but you're also building that mind/body connection as far as being aware of every movement - what your body's doing, how your body's feeling." —Miranda Rae Mayo

My mother was an avid follower of yoga, long before it became popular in North America. As a young child, I watched with wonder as my mother stretched her body into difficult, contorted positions on the living-room floor. Mid-pose, she would reach for her black-and-white yoga book to refer to specific poses. The book, *The ABC of Yoga*, was written by Karen Zebroff, a yoga instructor and TV personality.

I was too young to understand the health benefits of yoga; I thought it was slow and silly. Little did I know how powerful it was, and I didn't discover its importance until adulthood.

Yoga is a beautiful form of exercise that combines the breath and body with the mind. If one holds their body in steady poses and controls their breath, they will feel harmony and find a quiet place within.

It is a group of basic movements used to stretch and exercise the body; the poses often use common names such as the cobra, fish, or downward dog.

Yoga is so popular because of its many benefits; it helps you be fit and supple, reduces stress, and balances emotion. You don't need to visit the gym; you can do it in the privacy of your home. Before you begin a yoga program, consult your medical practitioner. Some exercises may not be safe. For example, if you have had a back injury, you may need to avoid certain poses, but there may also be beneficial poses for your back. It is always important to be careful before engaging in a new exercise program.

If you are new to this exercise, you want to research the best alternative. You may wish for a physically demanding class, something more relaxing and meditative, or a yoga program in between these classes.

To get you started, here are eight popular types of yoga:

Hatha is a standard term including many yoga styles that combine breath work with physical postures.

Vinyasa is a term that refers to yoga postures. The movements coordinate with your breath, and the movements flow from one pose to another.

Asthana. The term means *eight-limb path* and refers to a physical and demanding sequence of postures. This style is not for beginners.

It begins with five sun salutation As followed by five sun salutation Bs and evolves into a series of floor postures and standing poses.

Iyana focuses on detailed and precise movement and alignment while performing many postures and controlling the breath. Props get used to help perfect poses. This style is appropriate for those who have had injuries and need to go methodically and slowly.

Kundalini is spiritual and physical and releases kundalini energy trapped in your lower spine. The classes work your breathing and core with fast, invigorating postures using a mantra, meditation, and chanting.

Hot yoga features a sequence of specific poses in a room heated like a sauna, with 40% humidity and 26 basic postures performed twice.

Jivamukti incorporates Vinyasa-style flow using movement and themes, Sanskrit chanting, readings, affirmations, and meditation. Classes often begin with a standardized warm-up sequence, and students continue to educate themselves.

Yin/Restorative is slow-paced with seated postures that get held for a while. Yin is a meditative and slow-paced yoga that allows you to find inner peace.

A final note about the types of yoga

There are lots of yoga practices, and they offer something for everyone. You may ask friends for recommendations or research online to find a suitable yoga practice. When you discover a type or instructor style that is effective for you, stick with it.

When you start something new, have an open mind, and if you're attending a session in person, let your instructor know if you suffer from chronic pain, a health condition, or an injury that would require further modification. Instructors are happy to accommodate you. Yoga provides numerous benefits and is a beneficial practice to add to your life for spiritual, mental, and physical balance.

TRY THIS

TIME: For this escape, you need at least 30 minutes of uninterrupted time to enjoy a yogic session.

METHOD: When you practice yoga depends on you. You may start your day with stretching poses, do yoga in the middle of the day to alleviate desk sitting, or engage in a routine to help your body and mind unwind later in the day. It's up to you.

A couple of quick exercises to get you started:

Your space should be warm and inviting, and you may want to add an exercise mat or a soft blanket on the floor. Make sure you wear loose and comfortable clothing to allow freedom of movement.

Next, sit relaxed with a straight spine in a chair. Close your eyes and imagine you are at your favorite spot; it might be a beach, a camping spot you love, or another magical place. Begin your session with deep breathing. You should see your lower abdomen rise and fall when inhaling and exhaling.

Feel your breath as you let it become longer and longer. After 15 repetitions, let your breathing return back to normal. You should begin to feel more relaxed and calmer.

Begin the yoga session with your hands and knees on the floor (dog position) and keep your hands in front of your shoulders and legs hip-width apart. Inhale and tilt your tailbone and pelvis up and allow your spine to curve down, dropping the abdomen low, lift your head. Stretch gently.

Move into the cat pose by exhaling and reversing the spinal motion, tilting the pelvis down, drawing the spine up, and pulling in your chest and abdomen. Repeat 10 to 20 times, making the movements flow from dog to cat and cat to dog. This exercise is especially great for people who suffer from back pain.

If you wish to learn more about yoga, ask others who regularly attend classes and review types of yoga and how to practice.

Before you know it, you will relax to the magic of yoga.

SHORT STORY

> "Not that the story need be long, but it will take a long while to make it short." —Henry David Thoreau.

Have you ever read a short story that was so riveting you wished you had written it? From the moment you read the first lines until you finished, you felt entranced; the appeal was that it kept your interest and was a quick read.

Since our world is so fast-paced and people may not have time or patience to read a long novel, they may be interested in a short story that satisfies their interest in fiction. The appeal of a short story is you may read it while your wait at a medical office, on a bus or subway, or during a lunch hour. A great time to read a short story is at night just before you go to sleep; it's a great way to unwind and slow down your mind while taking you away from blue screens.

As a reader, you have many options for short stories. Novellas and short stories are abundant in the marketplace, so there are many choices for the genre. Anthologies are popular as many authors enjoy collaborating with other authors; this is a great way to find many stories wrapped into one book.

E-books have grown in popularity, and this interest has led to a growing market of numerous titles available for avid short-story readers.

What if you're not just interested in reading short stories? What if you've had a dream of writing a book? Many people dream of writing a book but don't do it because it feels too daunting and overwhelming. Many people live busy lives, and writing a book seems too "far-reaching" and "not realistic." Writing short stories is more appealing as it takes minimal time to craft than writing a book.

Short stories and novels may seem very different but what they have in common is they must tell a story, have proper grammar and spelling, and be coherent. The plot has five parts: an introduction, inciting problem, rising action, a climax, and falling action toward a conclusion.

When a novelist writes their book, they decide on the length, while short-story writers need to consider how many words their manuscript will be and work within these confines. Therefore, short stories generally focus on one part of a character's life or a relationship or challenge in a character's life.

Being aware of the structure and format for writing stories makes it easier to think about stories you want to write.

Writing a great short story also involves putting the majority of the story into the beginning with an obvious plot, thus allowing readers to be "pulled in" and inspired to keep reading the story.

You may include a bit of a backstory but make sure it's not too elaborate; there needs to be a reason for a character's motivation.

When writing a short story, there should be a small number of characters, and you may include a protagonist, antagonist, and a relationship character. To advance the antagonist or protagonist character, readers need to have someone to hate, like, and another character to move the antagonist or protagonist character.

However, if you want a simple short story, you may focus on one main character. You'll want to create a protagonist that readers appreciate if you choose just one character. It is effective for your character to have weaknesses readers understand, the determination that drives the person, shared by your reader.

Once you decide on your character or characters, there will need to be friction that adds tension for the character; bad things need to happen to test them and their strength. The conflict in the story may consist of a decision, dilemma, or revelation.

To make the reader feel like they are in your story, you need to use five senses to give them this experience. It's the concept of showing and not telling. For example, you may write, "The smell of large, barbequed steaks sizzling on the barbeque made John's mouth water and his stomach growl."

While these tips and strategies add to creating a short story, nothing makes the story come alive until you add convincing dialogue. One of the best ways to make this happen is to ensure tight dialogue, and you need to read it aloud to ensure it feels in-character and realistic.

Once you've done all this, the final step, editing, is the key to a tight, well-paced short story. Eliminate repetitive words, make all sentences count, "show," and eliminate unnecessary adjectives and adverbs. Having another person read and edit your story is all the better.

TRY THIS

TIME: For this escape, take 30 minutes and read a short story or a few pages from an anthology.

METHOD: If reading a short story inspires you to write, consider writing a short anecdote.

While it's tempting to write your story on a computer, challenge yourself by writing a scenario on loose-leaf paper or an old journal book.

Not sure what short story to write? Consider some of your dreams or events that happened during a busy week. Embellish the story, add interesting characters and challenges, and start writing.

For example, if you picked up a lotto ticket on the way home from work, you might create a short story around discovering that you just won a million dollars.

Or you might start with a sentence and then create a story. For example, "As Zachary walked away from an ATM after grabbing several hundred dollars, he quickly became aware of a dark, hooded figure following him toward his car."

With this sentence, you could create an intriguing, spell-bound short story.

PHOTOGRAPHIC MEMORIES

> "Not everybody trusts paintings but people believe photographs." —Ansel Adams

Have you ever taken a photograph that held deep meaning for you? Years ago, I took a photo of my grandparents at my cousin's wedding. It was a beautiful, sunny day, and my grandparents were happy, and the background was exceptional—gorgeous ocean views. I never realized how precious that photo was until years after my grandparents passed.

Years after I found this photograph, I was spring-cleaning my basement and found an old cardboard box filled with black-and-white photography; they were photos of my grandparents when they were young children, and these pictures were over 100 years old. I loved how my family seemed immortalized in these ancient black and white images.

Photography adds value to our lives. We capture many moments in time— vacations, people, special occasions, hobbies, and more. From your birth, first tooth, visit at kindergarten, grade school, graduation, and other events, these moments were often recorded in time using photographs. You're able to share your life experiences in meaningful ways through images, printed or online.

Photography also sparks your imagination, and it's a great stress reliever. When taking photographs, you mentally slow down when you study the environment. Your mind looks for creative, artistic shots you might not typically notice.

If you're talented at taking photographs, you may turn your passion for pictures into a part-time or full-time business. There are many ways you can sell photography online.

One of my favorite escapes is taking photographs. I love to focus on nature and specialize in macro photography. Viewing plants, animals, and insects up close makes me slow down and relax. I love this escape.

I took some of my photos and transferred a photographic image onto canvas, and then added oil paint to the picture to create a unique mixed-media painting. I have quickly sold these because the effect is dramatic; one painting was a close-up macro shot of a bumblebee straddling a flower and obtaining nectar. This photograph was a one-in-a-million shot.

In the past, photography was more cumbersome as you used a large camera and lenses. Now, the digital revolution has made it easy to be a photographer because you can use your portable smartphone.

There are many free and paid online courses for aspiring photographers.

The popularity of visual imagery continues to grow; technology allows more people to take professional photography, using filters and other effects.

TRY THIS

TIME: For this adventure, you want 30 minutes or longer to enjoy the activity.

METHOD: When you're feeling stressed, anxious, or "out of sorts," grab your smartphone or camera and consider exploring your world.

You may go out in nature and consider taking photographs of trees and branches, leaves, driftwood, grass, flowers, fields, orchards, and more. When you photograph the outdoors and nature, consider lighting—early morning, golden hour, and sunset. Seasons, times of the day, types of weather also make a difference in photography.

If you consider using a water theme for your picture-taking, take pictures of rain, waves, ice, snow, steam, creeks, and rivers.

Many of us enjoy taking photographs of others, but we take the same photos each time. As well as taking posing pictures of people, try candid shots; these are often more interesting as they capture an unexpected moment. You might take photos of your family or friends.

Our pets are considered family, and many people take pictures of their cats or dogs and post the photography online.

If you need something to photograph, special events such as weddings, sports events, festivals, parades, markets, and concerts are good subject matter for photographs.

Architecture is also a great subject matter for taking photographs. You might focus on old buildings and ruins, interiors, exteriors, and barns.

Photographing images of food, crafts, artwork, and objects is also fun to do.

The technique is crucial when capturing your images. Consider whether you will photograph your image in black and white, use silhouettes, close-ups, shadows, reflections, angles, and specific lighting.

A good exercise is to choose ten things you see in front of you but never really notice. Take one of these subjects and practice taking photographs of the person, place, or object.

Another fun project is choosing a favorite outdoor spot and taking a photo every month, paying attention to the changing of the seasons and the effects. Over time, you'll also notice how your skills and inner creativity are growing.

Once you have images you enjoy, the fun begins. With the advance of technology, images can be altered, changed, and transferred to products such as canvas wall hangings, calendars, duvet covers, digital frames, mousepads, rugs, furniture, and much more.

There is power in photography as art as it inspires us to see the world in new ways.

FARMERS' MARKET VISIT

> "What makes the farmers' market such a special place is that you're actually creating community around food." —Bryant Terry

A great and unexpected escape may be visiting a farmers' market. There are many benefits to visiting a local farmers' market, including access to healthier and tastier produce, supporting your local community, food that doesn't travel far from field to table, more affordable organic produce, and knowing the history of the food.

A great reason to buy produce at the farmers' market is that even the freshest vegetables and fruits at a grocery store are still a few days old, while the farmers' market produce may only be a few hours or a couple of days, and the food will be more nutrient-rich. Nutrients start to diminish as produce sits on a shelf. You may get organic produce cheaper as the farmer may avoid shipping and other added expenses.

If you have children, taking them to a farmers' market is integral to their learning as they can study healthy food, where it comes from, and how to grow it. Children should learn about growing food; it may inspire them to be more environmentally responsible as they grow up.

Learning where food comes from and how to grow it is more important than ever. In the past, we may have experienced food insecurity. When you visit a farmers' market, you help support local farmers and their families, and the money you spend directly impacts the community, allowing growers to continue the cycle of providing fresh, local food. Supporting the markets helps the environment because the food does not have to travel far from the farm to your table, so transportation costs, fossil fuels, and packaging for shipping are less expensive.

The benefit of attending farmers' markets is that you can speak with the growers and get inside information, recipes, and tips to prepare the food. Farmers will often show you foods you might not get in the local grocery store.

Another great reason to escape to a farmers' market is being outdoors as you walk from vendor to vendor, experiencing the sights, fresh air, and sunshine.

While you may visit a market for fresh produce, you may also experience live music and entertainment, and you may see arts and crafts, furniture, clothing, beauty products, and more. Sometimes you discover products you would never see at any retail store.

TRY THIS

TIME: For this escape, take two hours or longer to enjoy at a farmers' market.

A great way to make this fun is to make a list of upcoming and regular farmers' markets in your town or city and surrounding areas. Write down the dates and times of the events, and plan to attend.

To make this more of an adventure, bring family or friends. It is more fun to have someone with you to share the experience.

Happy escaping!

LIKE A TOURIST

"Not all those who wander are lost." —J.R.R. Tolkien

Years ago, my family had the honor of hosting a traveler from Finland as part of a Rotary Club program that focused on sending young professionals to other countries to study how people in other countries worked in the same industries. This traveler was a curator for a famous museum in Finland.

Having this young woman stay in our home for a week was inspiring as we learned first-hand about Finland. I had time to spend with her, and she wanted to see the sights and experience the sounds of my small city. I'd been living in my hometown for a few years and never thought about places to visit; I just lived and worked there.

While I was planning activities for her, I saw things from her perspective—the eyes of a tourist—and I started planning fun and unusual excursions for us to do.

It was enjoyable to spend time with her and see things in a "new" way. I'd taken my city for granted and hadn't engaged in fun and touristy things. Her enthusiasm was addictive, and I found myself doing tourist-type activities after she returned to Finland.

I hadn't visited my local museums—a military museum and a museum dedicated to the history of my region. Spending a rainy day visiting these places was well worth the time, as I learned a lot about the local area and had a "great escape" as a tourist in my town. My museum tourist day was fun, and I created "theme" tourist days.

You don't have to travel a long distance to enjoy relaxing, sightseeing, adventure, and culture. Being a tourist in your hometown is a great way to enjoy your day, and you can plan the excursion or go and explore.

An article by Stacey Leasca called, *New Study Suggests Exploring Your Own Town Can Be Good For Your Mental Health,* on the *Travel + Leisure* website, states, *"The experiences didn't need to be large. Instead, the findings simply found that those who traveled around their own neighborhoods rather than sitting at home all day were happier."* (21)

If you decide on new places to visit, go online to find coupons, discounts, and specials on restaurants, events, and activities. Grab a copy of your local city guide as it often lists many tourist attractions that you may have forgotten to consider.

Try out new restaurants you haven't eaten at, visit museums in your area and find the best parks, wooded areas, lakes, rivers, bridges, and outdoor areas to visit and possibly enjoy with a picnic.

If you plan to see a music concert, book a hotel ahead of time so you can relax and enjoy the music and later return to the hotel. You'll feel like you're away on vacation and not have the hassle of traveling home.

If city walking or bus tours are available, consider attending them to view your city from a new light. City tours may include food tours, artist, and wine tours.

Like many, I enjoy a good glass of wine and love traveling on wine tours to vineyards on Vancouver Island. The best days consist of going with friends, planning the lunch ahead of time, and then visiting other vineyards along the way, purchasing wine at the vineyards.

As well as the personal benefits of being a tourist in your region, you are doing something important for local businesses; the pandemic was unkind to many industries, and having the support of locals is the key to recovery. Some attractions that enrich our lives also exist because of a charitable model; supporting them ensures they may survive and strengthen the local economy by providing jobs and keeping money in your local region.

TRY THIS

TIME: For this escape, you may take two hours or a day to be a tourist in your home town.

Check with your friends, neighbors, or colleagues on places to go and make sure you keep track of their suggestions. You may wish to keep an inexpensive journal that you can use to write down ideas and inspiration for your next adventure.

Try new food at a different restaurant, see a sports event or a play or participate in local customs in your city. Even just walking downtown can be an adventure, depending on your city.

Whether you plan or take a few hours to explore your region, you will learn about that area's history, culture, art, and industries. You may experience new sights and sounds, and it may be a great escape that takes you away from the everyday.

FRIENDLY ESCAPES

> "Having a best friend is like having your own little corner of the world to escape to." —Unknown

Do you remember your childhood friends? Do you remember those endless days when you had adventures with them and sat and talked into the wee hours of the night? How about now? Do you have a close group of friends or one or two people you spend a lot of time with? Is there someone who knows you better than others?

True friendship adds a lot to our lives, and we need those friendships from our teens to our old age. While we may not have as much time to nurture our friendships during the years when we're working and juggling family obligations, we still need them.

Friends help share our sorrows and joys and the inevitable ups and downs in life. They often witness rites of passage like marriage, having children, deaths, and other important milestones. They are there to see that you are living and experiencing life; they may become like family and maybe easier to speak to as they may not be as judgemental as family.

Friends inspire you to be active, have fun, and introduce you to new ideas or experiences. They hear your secrets, boost your self-confidence, love you, offer honesty, improve your mental health and relationships, mitigate stress, motivate you, help you be more social, and add more meaning to your life.

I remember reading an article about how the elderly regretted not spending enough time with their friends.

In an article by Kira M. Newman, *Why Your Friends Are More Important Than You Think,* in *Greater Good Magazine by* the *University of Berkeley,* the author states, *"A similar thing happens in our own lives, writes science journalist Lydia Denworth. When something's gotta give, it's often our friendships, which take a backseat to our family and work obligations—or our latest fling.*

But that's a mistake, she argues in her new book, Friendship: The Evolution, Biology, and Extraordinary Power of Life's Fundamental Bond. In fact, research suggests that friendships can help us find purpose and meaning, stay healthy, and live longer. The intimacy, support, equality, and emotional bonds we have in our friendships are unique." (22)

When we get challenged in our lives, we need our friends. While reaching out to family is important, sometimes we find it a challenge with some family members, and our friends may offer us understanding and lack of judgment. As the saying goes: You can't choose your family, but you can select your friends.

TRY THIS

TIME: For this activity, you want to have 60 minutes or longer to spend.

METHOD: Spending time with friends is always important, especially when feeling challenged. Look at your week ahead and see how you might reach out to a friend—either video chatting or meeting up.

You might spend one week updating your friend contact list to ensure you have the latest ways to reach them. Create a list of friends you wish to visit, and then add them to your calendar to ensure you make time to talk to them and not feel rushed.

Next, you might phone or video chat with friends you haven't spoken to in a while.

Plan an event you and a friend can do together. The activity might be a picnic, going for a tea or coffee, walking through a park, hiking through a forested area—whatever it is, make sure the activity is enjoyable for you both.

Next, make a list of things you can do with your friends. Here are just a few ideas; you will likely have more after reading these:

- Explore a new city together
- Volunteer at a cause you both appreciate
- Enjoy lunch at your favorite spot
- Picnic somewhere beautiful
- Take a funny selfie of each other
- Go on a camping trip
- Enjoy a beach day—picnic optional
- Throw a dinner party
- Go on a wine-tasting adventure
- Play mini-golf
- Enjoy a board-game night
- Face your fear— try something new like bungee-jumping
- Enjoy an arts and crafts day
- Create vision boards of your dreams
- Attend an outdoor music festival
- Hike or backpack somewhere you haven't been to
- Play music together
- Learn a new language and practice together
- Learn to write a funny screenplay together
- Take an online cooking class together
- Learn to juggle

Great friends make the world go around!

PRECIOUS PETS

> "We may have pets, but when it comes to unconditional love, they are the masters." —Donald L. Hicks

Did you grow up with pets? Or did you spend more time with your pet during the pandemic? Perhaps you didn't have a pet but challenging times inspired you to adopt one.

As far back as I can remember, I've been fortunate enough to grow up with pets—dogs and cats. When my parents moved to acreage, we also had geese and chickens at one point in time. Spending time with animals was a wonderful experience as a child.

My first memories of having a pet were when I was two or three years old, and my parents had a cream-colored, fluffy cat. I loved following around the cat and cuddling with it.

When I was five, I remember having a Labrador Retriever named Frodo. My parents loved *The Lord of the Rings* books, and that's where he received his name. I used to go on hikes with him up a mountain behind our house; he was a very faithful companion.

Over time, I had a few other dogs as we moved to another city and had property, and a couple of the dogs either ran away or got sick and passed away. My mother loved Bearded Border Collies as they were affectionate and intelligent dogs, so we owned one for a few years, and when he passed away, we got another one.

During my formative years, I considered being a veterinarian. However, that was before one of my dogs, Chico, a Doberman Pinscher cross, was shot with a 22-caliber gun because he was stealing chickens from a neighboring farm.

I remember Chico's chest wound, and after taking him to the veterinarian, receiving news that the bullet missed his internal organs. My mother saved me countless years of vet school and bills by doing me a favor—getting me to take care of Chico while he healed. It wasn't a pleasant experience changing very nasty dressings and witnessing his pain. After a couple of months of doing this, I decided against attending veterinary school when I graduated.

On my childhood property, we also had cats, and they would have kittens. I recall seeing the kittens all nuzzled up with the Bearded Border Collies, resting on the grass. It was the sweetest sight.

There are many health benefits to having a pet as they may increase your chances of exercising outdoors and socializing. From a health standpoint, regular walking with pets helps to decrease your cholesterol levels, blood pressure, and stress levels. Having a pet in your life can help minimize loneliness and anxiety.

According to an online website, *webmd.com,* pets improve your health by boosting your mood, increasing your exercise levels, giving you stronger immunity, and so much more.

If you have a pet in your life, think about how you spend your days with them. What can you do to spend more time and do more with your pet?

TRY THIS

TIME: You want to spend as much time as you can allot with your pets for this activity.

METHOD: If you own a cat, there are many things you can do to improve and strengthen your relationship and have more fun with them. Some activities you may try include: getting cardboard boxes and putting holes in them for the cat to go inside, buying catnip toys, a feather and string toy, food hunting, hide-and-seek, or taking your cat for a walk outdoors.

- Other things you can do include:
- Cuddling with your cat.
- Creating a cat treat puzzle.
- Teasing your cat with a laser pointer.
- Making some homemade cat treats.
- Getting a cat climber and placing it near a window.
- Getting some interactive toys.
- Playing with your cat.

If you have a dog, you can do a lot with them, including going for a walk, throwing a ball or a stick, hiding treats inside or outside, going on a road trip with them to a new environment, running or swimming at a beach, lake, or river. You can also visit an off-leash dog park, take an obedience or agility raining class or create a dog puzzle. Other activities include: teaching your dog a new trick, running through a sprinkler, throwing a Frisbee, or cuddling on the couch with your dog.

CHAPTER 6

Fun and Creative Pursuits

Do you remember having fun and being creative as a child? Do you feel like these abilities have drastically dwindled due to never-ending adulthood concerns?

It is crucial to allow ourselves to be creative and have fun. We learn more quickly, feel less stress and anxiety, connect to creative activities and people, and have fun.

If it has been a while since you experienced this, you owe it to yourself to begin today.

TRY SOMETHING NEW

> "I like to challenge myself. I like to learn – so I like to try new things and try to keep growing." —David Schwimmer

Here's a question for you. In this last year, did you try something new? If you haven't tried anything new in a while, it's time to do so. You don't have to get into extreme sports but experiencing something different is good. It takes courage and allows you to explore and grow and break free of a boring routine.

We are creatures of habit and do the same things day after day, but if we become aware of the importance of trying new things, we may add new adventures to our lives. Trying new things allows us to learn more about new ideas, break up boredom and routines, and discover new things. We also boost our confidence and grow as a person.

Harvard Health Publishing published an article, *Rev up your thinking skills by trying something new.* The report states, *"It turns out that the human brain has a great potential for something called neuronal plasticity—that is, it's malleable. It appears that challenging our brains—for example, learning a new skill—leads to actual changes in the adult brain. 'It may create new connections between brain cells by changing the balance of available neurotransmitters and changing how connections are made,' says Dr. Papp."* (23)

Trying new things and going outside of your comfort zone may lead you to many interests or even a brand-new career.

When I worked in employment services, I took a chance outside my comfort zone to facilitate a workshop for job seekers after a colleague stated they were unavailable to attend. The first workshop I facilitated was terrifying, and I experienced anxiety. The participants seemed to learn a lot from the session, and after several weeks, management created a full-time position for me to facilitate workshops. I never imagined my job role would change from venturing out of my comfort zone; I discovered untapped skills.

When you take a chance and try something new, you may discover new interests, skills, and "hidden" talents you possess. Your life gets enriched, and others will also gravitate to you more if you have many interests.

Consider activities that allow for brain stimulation and social and physical activity if you're unsure where to begin. You might play a new sport, learn a new language, discover dance steps, engage in an art form, or take a new course.

If you're unsure about new things to try, see if there's something from this list that may inspire you:

- Take singing lessons or learn a new instrument
- Learn new dance moves and practice
- Start learning a new language
- Take a yoga class
- Take a martial arts course
- Plant a garden and plant new things
- Try kayaking or stand-up paddleboarding
- Camp under the stars
- Learn to ride a motorcycle
- Take a course in a subject not related to your career
- Visit a new restaurant or order takeout from the restaurant
- Meditate or try a new way to meditate
- Try a new hobby—sewing, woodworking, restoration, etc.
- Try a new way to exercise—be sure to get medical advice or professional advice to exercise safely and efficiently
- Visit a different grocery store and buy foods that you never eat
- Learn and practice a new art form
- Try a new sport such as badminton, lacrosse, tennis, pickleball, etc.
- Take photography lessons and practice
- Take dancing lessons
- Write an article, blog, submit a poem, etc.
- Take cooking lessons or try new recipes
- Do a video cooking lesson online with other people
- Get to know a neighbor
- Read a book that you would not read

- Listen to music that's not on your playlist

Write out a new things-to-do list you can review and check things off that list.

Enjoy!

TRY THIS

TIME: You want to have at least 30 minutes for this activity.

METHOD: Whether you take cooking lessons, try learning a new instrument, or learn a new language, you will need to be patient and dedicate a specific amount of time to learning.

Learning new things makes you get outside your comfort zone, face your fears or insecurities, and boost your immune system. Doing new things helps you be more creative and break out of ruts, so enjoy the process.

NEW NOVELTIES

> "I hope that in this year to come, you make mistakes. Because if you are making mistakes, then you are making new things, trying new things, learning, living, pushing yourself, changing yourself, changing your world. You're doing things you've never done before, and more importantly, you're doing something." —Neil Gaiman

Have you done something new recently? How did that feel? Was it scary and invigorating at the same time? In life, unexpected events can change even the most organized people.

I always planned to offer in-person workshops to job seekers. However, after an unexpected global pandemic, I was suddenly learning new online platforms, so I could continue working and helping clients. All of this was new and exciting but also scary. I was reluctant to be on camera as I preferred to be behind the scenes, and this new way of working was a steep learning curve. Like many people, I had to get used to seeing and hearing myself on camera; this was very uncomfortable. However, after several months, it became routine, and I gained new skills, which allowed for valuable information to reach more people.

I discovered that learning new things seemed to make time slow down; I paid more attention to my days because there were more novel things to enjoy. This idea sparked interest in adding more new activities to my life. I wanted to gain new skills and improve my abilities.

In an article by Steve Taylor, *The Conversation, Feel like time is flying? Here's how to slow it down*, the author states, *"In my book Making Time, I suggest a number of basic 'laws' of psychological time, as experienced by most people. One of these is that time seems to speed up as we get older. Another is that time seems to slow down when we're exposed to new environments and experiences.*

These two laws are caused by the same underlying factor: the relationship between our experience of time and the amount of information (including perceptions, sensations, and thoughts) our minds process. The more information our minds take in, the slower time seems to pass." (24)

There are so many positives to learning new things.

What have you learned in the last year or two? What is your takeaway?

TRY THIS

TIME: For this escape, you can take an afternoon or longer, depending on your new passion.

METHOD: If you don't know what new things to incorporate into your life, see if any of these ideas inspire you:

- Learn a new language
- Travel somewhere new
- Try a new profession in a different industry
- Train for a marathon or triathlon
- Write a song
- Learn to play an instrument
- Be a guest on a podcast
- Try a new sport
- Try a board game or strategy game
- Volunteer or mentor someone
- Pursue a long-enjoyed passion
- Start your business or a side hustle
- Sing to an audience or play an instrument
- Dance in the rain or walk barefoot in the grass
- Get a new pet
- Write and publish a book
- Public speak in front of an audience (in person or online)
- Get a complete makeover
- Take a course or enroll in a program
- Learn new dance moves
- Learn martial arts
- Road trip somewhere
- Act in a film (self-produced or otherwise)
- Get featured in the media for an accomplishment

- Listen to music from another country or a new genre
- Read a book about a new subject
- Send a great review to your favorite company—write an old-fashioned letter and send it
- Have a "strange food" week—buy unusual food and figure out how to prepare it
- Face the biggest fear and work on improving
- Picnic somewhere unusual
- Design/Create a new "superhero"—draw it, create a costume, write a comic, etc.
- Meet someone you only dream of meeting
- Learn sign language and teach others
- Wear a superhero costume to work for a pick-me-up and to add "fun" to work for you and others
- Start a website or blog—use your talents and help others
- Look into "living off the grid"—if you're more interested, start doing more research
- Create art—photography, painting, video, etc.

Want to add more excitement to your life? Try something new – you will walk away learning so much about yourself and the world. Enjoy!

INCREDIBLE INNOVATION

> "I think all great innovations are built on rejections."
> —Louise Nevelson

Years before computers were our mainstay, my grandfather, an electrical engineer, drew designs for innovations on paper. He loved the idea of creating a solution to fix something in his life.

My grandfather had an attic storage space that annoyed him because he had to get a ladder; it was unstable when he climbed up to the attic. In his studio, he drew out a design for a fold-down ladder. After a few days, he created a ladder that folded down from the ceiling; the concept was simple, slick, and convenient. My grandfather always invented something to make his life easier; I mentioned he could market his ideas, but he didn't care as he liked a challenge and enjoyed making things better in his life.

Innovation may happen in your life when you notice a problem or challenge that needs to be solved, and you believe that "there has to be a better way."

For years, there have been shows on television such as *Shark Tank* or *Dragon's Den* that cater to entrepreneurs that have created something that's turned into a business. People may not have planned to be entrepreneurs, but they solved a personal problem and discovered a market for their products or service. Many parents have faced challenges while caring for their children; products evolved to improve their lives: carrying cases, new bottle holders, heated baby wipes, creative toys, and more.

You don't have to create a new invention, service, or run a company to take advantage of the innovation escape. Innovation refers to devising a new idea, product, or service to improve efficiency or effectiveness. Being more innovative may help with your personal development, self-employment, or if you currently work for an organization or company.

So, what do you do if you don't feel very creative or innovative? There are many things you can do to reignite that spark in you. The first thing to do is to think like a child. Children are curious, ask many questions, and aren't afraid to make mistakes. These two concepts alone allow them to create and have an innovative mindset. As we grow up, we often don't ask enough questions and fear making mistakes (which allow for learning and growing).

Have a journal (paper or online) to write down your ideas and thoughts as they come to you. It may include words, drawings, phrases, and more. When you write down your ideas, don't edit them right away; record the information and avoid judgment. The craziest ideas sometimes spark inspiration and may be the missing piece in a challenge or solution; these ideas may lead to even better thoughts.

Doing things the same way all the time doesn't spark new ideas; your thinking is limited, and you're living in your comfort zone and not learning or doing new things. The best way to spark innovation is to seek new experiences such as traveling, eating or cooking foods, learning a new language, playing an instrument, trying new hobbies or sports, reading books in new genres, or listening to new music.

If you have a big idea and aren't sure how viable it is, share it with those you trust; running your thoughts by someone you respect and admire will help when you see if it's worth pursuing.

Make mistakes and be persistent; many innovations take many "tries" and "fails" before working. If you feel frustrated, take some breaks to relax your mind; even getting bored can lead to innovation.

TRY THIS

TIME: For this activity, take at least 30 minutes or longer.

METHOD: This escape can happen anytime you keep your mind "open" and "think like a child and engage your curious side."

To start this escape, ask yourself: *What can I do to improve or add something great to my work or personal life?* This question may spark some ideas so ensure you have a way to record them.

Keep a journal nearby and ensure you write down ideas as they come to you. If you're a three-o'-clock idea person, make sure to write down your thoughts while you still remember them. They may seem crazy at the time, but you never know what the ideas may lead to as you look to solve a challenge or problem.

CREATIVE VISUALIZATION

> "Creative visualization may be described as an extended meditation session that reaches beyond passive contemplation and achieves transformative action. The uses to which it may be applied are limited only by an individual's imagination." —Aberjhani

Have you ever thought about something you wanted, and it showed up in your life? Maybe you recorded your ideas in a journal, created a goal sheet, and displayed it where you could see it every day. Were you surprised this person, place, event, or object showed up in your life? Did it seem like a coincidence or luck?

Creative visualization is a mindfulness technique that uses your imagination to create your reality. Imagine Olympic athletes preparing for their event if this sounds hard to believe. What do they do to get ready?

Athletes take time to meditate, and they visualize winning the event; they imagine every moment from putting on their uniform to the moment they are standing on the podium.

For example, in an experiment conducted years ago, scientists hooked up electrodes to the brain of an Olympic sprinter athlete in the hopes of measuring brain activity as the athlete imagined running their race. They visualized putting their feet on the starting blocks, hearing the sound of the gun, racing down the track, coming across the finish line first, hearing the cheers from the crowd, feeling a cool breeze across their face, hearing the pounding of their chest, and finally receiving a gold medal on the podium.

When scientists studied the athlete visualizing running a race, the study indicated that the same brain regions that lit up when the athlete was doing the activity also lit up when they imagined the event. This experiment proved the unconscious human mind couldn't discern between reality and thoughts about reality.

Creative visualization helps you use your imagination to create what you want to happen in your life, and it is a type of mindfulness exercise that can inspire success in all areas of your life. It uses your thoughts to imagine, design, and attract what you want in your life. You have direct control over your subconscious thoughts and using visual imagery helps you manifest what you desire. Adding emotion to this technique helps tap into your deeper feelings and subconscious thoughts.

If you're new to practicing creative visualization, you'll need to practice it frequently to gain benefits. You are training your brain and rewiring new neural networks, and it takes time to make changes. Mastering this process allows you to make changes more quickly than many other methods.

TRY THIS

TIME: For this escape, you want to put aside approximately 30 minutes to find a quiet, undisturbed place to practice creative visualization. You may practice in your parked car, empty office, bedroom, or outdoors—wherever you can think quietly and focus.

METHOD: Calm down and relax by finding a comfortable place to sit. Start by emptying your mind and body and do this by sitting upright, breathing deeply, and counting slowly from 30 to 1 while relaxing your body from head to toe.

Next, imagine your outcome and think in the present tense by visualizing the plan like a movie; concentrate on the picture and engage your senses. For example, if you imagine you have a new job, visualize the first day of work. What are you wearing? What do you see when you enter the building? Who greets you, and how does the staff treat you? What do you do for that first day of work? What is your role in the company? Imagine feeling happy, excited, and inspired. Imagine the office has an essential oil diffuser infusing a light aroma of lemon into the air. The more senses you engage in your imagination, the more you will feel and the more it will resonate on a deep, subconscious level.

In the next step, feel the excitement of achieving your goal. What are you feeling? Are you excited and happy? Your emotions create energy in motion—they inspire you to take action.

To create power in this method, you need to believe you've already achieved what you want. It's not about lying to yourself or wishful thinking; it's the idea that "what you believe the mind can conceive." Bob Proctor, a motivational coach, world-renowned speaker, and Law of Attraction teacher, once mentioned in a speech that everything you see was created twice, first in the mind and then in physical form.

If you consider this, you realize this is true. Everything around us started as a thought in the mind before it appeared in reality. Any time you put on your clothes, eat from a bowl, drive a vehicle, decorate your space or hang pictures on walls, this law comes into effect.

Finally, once you visualize an outcome you desire, you need to detach from the final result. It may not occur if you hang on too tightly to an idea because you strip yourself of your power to create your outcome.

Don't believe me? If you're single or were and you found yourself desperately looking to find a partner, it probably didn't happen quickly.

The moment you start dating someone, you probably find other people wanting to spend time with you. Where were they when you were single?

Once you practice this process, be sure to practice every day—preferably early in the morning and then the evening before you sleep. These times are powerful as the mind is in a semi-relaxed state and is more open to suggestions.

Finally, when you complete creative visualization, get back to your day and think positive.

POETIC PASTIME

> "For this reason, poetry is something more philosophical and more worthy of serious attention than history." —Aristotle

Does your life flow like elegant prose or fall like a shattered limerick? If your life's pace is scattered and stressed, you may need to escape to poetry. Poetry has been used for centuries to express deep feelings and help lovers impress their beloved. If poetry conjures up thoughts of failing high-school literature class, be patient—poetry can be fun.

Whether you read Robert Frost or poetry written by a family member, you'll feel your mind switch to a lower gear when you follow this poetic escape.

If you order a poetry anthology online or find an old book at home, flip through the pages and find a poem that speaks to you. Study it and decide what the verse is saying. Why did you choose the poem? Why does it resonate with you? Make this escape fun by thinking of exciting and creative places to read your poetry; you may choose to read it outside in a park or at home, cuddling on your couch with your dog and a fluffy blanket. You can take this poetic activity further by writing your original poetry. If you have experience writing in a specific style, challenge yourself to write about a subject.

If you are unsure what style to write, review poetry books, and study the poetry styles you enjoy. Do you like limericks, sonnets, haikus, epigrams, ballads, odes, or free verses? There are many different styles and what can make this mini-vacation enjoyable is to study the various poems and choose one that appeals to you and then write in that style.

To get you started, I've written an original poem that reflects this great escape:

Life's Not a Race

Our busy lives and hectic pace
do us no good, life's not a race.
We need to stop and behold nature
and give our thanks to our creator.

To view a flower in all its splendor,
may slowly guide us to our center.
To hear the sound of falling water,
will make our life feel that much broader.

Our precious moments with family and friends,
create the time that never ends.
We value hours with cherished pets,
for playing with them is no regret.

We treasure peace to chase our dreams,
our passions, hobbies, and life themes.
Our busy lives and hectic pace
must be balanced with vacations, calm, and space.

(Poem credit: *Life's Not a Race* by Lisa Rickwood)

TRY THIS

TIME: You want to have 30 minutes or longer of uninterrupted time for this activity.

METHOD: The style of poetry you write will depend on what you enjoy; choose a type you like and then focus on a subject you want. Once you decide, start writing without editing; you may lose the poem's essence if you edit as you progress.

COOL WORDS

> "Words have the power to destroy and heal. When words are both true and kind, they can change our world." —Buddha

Have you ever verbalized something to someone important you wished you could take back? Did you obsess over what you expressed and wonder what would've happened had you not uttered those destructive words?

We've all spoken things we regret—we're human. And, as many of us have discovered, once those words are said, they can't be taken back. The power of words written or spoken in good order may bring us money, respect, and love, or when said the wrong way, may lead a country to war. The best world leaders and thinkers used the power of the word to inspire people to see their vision and create actionable change. Whether it was Martin Luther King, Jr.'s 1963 speech, *"I Have a Dream,"* or Winston Churchill's famous 1940s talk, *"Finest Hour,"* words have impacted those who listened. Words shape our lives, and they can inspire change and action and improve our lives.

We use words to express and share our experiences with others but may not be aware of the far-reaching impact when used daily. Just like positive affirmations, it's nice to have a toolbox of "cool" words in your mind or that you have on display in your environment.

The popularity of words continues to grow as many products in the marketplace are adorned with words, such as T-shirts, posters, pictures, mugs, pillows, and more.

Whether you have a large project or small goals, using words, words, or phrases you see every day will inspire and motivate you. These words may appear on a tattoo, ring, bracelet, necklace, poster, sticky note, or screensaver—the choice is yours. By placing visual cues in prominent places, these words act as positive environmental triggers to help your mind stay on track.

Affirmations are more of a phrase, and "cool" words consist of one or a couple of words to inspire and motivate.

TRY THIS

TIME: For this activity, you can allow as much time as you wish.

METHOD: When you want to get motivated, achieve a goal or large project, consider adding motivating words to your work and life environment. If you are not sure what words to use, pay attention to words you see around you; you may notice a quote on the back of a vehicle, a poster at work—look for signs or words that speak to you.

Place words by your desk, by a mirror, wear words, or add them to areas you frequent throughout your day. Have fun deciding how those words will show in your work and home environment. Make sure to use positive words and phrases to keep you energized and motivated.

If you are unsure what words to use, here are a few to get you started:

goals, challenge, truth, laughter, determination, perseverance, freedom, faithful, tenacity, endurance, learn, courage, hope, time, love, power, enjoy, fun, best, adventure, achieve, accomplish, action, alive, attitude, believe, bliss, clarity, commitment, courage, create, dare, dreams, empower, encourage, energy, excellence, envision, fearless, fulfillment, goodness, gratitude, imagination, inspire, joy, kindness, life, live, meaning, move, now, opportunity, passion, peace, plan, positive, possibilities, risk, spirit, strong, teach, wise, yes.

When you surround your life with uplifting and motivating words, you see how positive changes start to happen. Have fun!

LIFE-LIST COLLAGE

> "Your brain will work tirelessly to achieve the statements you give your subconscious mind. And when those statements are the affirmations and images of your goals, you are destined to achieve them!" — Jack Canfield

Do you remember making colorful collages as a child? Many of us remember the moment when our teacher handed us colored construction paper, glue, and scissors. This art activity was an exciting moment to get creative and make a mess.

Wikipedia describes to word collage as *"a technique of an art production, primarily used in the visual arts, where the artwork is made from an assemblage of different forms, thus creating a new whole."*

The word collage originates from the French word, *coller*, which means "to glue." This art form often uses newspaper and magazine clippings, paint, colored paper, quotes, words, photographs, and other objects glued to canvas or paper. This process dates back hundreds of years and reappeared in the early 20th century as a novelty art form.

While many of us have heard of vision boards, collages are a little different as they tend to appear more "artsy." However, for this chapter, I want you to think of the collage as a "life list." You'll focus on what you'd like in your life, and you'll be creating a collage to reflect your dreams and goals.

What you want to do is have fun, be creative, choose images and words that speak to your heart (don't overthink things), and place them on a piece of paper; this will become your life map or your vision board.

Whether you believe it or not, we know visualization works to achieve goals. Olympic athletes use it to improve performance. Science proves that brain patterns triggered when a sprinter runs the 400-meter relay are activated when the sprinter imagines (visualizes) winning the relay.

What is the secret to creating a life-list collage that is effective? It's simple: Your life-list board should pinpoint what you wish to feel, not just things you want to get. It's the feeling that will propel you to your goals and dreams.

TRY THIS

TIME: For this escape, take as much time as you need to find materials to create the collage.

METHOD: Grab scissors, glue, poster board, colored paper, stickers, and other items.

Next, take at least 60 minutes to get lost in this escape. Collect all the materials you need for this project. Fold, tear, or cut the paper into different shapes, add embellishments, develop a theme, assemble the pieces in place, and glue them to the material when ready.

Once dry, study your collage. What is a common theme? Do you have many pictures or words about being outdoors? Do you have a family theme? Are there pictures of places you wish to visit? Study the collage and then place it where you can see it all the time.

UNBIRTHDAY SURPRISE

> "May your birthday be bright as your smile, warm as your heart, and as sparkly as your accessories."
> —Anonymous

Have you heard of the word "unbirthday?" While it may seem like a modern term, it dates back to 1871 and was referred to in the novel *Alice Through the Looking-Glass* by Lewis Carroll. Carroll wrote four books, and they were in order: *Alice in Wonderland, Alice Through the Looking-Glass, Hunting of the Snark,* and *Alice Underground.*

In his book, *Alice Through the Looking-Glass*, Carroll devised a new word called: unbirthday. The term refers to an event that can be celebrated and doesn't fall on a person's birthday. Some people consider an unbirthday calculated by adding six months to a person's birthday to determine the unbirthday date.

It doesn't matter how you set this up except that you want to choose a time to celebrate no birthdays.

For example, if you live in a household with others, you may take their birthdays and then choose one day to either celebrate one unbirthday for the year or have a celebration for every person in the household. This escape is fun if you live in a household where the birthdays are close together, and there's nothing to celebrate for months and months.

You can have fun with this escape—buy balloons, get a cake with candles, put up decorations in your home, buy a present. There's no limit to how fun and silly you can make this event.

This exercise can be gratifying if you're going through challenging times if you live alone. Pick up bright, fun decorations, a cake, and a present, and you might even invite some family or friends over to get silly and play a board game.

TRY THIS

TIME: For this escape, take at least 60 minutes to celebrate with family or friends.

METHOD: To prepare for an unbirthday, ensure you have the materials you need such as birthday cake, icing, candles, balloons and signs, lunch or dinner for the occasion, and presents. You will be celebrating as though this was a specific person's birthday, so enjoy the moments.

Be sure you plan and get all supplies you need so you don't have to go out and pick up last-minute items. You want the mini-vacation to be easy with minimal hassles.

SUPERHERO DAY

> "What is a superhero? They're supposed to represent hope, opportunity, and strength for everybody." —Aldis Hodge

Do you watch superhero movies, or did you pretend to be a superhero when you were a child?

I remember being ten years old and pretending to be Wonder Woman outside at a neighbor's yard while my friend acted out movie scenes as Captain America. We spent hours concocting stories, running through fields, and climbing small mountains—it was a fun and free time in my life.

Why do we like superheroes? I believe a lot of the appeal is because when we watch them in a movie, it's a great form of escapism from troubles we may be experiencing in the world. Also, the characters often show strength and vulnerability, and we may relate to them.

Finally, they instill a strong feeling of hope we gravitate toward when things in our life seem chaotic or challenging.

Another reason we love superheroes is we see that one individual can make a tremendous difference in the outcome of a situation. They represent more idealistic and valued personality traits and a sense of justice.

In an article in *Smithsonian Magazine*, *The Psychology Behind Superhero Origin Stories,* clinical psychologist Robin Rosenberg writes, *"As a clinical psychologist who has written books about the psychology of superheroes, I think origin stories show us not how to become super but how to be heroes, choosing altruism over the pursuit of wealth and power. I've learned this through hundreds of conversations at comic book conventions, where fans have been remarkably candid about their lives and the inspiration they draw from superhero stories."* (25)

Although comics depicting superheroes have been around since the 1930s, the surge in popularity occurred in the 2000s with the release of movies and television shows such as *Iron Man, Spider-Man, Agents of SHIELD*, and other forms of entertainment. Movies in the 2000s were so prevalent because technology allowed for better and more realistic effects. Audiences enjoyed, craved, and demanded more detailed and action-packed entertainment, and Hollywood was up to the challenge.

The appeal of superheroes has also translated to a special day in the US called *National Superhero Day*, and this day was created on April 28, 1995, by Marvel Comics employees. Every year on April 28, people have a chance to honor their favorite superheroes—real or fictional—and they can get dressed up, treat a real-life hero to lunch, or celebrate a person in their lives.

In the last few years, we all became aware of the true superheroes—teachers, frontline workers, truckers, farmworkers, medical professionals, scientists, people working tirelessly behind the scenes and not taking any glory.

You can celebrate Superhero Day any time you want and do it in a way that makes it fun. Perhaps there are medical professionals you wish to thank; you might send a heartfelt card to them. Or, you might work for a company that encourages its workers to have fun and dress up as a superhero.

While I wrote this book, my youngest son worked as a cashier at a grocery store where the company encouraged their workers to dress as they liked on Fridays. On a Friday, my son donned a Batman t-shirt, cape, and mask and went to work and cheered up his colleagues and customers who came through his till to pay for groceries. He said, "I'm raising the bar at work, so all my colleagues will have to dress up on Fridays!"

I admit I've had fun with this superhero concept while facilitating video webinars to clients. In a webinar career series, I wore a Wonder Woman tiara and bracelets and talked about the epic journey of building and creating a successful career.

TRY THIS

TIME: For this escape, think about the heroes you like and decide how you want to create your day. You can dedicate as little or as much time as you wish to this activity.

METHOD: Perhaps you decide to wear Batman socks or a Wonder Woman bracelet to instill a little "hidden superhero" magic into your day. Or maybe your company dedicates a day to being a superhero, and you can get dressed up at the office or in a video conference.

You might take some time to read fairy tales or poetry or even create art that's focused on being a superhero.

If you've experienced excellent medical care from a medical professional, you might send them a card of thanks and appreciation.

If you're a parent with children, you might have a superhero birthday party or create a superhero night where you dress up like a superhero and sit down and watch a series of movies with them. Children love creating, so you might create a superhero costume with them.

Creating a superhero takes creativity and time, and if you're working on this theme with children, there are some key questions to ask that include: the superhero's name, a description of the superhero (costume and appearance), superpowers, how they got their superpowers, secret identity, good things the superhero does, the superhero's enemy, their weaknesses and vulnerabilities, and if they own any gadgets.

Have fun and enjoy this superhero escape!

CARTOONS AND COMICS

> "Comic books to me are fairy tales for adults." —
> Stan Lee

When you were a child, did you read comics or watch cartoons on television or do both?

If you were like many people, you did engage in these activities, and as an adult, you may still be interested in comics or cartoons or both. Many people enjoy cartoons, and this concept is evident when we study one of the longest-running television cartoons in history.

Consider the incredible success of the half-hour television cartoon, *The Simpsons.* In September 2020, the series entered its 30th season. This fictional series is about a family, the Simpsons, who live in the imaginary town of Springfield, USA, and consist of characters including Marge, Homer, Bart, Lisa, and Maggie, the baby. The series is a sarcastic and satirical look at American life and humanity, and its humor and relevance still resonate strongly with its viewers.

Matt Groening created the fictitious family while working with film producer James L. Brooks on a series of shorts. These shorts appeared for three seasons on the *Tracy Ullman Show* and later became a half-hour show which appeared on *Fox Television*. Groening named the characters after his own family but substituted his name for Bart. For over 30 seasons, people have had front row seats to the Simpson family.

Whether you watch this cartoon sitcom or not, the appeal of cartoons and comics for adults is not diminishing. Witness the popularity of the *DC Comics* and movies or the *Marvel Comics* and movie series—we love comics, cartoons, superheroes, and escaping to imaginary worlds.

This fascination with fantasy is not going away because many of us got our passion for reading comic books and cartoons when we were children; we were positively affected by these early influences.

I remember spending hours watching television cartoons and reading comics in my spare time when I was a child and preteen. I had amassed a 400 plus comic book collection that might be worth a lot now, but when I was 17, I had to leave my comics as I didn't have room to take them with me when I went to university. I left them with my parents, and my younger sister and brother had fun with them. The comics didn't survive. I always wonder what would have happened if I could have taken them and kept them in good condition.

If you haven't read a comic or watched cartoons for a while, you may want to consider this great escape. Opening a comic book and sitting back and getting lost in it helps you relax and calm your busy mind. If the comic is a series that you remember as a child, this brings back those nostalgic feelings and may make you feel happy and positive. We often associate those early memories of reading or watching cartoons with more innocent, carefree times.

TRY THIS

TIME: For this activity, take at least 30 minutes.

METHOD: Make sure you have a comic or cartoon series you enjoy viewing. Turn off all other distractions and take at least 30 minutes to watch a cartoon or read a comic book; choose a quiet, comfortable place to engage in this activity, and you'll feel multiple benefits.

Enjoy!

JUST JOKING

> "Humor is the great thing, the saving thing. The minute it crops up, all our irritation and resentments slip away, and a sunny spirit takes their place." — Mark Twain

Most of us have heard the line laughter is the best medicine, a proverb derived from the Wisdom of King Solomon. The original line was: *A merrie heart doth good like a medicine: but a broken spirit drieth the bones.* Over the years, the line changed to the quote we all know and understand.

When life gets challenging, frustrating, and gets on your last nerve, fight back using humor.

It's not easy to practice humor when everything around you seems to be crumbling or imploding. How can you possibly crack a joke or have a good laugh? But you need to.

In an article called: *The Importance of Humor Research: A serious non-serious research topic,* by Peter McGraw, Ph.D., for *www.psychologytoday.com,* the author states: *"Humor appears to help people's psychological and physical well-being - for example, helping folks cope with stress and adversity. Humor even seems to help people grieve: Dacher Keltner and colleagues found that people who spontaneously experienced amusement and laughter when discussing a deceased spouse showed better emotional adjustment in the years following the spouse's death.*

But humor has physical benefits, too. Laughter - especially a hearty laugh - has been shown to benefit your circulation, lungs, and muscles (especially those around the belly area). Humor also helps people deal with pain and physical adversity. Hollywood even made a movie, Patch Adams, about the benefits of humor in clinical settings." (26)

While I agree with the importance of humor, it wasn't something that came to me quickly because life handed me many challenges all at once. Maybe you can relate.

I lived through the 2008 global economic crisis, closed a high-end retail store shortly after, had creditors show up on my doorstep, call me at home and work, threaten to garnish my wages, and more. My nine-year-old Jeep had no market value, so I got to keep that as well. I also managed to go a couple of weeks not eating, so there was enough food for my children; just having enough money for food was a challenge for months. During this period, I lost a father-in-law and my father at a young age. I didn't laugh a lot during that time.

Then, after years of attempting to catch up, the pandemic hit and affected my family. I decided that life was too short to feel miserable, and we needed to use humor despite the craziness of the world and the challenges that were happening all around us.

Our short-term solution? We started watching more comedies. I'd look for funny jokes and practice these on friends and family. I also thought about a friend I knew many years before working as a comedian; she would mention that humor is a perspective, looking at situations and asking yourself, "What is funny with this?" There are some moments where humor is not appropriate or won't work to ease the pain of the situation.

It wasn't easy, but switching the way I looked at life helped improve my mood. On several occasions, I've had a great laugh with friends or family—the kind where tears stream down your cheeks.

While writing this book, my son and I stayed up late to watch a cult classic movie, *Office Space*, a brilliantly written movie released in 1999. Although the movie came out quite some time ago, it has a strong appeal to those who've worked in an office or anyone who didn't like their job. The movie was a satire about work-life in the 1990s and featured three main characters who wanted to get even with their greedy boss.

One of my favorite scenes that made me laugh until I cried had happened when the three main characters, Peter, Michael, and Samir, stole an old, antiquated fax machine from their office that kept jamming papers every day. They drove out to an open field, and they proceeded to pound on the old machine. I completely lost it, and tears were streaming down my cheeks. They were kicking and punching the photocopy machine as though it was a bad guy, and Michael finally had to be pulled away from the photocopier.

I laughed hysterically because I'd experienced a jamming fax machine in an office where I'd worked, and management didn't replace it; I dreamed of smashing it to bits. What made this all better was that I was sharing this movie with my son, and he was laughing so hard he told me his stomach hurt after we finished.

Humour is so positive and what makes it so appealing is sharing it with others, so it becomes a social event. While we may laugh at something when we're alone, it is more entertaining with family or friends.

Humour is something that even young babies possess. As a new mother, I remember watching everything my first-born child did. On one occasion, my son was only four months old and sitting in a baby seat on the kitchen floor by the fridge. I looked down at my young son, and I felt like I should be silly with him for some strange reason. I stood above him and said, "I'm a big boy!" and I beat my chest. I didn't know how he would react, but he instantly started laughing—a deep, belly laugh. I couldn't believe that someone so young could have a sense of humor; it was incredible to witness an infant's first big laugh.

I went to a comedy night with my husband, and we saw the actor, Jon Lovitz perform in our city. I'd seen him on *Saturday Night Live* and watched him in *Rat Race.* But I was still so impressed by his comedy—I laughed for most of his almost two-hour performance. It was certainly worth the money we paid for the tickets; you can't put a price on humor.

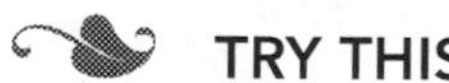

TRY THIS

TIME: For this escape, you need very little time, which can happen anywhere. The idea is to "prime" your mind to think of funny situations and make it a mission to look for funny things.

METHOD: Here are some ideas to get you started:

- Tune into sketches or sitcoms on TV or radio
- Write in a gratitude journal
- Spend time with children
- Spend time with pets
- Ask yourself what your favorite character or comedian would do about a stressful situation you are experiencing
- Create a funny file—online or paper and include: cartoons, funny photos, greeting cards, jokes
- Have a "funny bone" jar—write down something funny that happened today and put it in the jar
- Funny movie night—look for comedies and only watch these
- Visit a comedy show when you can
- Tell something funny about yourself to a friend
- Find humor in something serious
- Visit your funny friend
- Try something new that you're not good at
- Write a humorous short story
- Study your friends or family members and think about something funny they do
- Go ahead and get silly!

SILLY SKILLS

> "We don't stop playing because we grow old; we grow old because we stop playing." —George Bernard Shaw

Do you remember the kid at school who could wiggle his ears or the one that could do the splits on the floor? You probably remember someone who possessed some unusual talents, or perhaps you were the one with an obvious or "hidden" talent.

When we were young, nothing was too crazy or silly, and we'd try all kinds of things to have fun and learn. We had a lot of spare time, and we'd often see who was the weirdest, fastest, most disgusting, or strangest performer.

I remember learning how to print and write backward and send notes to friends in the classroom. I also got pretty skilled at wiggling my nostrils.

You may also have some funny talents that don't become obvious until you've had one too many at a party or when you're acting silly with a dear friend.

We don't spend much time thinking or doing silly tricks; we're busy with work, family, and other responsibilities. However, these skills we learned as children are more than ridiculous abilities; these abilities often helped us infuse humor into our lives and cope with the challenges of being a little person in a grown-up world. Silly skills shouldn't end when we grow up. These skills are beneficial when you're parenting as you can better relate to children.

These skills also help you be creative, productive, and they boost your energy levels and make it fun to bond with your friends. You probably have friends who make you laugh. When you try new things or do silly things, you take the pressure off yourself and get less serious.

This relaxing way of acting allows you to decompress and feel like a young child.

Children think and act in a certain way, and adults can learn from this. While we want to avoid being immature thinkers, we want to embrace more creativity and fun in our lives. We want to have that childlike essence but act by being an adult. We need to have fun and still be an adult; there is a lot we can learn from observing children.

One way children surpass adults is with their imagination. Don't believe it? Remember a time, probably before the age of eight years old, when you thought you were a superhero or a firefighter, a vet, or an artist—you were whatever you wanted to be. You could easily imagine a whole different world, and while you knew the difference between your daydreaming and reality, your mind was open to possibilities.

The other benefit of thinking like a child is that they don't tend to overthink because they learn new things by watching others. Children don't waste time by overanalyzing everything; they go ahead and act on impulses. They also aren't afraid to reach out and ask for help when they're stuck.

Children love to have fun doing silly skills, and they tend to live in the moment and don't get stuck worrying about the future.

TRY THIS

TIME: You can spend as little or as much time as you wish on this fun activity.

METHOD: Revisit your "silly skills" and see if you can add them to your day. Is there a skill you can showcase at work to cheer up your colleagues? If you parent younger children, can you learn a new "silly skill" from them? What can you do to add more fun to your days?

Take time and get a blank journal. Write down some funny skills you had as a child.

Some silly skills include: juggling, wiggling your ears, tongue acrobatics, going cross-eyed, whistling, doing backflips, etc.

JUGGLE AWAY STRESS

> "I'm happy when I'm juggling, but I feel like I've gone from, like, 3 balls to 10 bowling balls. But, that's a good problem. I don't really have a complaint about that." —Kirstie Alley

You're awake most of the night as your mind is racing—you're upset about your employment and career challenges, health issues, and sleep does not come. When morning arrives, you're stressed and jittery and ready to kick someone or something.

If you've ever been angry, stressed, or anxious, you may benefit from blowing off steam by juggling. You may wonder how this could be a great escape to diminish stress. Many studies show the benefits of this fun exercise.

In a *Huffington Post* article by Alena Hall, titled, *How Juggling Can Relieve Stress and Still Your Mind,* professional juggler Jennifer Slaw joined HuffPost and discussed how juggling was a form of stress relief. *"I've gotten to that point where it is kind of zen-like where you get into this rhythm," said Slaw. "I actually get up in the morning and juggle for a few seconds or minutes with my eyes closed just to sort of be at peace and have that moment in the morning to sort of reflect on what's going to happen for the rest of the day."* (27)

If you wonder if juggling calms your nerves, rest assured, it works. When you focus on performing a new task that requires patience and skill, your mind is distracted from stressful thoughts; juggling requires intense concentration, so your worries disappear while you do this.

If this doesn't convince you that this might be a beneficial activity, nothing will.

If you tried to juggle as a child, you probably gave up as you knew it would take time. For this escape and a great way to blow off stress, you may want to take some time alone to learn how to juggle away stress.

TRY THIS

TIME: For this mini-vacation, take at least 30 minutes.

METHOD: For this escape, you want to begin with equipment that makes learning easy. Some people start with scarves to learn quickly and avoid the frustration of bouncing balls. Others use bean bags and practice learning the correct technique for juggling. There are plenty of online videos—feel free to watch these and practice along with the video.

As you learn, it will be a great distraction, possibly a little frustrating, but it will take your mind off stressful events.

Happy juggling!

MAKING MAGIC

> "The world is full of magic things, patiently waiting for our senses to grow sharper." —W.B. Yeats

When you were a child, did you enjoy watching magic performances? Did you ever try to create magic tricks on your own?

I still remember being five years old and watching my cousin, Billy, as he showed me a magic trick. He took an old, crumpled paper bag and held it in one hand, and then he put an uncooked egg in its shell into the bag. I watched him shake up the bag and then take his palms and crush the bag; I expected there to be a mess inside the bag. When he opened the paper bag to show me, there was no egg or egg yolk to be seen. I still can't figure out how he did this trick. I was obsessed with learning how to create magic tricks from this moment.

Many children express interest in learning magic tricks, and I bet you were one of them.

Even though you may not be a child anymore, you may still enjoy watching magic or learning magic tricks. Why do we love magic so much?

An article on *www.bbc.com* by writer Sean Coughlan, *Why do we like magic when we know it's a trick?*, mentions, *"Everyone knows these are tricks and not "real." It's not as though we don't know our senses are being deceived. But we still watch and wait for the reveal.*

It might be more of a surprise to find there is a university laboratory dedicated to understanding magic - the Magic Lab, part of the psychology department at Goldsmiths, University of London.

It's part of a growing interest in putting magic under much more rigorous, scientific scrutiny." (28)

Magic uses principles of distraction or misdirection and where we focus our attention and process information. As well as misdirecting us, magic takes advantage of our flaws in how we see; optical illusions and other tricks get created to manipulate our senses.

I went to Las Vegas, Nevada, with my husband for one of my birthdays. We spent time walking around and exploring, went for dinner, and went to many shows and performances such as *Cirque du Soleil* and magician *Lance Burton.*

I remember being blown away by Lance Burton's show's large scale and professionalism. Like many magicians, Lance became interested in magic as a child of five years old, and he went on to practice and won his first magic contest at the age of 17. He performed over 15,000 shows over 30 years for more than five million people. I was lucky enough to see him three years before his contract ended.

The show was mesmerizing—bright lights, colorful dancers but mostly how he managed to make a red sports car disappear in front of an entire audience. I saw it at the front of the stage, Lance placed a giant cloth over it, and then in a brief moment, the car was gone. There was a hush over the audience. No one could figure out how he did it.

Watching professionals perform magic is truly a great escape, but learning to do small tricks is fun.

TRY THIS

TIME: For this activity, take at least 30 minutes to enjoy the moment fully.

METHOD: For this escape, decide if you will watch magic or perform magic. Both activities are great ways to take your mind off present-moment problems and challenges.

If you decide you would like to learn magic, do your homework and seek out people to show you tricks. Do you have friends who know great card tricks? Are there any workshops that offer you how to create magic? Why should kids have all the fun?

If you don't succeed at finding someone to show you magic tricks, invest in a good book or a magic kit with instructions. Then, take time to read through and practice, practice, practice.

You don't have to be Lance Burton to bring fun and creativity to a meeting or event. All you need is a bit of good old-fashioned magic.

CHAPTER 7

The Great Outdoors

If you feel stressed or overwhelmed, one of the best ways to remedy this issue is to spend time in nature. Nothing is more relaxing, calming, and satisfying than being outdoors in the fresh air and away from four walls.

When you get outdoors, you are spending time away from your usual environment, which wakes up your senses and allows your body and mind to recalibrate.

Unplug from your digital devices for a while, and engage all of your senses outside to enjoy the outdoors. When you spend time with family or friends and are physically active, this helps your body, mind, and spirit.

As soon as time permits, get busy being outdoors.

THE ELEMENTS

> "Everybody talks about weather, but nobody does anything about it." —Mark Twain

We live in an artificial world with heated homes, air conditioning, electricity and appliances, and technological gadgets. We'll hop in our cars, walk into air-conditioned shops, and occasionally get a taste of Mother Nature.

We slather on sunscreen to prevent sunburns, carry umbrellas to keep dry from rain, and curse the falling of snow. In short, we're "wimps" and disconnected from nature.

If you're spending most of your time between four walls, it's time to immerse yourself in the great elements outdoors—wind, rain, snow, and sunshine. When you spend time outdoors in less-than-ideal weather and feel the power of the wind, for example, you feel free and relaxed.

I felt that "free and wild" feeling when I sailed on a 27-foot Vega Sailboat in the Pacific Northwest with my grandparents, who were seasoned sailors.

On one particular day, we crossed the Strait of Juan De Fuca in the Pacific Northwest, and the wind became intense. We were caught in a bad storm and noticed sailboats that had been out in the Pacific Ocean were no longer visible. We quickly took down our sails as the storm became more intense, and we turned on our motor to get safely away from the storm. At one point, the boat lurched to the right, tipping toward the ocean, the seawater flowing into the cockpit. It was a crazy, intense time, but we all felt alive while the wind whipped around the boat. We managed to get far enough away from the storm, and we continued to motor back to our marina.

We won't get outside as much as needed if we wait for perfect weather. Therefore, we need to consider feeling uncomfortable and dressing to suit the weather but knowing we may be wet or cold. When we spend time outdoors, we feel the power of the elements and can feel energized. Of course, we will use our common sense and avoid extreme weather that risks our health.

An online article, *How Does Nature Impact Our Wellbeing?*, posted by the *University of Minnesota*, stated, *"One of the most intriguing areas of current research is the impact of nature on general wellbeing. In one study in mind, 95% of those interviewed said their mood improved after spending time outside, changing from depressed, stressed, and anxious to more calm and balanced. Other studies by Ulrich, Kim, and Cervinka show that time in nature or scenes of nature are associated with a positive mood, and psychological wellbeing, meaningfulness, and vitality."* (29)

I'm sure you realize you don't need scientists and research to tell you that you'll feel better outdoors; you already may be traveling, camping, exploring, and feeling the positive effects of Mother Nature. You know your mood improves when you escape the four walls you routinely surround yourself with.

TRY THIS

TIME: For this mini-vacation, make sure to take at least 60 minutes or longer to enjoy the effects.

METHOD: When you get cabin fever and need to escape the four walls, choose a day when it's windy, rainy, or sunny, dress appropriately, and immerse yourself in the weather.

If you don't go out much in rainy weather, try bundling up to stay warm and dry and taking a walk in the rain. Notice the sounds, sights, and listen to the sound of falling rain. Let a few drops of rain land on your cheek. Lose yourself in the moment.

When you're outside and cold, how long does it take before you feel uncomfortable?

Or do you even feel uncomfortable? Do you feel energized instead?

SUNRISE, SUNSET

"'Sunrise Sunset' is about trying to get to a place where life is simple and not letting the stress and happenings

in the world get in the way of your happiness." —
Benny Cassette

There's something magical about sunrises and sunsets—blazing colors of yellow, orange, red, bronze, and gold light the sky on fire, and everything seems drenched in a beautiful brush.

Witnessing sunrises and sunsets can make time appear to slow down for you, and it takes only moments to feel the awe and beauty. It may motivate, inspire or make you feel gratitude and take your mind's focus from your challenges to considering the world where we live, where there is something bigger than you.

In places such as Hawaii, Australia, and Greece, the sunset is part of a nightly celebration, and crowds gather to view and appreciate the beauty unfolding in front of them and be thankful for their day.

I remember sailing with my grandparents in the Pacific Northwest and dropping anchor near a small island when I was a teenager. Viewing a sunset on a boat was a treat; I loved how the sun reflected off water and sank behind a small mountain, leaving an iridescent color painted across the summer sky.

My grandfather would use the phrase, *Red sky at night, sailor's delight. Red sky in the morning, sailors take warning.* There seemed to be some truth to this, and when we slept on the sailboat and saw a red sky at night, we awoke to a beautiful morning.

I spent many summers enjoying new experiences on board my grandparents' 27-foot Vega sailboat as we planned day trips, overnight trips, and explored. We had moments of witnessing schools of dolphins, orcas, humpback whales, sea lions, getting caught in unpredictable storms, and viewing nature.

Cinematographers use sunsets and sunrises to film a movie; they often add more drama to a particular scene.

If you have a camera or smartphone and enjoy taking photographs, pay attention to sunrises and sunsets and look to capture some sights. If you don't live near an area to get a good picture, make it part of your great escape to get to a place where you can take great photos.

For many photographers, the quality of the light is as important as the subject. We know the light is crucial as our eyes only register objects bathed in light.

Not all mornings and nights are the best for capturing impressive sunrises and sunsets. We often do not realize the beauty of the sky, and if we are not ready to photograph it, we quickly lose the impact. It takes mere seconds to move from a dramatic image to an ordinary one—light changes that fast!

An article by Kate Doyle on the website, *www.abc.net*, titled, *How to predict a good sunrise or sunset so you can brag about it on social media,* mentions an aspect of predicting the best time to capture a photograph: *"Gregory Dunbar, founder of the sunrise and sunset predictor app SkyCandy, said he took into account: Humidity—best when humidity is low but not too low. Cloud coverage—best when between 30 percent and 70 percent. Not good if below 30 percent, and terrible if above 90 percent. Prior rainfall—2–6 hours before sunrise or sunset is okay, but not during sunrise or sunset. Visibility—the higher the better. Wind speed—best if the wind speed is low or non-existent. Fog—no fog … this should go without saying.*

These are some of the factors. He was not silly enough to give away the whole story." (30)

I notice sunrises and sunsets are dramatic during the changing of the seasons when the weather may be volatile and unpredictable.

For example, in mid-February in the Pacific Northwest, we get storms, snow, four-season weather (rain, hail, wind, snow, sun in one day), and is often when sunrises and sunsets are unpredictable and filled with dazzling colors.

TRY THIS

TIME: For this activity, take 30 minutes or longer. This mini-vacation is more enjoyable when you have more time to practice.

METHOD: For this escape, pay attention to the weather in the next day or two and choose to either get up just before sunrise or focus on taking sunsets (pay attention to sunrise and sunset times—usually available in the weather app on your smartphone).

During your escape, ensure you have a camera or smartphone with you and watch the sky; breathe slowly, quiet your mind, and take in the moment. Anticipation and watching the sky's changing is enough to make you feel calm.

You may or may not see what you consider an impressive sunrise or sunset, but the point is to make time to notice this in your life. You might have a week where you get up earlier to see a sunrise.

It doesn't matter how you practice the escape; it just matters that you notice the sky around you—take a moment to revel in the beauty of nature.

STARRY-EYED

> "No pessimist ever discovered the secret of the stars, or sailed to an uncharted land, or opened a new doorway for the human spirit." —Helen Keller

Have you ever gazed into the sky at night only to see a shooting star, a comet, or some other celestial body? Have you ever questioned whether we were alone on Earth or contemplated the possibility of life in another solar system?

Many of us ponder the stars and space, especially when we were small children.

And civilizations have used the stars to navigate, tell stories, plant crops, place buildings, engage in celebrations, and more. Stargazing has been a part of our humanity for as long as we can remember.

After witnessing stars, solar eclipses, *Halley's Comet*, and other celestial scenes, studying the stars has always fascinated me. My father was interested in space, and his passion inspired me to explore the skies.

One summer night in the Okanagan in British Columbia when I was a teenager, I watched a summer rodeo with my parents, sister, and brother and drove to head home later that event. We did not get far before we pulled our car over to the side of the road to witness something very unusual for this time of year and area of the world—Aurora Borealis, the Northern Lights.

I have never witnessed this so far south in the summer—it was a once-in-a-lifetime vision. No one in this region of the world had witnessed such a bright sight as we saw this night. There may have been hints of Northern Lights but not to the extent of brightness and beauty.

After we pulled over to the side of the road to look at the Northern Lights, a police officer drove up to us and stopped his vehicle; he seemed confused why we parked to the side of the road.

The police officer walked over to us and said, "Is there a problem?"

My father replied, "No, we just pulled over the see the Northern Lights. They are beautiful."

The officer looked up into the sky, his mouth dropped open, and he said, "Oh wow… I did not expect that. Have a good night." He got in his vehicle, drove around the corner, and we saw him stop his car in the distance, his headlights still casting light.

We watched the Northern Lights for a few more minutes, and then the show was over, so we drove home. When we arrived home, we got out of the vehicle, looked into the sky, and saw dozens of shooting stars. It was an incredible evening.

TRY THIS

TIME: For this escape, take at least 20 minutes.

METHOD: For this escape, do a little homework and find out some things about the constellations in your region or download a constellation app. I have one on my smartphone, and when I step outdoors and hold it to the sky, I quickly locate some of the major constellations and planets.

At certain times of the year, there are solar eclipses, meteor showers, and other celestial shows. It is a great idea to check for upcoming spectacular events and ensure you have time to view them.

The best way to view stars is away from lights, so if you live in the city, you want to get away from the downtown core. Driving in the country or camping is a great way to experience the stars.

To make the most of the experience, use binoculars or a telescope and learn how to view the celestial bodies. You might add to the ambiance by having a blanket, a bottle of wine, and someone to spend time with while you view the stars.

When you are outside, look into the sky to get your eyes adjusted; there are differences in the color of the stars that derive their color from temperatures. Hotter stars appear bluish, and cool-toned stars look more yellow, orange, or red.

See if you spot any patterns and recognize a constellation such as *Orion's Belt.* This constellation consists of three stars spaced evenly, which appear midway in *Orion the Hunter's* constellation. Ancient civilizations saw this as the figure of a king who got shot (the three stars). Once you locate this constellation, it will be easier to find other constellations in the sky.

The Big Dipper is another constellation found in Canada, the US, the UK, and Ireland. You can locate this constellation by looking at the northern sky, and from the horizon, approximately a third of the way up, you will see it. It rotates around the North Star through the seasons. It appears like a bowl with a handle; three stars show up, and four stars make the bowl.

Once you start studying the stars in more detail, you will want to learn more, as it makes for a great nighttime escape.

Happy escaping!

RELAXING SPOTS

> "I love places that make you realize how tiny you and your problems are." —Anonymous

Do you have a favorite spot that you like to visit? Do you go there often? Why do you like that place? Most likely, your favorite spot is outdoors, and you feel relaxed and calm when you spend time there.

According to an article online, *Spending Just 20 Minutes in a Park Makes You Happier. Here's What Else Being Outside Can Do for Your Health,* on *www.time.com,* by writer Jamie Ducharme, *"Now, a new study published in the International Journal of Environmental Health Research adds to the evidence and shows just how little time it takes to get the benefits of being outside. Spending just 20 minutes in a park —even if you don't exercise while you're there —is enough to improve wellbeing, according to the research."* (31)

Spending 30 minutes outdoors in nature may significantly help with mental and physical health issues, including stress and depression.

It also helps lower blood pressure and heart rate and inspires physical activity.

I don't need experiments or scientists telling me this—when I step away from four walls, blue screens, air conditioning, and artificial lights to the great outdoors, I instantly feel my stress levels diminish.

Sometimes, the best way to cope and thrive is to escape to a relaxing and tranquil outdoor spot during challenging times. When you want to relax somewhere, what comes to mind? Do you enjoy a deserted beach, a river in a park, the ocean, a city park with lush grass and flowers, and an abundance of trees?

If you live in the city, it's not always simple to quickly find green space, so you may need to be creative to find a place to relax.

Relaxing spots tend to be outdoors where there's greenery, sounds of birds, fewer city sounds (honking, big trucks, etc.), and places to walk and relax. Finding well-maintained side streets with rows of trees may be very tranquil if you live in the city.

I walk to a nearby park in the winter to "get away from it all." This large central city park has a flowing waterfall, a duck pond, an outdoor auditorium by the duck pond, numerous paths, and areas to explore. I always take my Border Collie Labrador dog for a walk through this beautiful park, and I have time to exercise, slow down and decompress.

In the summer months on Vancouver Island, I have the option to create a portable spot to relax in my back yard under an apple and cherry tree in a large canvas hammock. Shaded from the sun, this is my happy place to relax and gaze at the clouds, visiting birds and other signs of nature. I may nap, read, listen to music, or daydream.

I love hammocks so much that I purchased a portable nylon hammock to take when I hike. I have one favorite spot I visit with family, and we set up our hammocks at the top of a small hill, overlooking the ocean, and then we let relax and take in the sights and sounds of nature.

Where do you go to "escape the pace" for a while? Do you have a favorite spot?

TRY THIS

TIME: For this activity, 30 minutes or longer ensure you time to calm down and relax.

METHOD: Think about having at least two relaxing spots in your world. You may have one outside and one inside when time and weather get in the way.

Your space doesn't need to be elaborate; it may be a simple as a bench in the park or a spot in your car at a parking lot. Space may be a room in your house, an area on your deck, or in your backyard. Once you determine what areas may be great retreat spots, you may wish to add objects to some of these spaces to help you relax.

If you designate your balcony as an escape spot, include cozy chairs, a table, and plants for privacy and add what soothes you.

A room in your home may include a comfy chair, flowers and relaxing music in the background, books, journals, and a cozy blanket to wrap around yourself.

Use your imagination to create a spot for you; be sure to add fun things, things that help you relax and rejuvenate. You deserve it.

RELAXING WATER ESCAPES

> "Water is the driving force of all nature." —Leonardo da Vinci

Do you find yourself more relaxed when you spend time near a creek, river, lake, ocean, or body of water? You are not alone. Science indicates we have a blue mind, a mildly meditative state that happens near or in the water.

In an online article, *Why Being Near The Ocean Can Make You Calmer And More Creative,* on *www.huffingtonpost.ca,* writer Carolyn Gregoire mentions Marine Biologist Wallace J. Nichols and his book called: *Blue Mind: The Surprising Science That Shows How Being Near, In, On, or Under Water Can Make You Happier, Healthier, More Connected, and Better at What You Do.* In Nichol's book, he mentioned we all have a blue mind, *"a mildly meditative state characterized by calm, peacefulness, unity, and sense of general happiness and satisfaction with life at the moment" and this is activated by the presence of water.* Nichols goes on to say, *"We are beginning to learn that our brains are hardwired to react positively to water and that being near it can calm and connect us, increase innovation and insight, and even heal what's broken."* (32)

I do not need science to inform me that being near water is beneficial. As a child, I always felt mentally and physically better after spending an afternoon in a lake or stream in the sunny Okanagan in British Columbia. I lived for swimming and would stay in the water until my lips turned blue (borderline hypothermia), and my mother would yell at me to get out of the water. I always slept better at night and had minimal stressful thoughts going through my mind after a day of swimming.

I love being on or near the water, and while writing this book, I finally invested in a kayak to use on the ocean and lakes; I rented kayaks for adventures over the years but wanted to choose a day and take off and explore. It was the best decision as I could paddle to new and beautiful places around Vancouver Island.

Research indicates our brain calms down when we spend time around water and not just ocean water. Our everyday lives fill with more sensory stimuli than our brains can handle; if we are not working, taking care of families, managing our households, we are obsessed with our technological devices. We do not give our minds a break—if we feel bored, we grab our devices.

Our minds get a break around water because fewer stimuli are happening, and your brain has a chance to slow down and enter a different brain wave state which is more relaxed and meditative. You experience less stress, anxiety, improved focus, mental clarity, and better sleep when you give your brain a break.

Being in nature near water helps your mind switch from future thinking to present thinking, and you may feel connected to nature when surrounded by water, trees, grass, and the natural environment.

Ever notice your best ideas come to you while out on a walk, driving for long periods on the highway, or showering? Our brain switches to a slower frequency of brainwaves; this triggers a default mode network—the network of the brain that is associated with: imagination and idea generation, daydreaming, memory consolidation, insight, and introspection. Creativity flows from this state, and this is why your best ideas may come to you at three o'clock in the morning, in the shower, or standing by a waterfall.

A problem you may have struggled to solve while tethered to your work desk may disappear once you take that lunchtime walk.

TRY THIS

TIME: Take at least 30 minutes to immerse yourself in this escape. Find a water source, even if it's your local park fountain. Shut your phone off and be present for your adventure.

METHOD: For your adventure, look to add water to your life—have a shower, swim in a lake, river, stream, or visit the ocean.

Being outdoors near water and exercising will add an extra boost to your mind and body.

Happy escaping!

OUTDOOR FITNESS

> "An early-morning walk is a blessing for the whole day." —Henry David Thoreau

It's a Friday afternoon, and you have three free hours to yourself with no work, errands, or responsibilities. You glance out of your front window and see the bright, shining sun amidst a turquoise blue sky. You feel an itch to get outdoors, and you put on shorts, a t-shirt, grab your hoodie, and put on your lightweight running shoes.

Birds are singing, and people are out walking. Your mood brightens with every step you take. While you walk, you look around and notice your surroundings—a statue, a new gate, and the way light rays hit a pond in the distance.

As you walk, you start to feel energized and pick up your pace to give your heart and lungs a great cardiovascular workout. You feel like you're eight years old again—full of energy and happiness.

Do you remember when you were little and played outside for hours? Perhaps you hiked with friends, rode your bike all over town, swam in lakes, streams, and rivers, and explored every corner of your little universe. Chances are, you had many moments where you were so exhausted from your outdoor exercise that you fell asleep the moment you hit the bed.

Now, with work and possibly family demands and everything that life throws at you, you may not be as motivated to get outdoors and exercise.

If you've ever been athletic, you know the rewards are endless; you may lose pounds and inches, build and sculpt muscles, increase your flexibility and strength, decrease stress and anxiety, and sleep better.

Many of us believe we need to exercise for a long time in a gym, but that's not true; we can get a great workout doing short, intense spurts of exercise. In 20 minutes, you might go outdoors and run intensely for a few minutes, take a break and then run again.

Or, you might decide to go hiking with friends, biking, rollerblading or swimming in a lake. There are so many outdoor activities that you may want to list all the activities you would like to do.

The quickest and easiest way to get exercise outdoors is to take a walk. You can decide if you want to walk to a specific location or start walking and see where your journey takes you—the choice is yours. To make your outdoor fitness adventure fun, plan and spend your time with friends or family and bring food to have a picnic after a great workout.

Exercising outdoors also benefits you as you enjoy the sunshine, vitamin D, fresh air, and a change of scenery.

TRY THIS

TIME: For this escape, you want at least 30 minutes to exercise outdoors.

METHOD: Decide when you will exercise and where you might do the activity. Also, decide if this is a solo event or if you wish to have family or friends join you.

Whatever activity you decide to do, be sure you are physically able to do it and that you have ample time to warm up your muscles and get ready. Starting with a quick walk is always a great way to get your body primed to be active outdoors.

Your escape might include a fast walk to a park, a bike ride, hiking with friends, playing tennis, jogging in the forest, or a quick dip in a lake. The choice is yours.

PASSIONATE PICNIC

> "A picnic is more than eating a meal, it is a pleasurable state of mind." —Dee Dee Stovel

Do you remember going on picnics when you were a child? Do you go on picnics now?

If you're like most people, you may not have many moments for picnics as family and work demands may leave you little energy or time.

There are so many benefits to eating outdoors with family and friends. First, being outdoors, breathing fresh air, and enjoying a beautiful view are beneficial. Second, this activity allows for more time to bond with family and friends. You build stronger bonds and friendships when you're outdoors with people and away from work and other obligations. You have time to get updated on other people's lives and have a chance to connect and learn from each other; this may help improve your relationships.

When we engage in picnics, we often prepare healthy and nutritious meals to take on our picnic; the most common picnic foods include fruit, vegetables, sandwiches, nachos, cheese, water, and juice. Sometimes, we stop by a grocery store and add snacks, but we tend to eat a little better when we take time to plan a picnic. The other bonus—food seems to taste better when we eat it outdoors.

In an article, *Why food tastes better outside,* on *www.medium.com*, author Julia Plevin, states, *"There's a scientific reason why food tastes better outside. Evolutionarily, we're programmed to relax in nature. The landscape elicits a soft focus from us to calm our nervous system down after being in a fight-or-flight scenario… As a species, we're not actually in fight-or-flight mode anymore but the demands of modern life trigger and trigger and trigger this. And so we need more time in nature to counter this. When we are relaxed, our parasympathetic system (known as the "rest-and-digest" branch) kicks in."* (33)

Just spending time outdoors allows us to take deeper breaths of fresh air, which may boost our metabolism, especially if we're active. We also may feel our mood lift, and this also stimulates our hunger response. If our nose feels plugged indoors, we may find our sinuses open up more, which allows us to notice more flavor when we eat food.

Don't believe me? Think back to when you camped as a child and had your breakfast on a picnic table outdoors. I bet you noticed so-called boring foods like bacon and eggs or boxed cereal appeared to taste better.

Depending on our picnic plans, we may have family rituals where we play different sports and games such as tug-of-war, flag football, kickball, soccer, badminton. If we picnic by a lake, we might kayak, canoe, water ski, or jet ski. Picnics may include a physical activity that relieves stress, boosts mood, and helps you stay active.

One of the best memories occurred when my husband and I celebrated our eighth wedding anniversary. One month earlier, we'd taken a risk and ventured into the world of entrepreneurship and purchased a high-end menswear store; we were shell-shocked, broke, and not in a position to even celebrate in a restaurant.

I wanted this anniversary to be unforgettable as this had been a challenging year to put together this huge deal, and I wanted to have special memories for our anniversary. I got a sitter for our young children, purchased a picnic basket filled with plates, cups, and cutlery, a bottle of red wine, specialty crackers, cheese, fruit, aged cheese, specialty meats, and other goodies. I packed the basket, picked up my husband from our store, and told him we would go for a drive before visiting a restaurant. I hid the picnic basket under an old blanket in the trunk of my car.

We drove to a breathtaking beach, and he figured we were going for a stroll along the shore and then heading home. After our walk, we arrived at the car where I reached for the blanket, picnic basket, and I mentioned we were staying there for dinner. My husband was surprised.

We walked up a small cliff that overlooked the Pacific Ocean, and we sat on a bench that was up on the top of this spot. We pulled out the food and put it down, making snacks before sitting on the blanket overlooking the bluff; it was a magical, beautiful West Coast night, and we watched the sun go from bright and shining to sinking behind a mountain. We both remembered this time.

What made this so funny was that two other couples were also up on the bluff with blankets and picnic baskets and food spread out all over the place. When they first saw us, they laughed.

TRY THIS

TIME: For this escape, you want at least two hours of uninterrupted time, and remember that your picnic can be sophisticated or simple as any feast.

METHOD: Next, think about who will attend and the theme or focus for the event. Are you just hosting a picnic outdoors for friends or family? Are you having a birthday picnic? When you plan your event in detail, this will determine the food and supplies needed.

Depending on where you host the picnic, you may opt for an old-fashioned picnic basket or backpacks with picnic accessories included. You should possess one container (or more) that keeps food chilled and insulated with the option to add ice packs. Plastic boxes and bins work well as well as coolers. If you are an avid camper, you'll have many picnic accessories you need.

Food is crucial to the picnic, and what you prepare and bring will depend on the theme, the number of guests, tastes of those attending, and easy-to-transport foods. You should also keep it simple.

Simple ideas include crackers and cheese, sliced bread, biscuits, jam, jelly, dried fruit, and nuts. Finger foods such as cookies and muffins, snack bars, cut-up vegetables and dip, nachos and guacamole, hummus, salsa, and chips are great additions to the picnic.

Other types of food include green lettuce salads (pack dressing separately), bean salad, coleslaw, pasta dishes, potato salad, and main courses. The main courses include grain dishes, potato salad, picnic sandwiches, vegetable wraps, grilled corn and bean salad, chicken and salad wraps, pasta salad, and cold cooked chicken.

CAMPING ESCAPES

> "A bad day camping is better than a good day working." —Unknown

Did you ever go camping as a child? What memories do you have?

I have many fond memories of camping in tents, trailers, and cabins—if you call it camping when you sleep in a trailer. My first memories were when I was two or three years old and spending time with my mother and father in their dark green camping van. Things like sitting on a chair with my father, eating cereal from small cardboard cereal boxes, and sleeping in a sleeping bag stood out in my mind. I remember my father put me on his shoulders, and it was so fun as he was 6'2" tall, and the view from above was mesmerizing interesting to a child who stood so close to the ground.

When I was twelve years old, I had the opportunity to attend a bible camp at the height of summer with my best friend, whose father was a minister. We filled our days with swimming in the lake, outdoor games like badminton, horseshoes, learning to cook, and telling stories. I remember one early morning, we were all resting in the cabin, and we started telling dirty jokes. I learned the best ones at that bible camp—who knew?

There's something magical about camping—seeing the stars at night, roasting food over a fire, breathing in the fresh air, walking and hiking, boating, fishing, riding a bike, and hearing nature's sounds.

Even if you haven't had many positive experiences from camping or you're not keen on bugs, you may want to consider this activity. You don't have to be in a tent if this isn't your thing. You can choose to rent or use your trailer or a cabin. There are so many benefits to being out in nature.

Camping is a great escape as it minimizes stress in your body; fresh air, exercise, a change of scenery, and spending time with family and friends are benefits. When you are outside, you breathe cleaner air than city air, your body clock gets more aligned, and you can exercise. You have time to disconnect from constant notifications and improve your overall health and mood.

If you decide to go camping, you need to plan well for a great camping experience. In particular, if you're going to use a tent, you'll want to ensure your tent is in good working order. It is recommended you put the tent up at home to ensure you have all the pieces and are proficient at setting it up; if you have children, you don't want to be fussing with building a tent while they're running around the campsite.

Campsites book months or even a year ahead, depending on where you live, so you want to do your homework and decide where you want to go and the time you want to camp. If you can, you choose to go during the week instead of the weekend as it won't be as busy and will be more peaceful.

Make sure you know what amenities are with your campsite booking. For example, does your campsite include hot showers, clean restrooms, picnic tables, water spouts, fire pits, level areas for tents, or Wi-Fi? What do you need to have?

A great way to plan meals is to take a piece of paper and write down the number of days you'll be camping and then the number of meals per day. Then, write down what you will eat for each day; writing it down on paper lets you see where you can buy items that work for several meals. Consider campfire-friendly meals and prepare these ahead of time to make it easy for yourself.

It's always a good idea to bring extra bedding and padding because a leaking air mattress is not fun.

I remember waking up at three o'clock in the morning to the pain of rocks on my hip; my air mattress had sprung a leak, and I was essentially lying on rocks - not a great way to feel relaxed and energized for the day. I could have used extra padding and bedding at that time.

Consider what you will be doing at the campsite. Are you athletic? If so, bring your bike, kayak, canoe, or hiking gear.

Most of us have a good idea of what to pack, but even the most experienced campers may forget to bring hiking shoes or runners, forget a hoodie or other items. The weather may look great but then unexpectedly change, so be prepared. If you pack a pair of shorts, ensure you have some long pants and maybe even leggings. If you have a t-shirt packed, throw in a hoodie. Make sure you have cozy socks included. If you bring a bathing suit, place it near the top of your clothing bag so you can pull it out if you see a place to swim.

As well as sports activities, games are always fun to play with family and friends. The games may be outdoor or indoor board games, card games, and other activities.

To make your adventure more pleasant, be sure to arrive before it's dark so you can see and set up your campsite. Also, avoid choosing the lowest area of the site because rain will gather under your tent, should it rain. It's always a good idea to keep your bags zipped up to avoid any uninvited bugs showing up in your bedding or clothes. Shake out your sleeping bag before you get into it if you're at all concerned. Many tents have mesh and other protectors to keep those pesky bugs out of your tent. Be sure to avoid leaving your shoes outside your tent; even the best summer day can have a surprise night rain. I had a mid-night rain drench my runners, and they were the only pair I brought on the trip.

Also, never leave food outdoors unattended; put it in your vehicle to not attract bears or other forest creatures.

There are many tricks and strategies for camping, and if you want to know more tips, do your homework and read books or go online to get the information.

TRY THIS

TIME: If you decide to go camping, be sure you choose at least a couple of nights or longer to go as it's a lot of work to get organized, pack, travel, and get your campsite ready to enjoy. Even if you have a trailer or rent a cabin, you'll want more time to enjoy yourself with family and friends.

METHOD: Book your time ahead for peace of mind; popular places get booked early, and there may be a year waitlist for some locations.

Plan what you have and what items you may need to purchase, borrow, or rent to ensure a great time.

Once you have everything packed, your family and friends with you, the adventure begins. Remember to enjoy the journey as well as the destination.

ROAD-TRIP FUN

> "It's not the destination, it's the journey." —Ralph Waldo Emerson

Have you taken a road trip lately? If not, you may want to consider this as there is nothing like taking a road trip and venturing to new places. It is a form of travel where the focus is the destination and the journey. The sights you see along the road, the people you meet, and the experiences you have added to your road trip. When you take a road trip, you may go off the beaten path, allowing you to see communities and natural wonders.

I remember the road trips I took with my grandparents. They knew how to vacation; they would plan the best road trips on Vancouver Island for my cousins and me. My grandparents had an Airstream trailer, and they would take me and my cousins on road trips where we would experience new things along the way before stopping at a campsite and spending time in the trailer.

Sometimes we stopped for ice cream and snacks at general stores along the highways. Other times, we took time along our journey and went for a walk along a beach or played mini-golf. These moments were precious.

The benefits of road trips are endless. As well as getting out of town and seeing new people and places, you have time to think; you get to engage your curiosity, learn patience, problem-solve, change plans, and experience unique moments.

A little preparation makes a big road trip enjoyable, and it all starts with your transportation. If you are embarking on an extensive road trip, you want to ensure your vehicle is fit for driving, and if you have kept your maintenance up to date, there should not be too much to do. It is a good idea to have a professional check it out to ensure the brakes and other components are safe to drive. You also want to have an emergency car kit on your journey.

Suggested items for your emergency kit should include a tire pressure gauge, jumper cables, safety cables, fire extinguisher, jack and axle stands, road flares, tow straps, pocket knife, Phillips screwdriver, and flat-blade, pliers, adjustable wrench, vise-grips, and wire cutters. Other items would be rope, an emergency blanket, sufficient water, and portable food in case of a challenge. You may add various items as well. It is always good to have an emergency kit in your vehicle at all times, as you never know when you may need the supplies.

Your road trip might consist of planned stops and places to sleep, or you might be more of an adventurer and only plan for overnight stays. Or, you might wing it and drive and figure it out as you go. It is up to you, but you want to consider the region, the season and availability of campsites, and other types of accommodations to ensure you have a place to sleep.

Navigation should be simple as many road signs are easy to understand, and many of us use a GPS or Google Maps. Electronic maps will use data or Wi-Fi, so ensure you have enough data and have Wi-Fi access. To avoid a possible issue obtaining the map, download it ahead of time. If you are adventurous and have access to a physical paper map and enjoy reading it, this may be an option. Plan your route around rest stops and accommodations to ensure you have a more relaxing trip.

Food is a crucial component of the road trip, so make sure you plan what you will take on the trip. If you are camping, you will want to consider how many days and nights you will be camping and traveling to your site; this will allow you to plan your food choices. It is always a great idea to have snacks for the road, especially when traveling with children, as they tend to get cranky when tired and hungry. Simple and healthy foods are best, but who does not love a bag of quality cheezies or chips? Have fun with your food choices. And be sure to bring enough water and drinks.

Things can get messy quickly when traveling, so ensure you have toilet paper and wet wipes, disinfecting wipes, hand sanitizer, and towels. Ensure you have allergy medication, prescriptions, pain medication, multi-vitamins, extra contact lenses, and glasses.

Accommodations are crucial, and what you bring on your trip will depend on whether you camp, stay in a cabin, guesthouse, hotel, or book another option. Sometimes, you will need to bring bedding, and other times you may not need to take anything; you want to double-check ahead of time. If you have a favorite pillow and blanket, it never hurts to take this with you on your journey, as getting a good rest is crucial.

Depending on the type of road trip you take, you will want to include items that make your trip more fun. If you are into sports, this might consist of kayaks, paddleboards, bikes, and other toys. You might take books, cards, board games, and hobbies if you also enjoy indoor activities. It never hurts to include a few extra toys on your trip as you may encounter opportunities to use them.

Once you are ready to go, enjoy your journey.

TRY THIS

TIME: For this mini-vacation, you will most likely take more than one day to enjoy.

METHOD: If you can't remember the last time you took a road trip, it is too long. For this escape, take time to decide where you would like to travel; it may take a while to finalize your decision. Ensure you book early to get the best choice if you need accommodation.

When you are ready, take another long escape and go on your road trip. Enjoy!

SWIMMING ESCAPES

> "While I'm swimming, I sing songs in my mind." — Alexandr Popov

Do you remember the first time you learned to swim? How old were you? Who were you with when you learned to swim?

I remember being six years old and spending time at a lake in the Okanagan in British Columbia. My parents and I enjoyed a hot, summer day and my mother was determined to teach me to swim. I had figured out the doggie paddle stroke but did not feel confident enough to swim in waters higher than my head.

My mother grabbed me, swam with me, and I held onto her, and then suddenly, she released me in the deep water. I felt uncomfortable and was ready to panic when practicing the doggie stroke and swam toward shallower waters. I swam to where I could put my feet on the bottom of the lake; it was a great feeling.

After that day, my mother struggled to keep me away from water. I swam in pools, rivers, creeks, lakes, and the sea. I could not fit enough swimming into my days; I even swam across a lake when I was 12. I was an agile swimmer with a lot of endurance, and I loved the feeling I got when I was in the water.

I recall many times I stayed in the water so long I was shivering, my lips were blue, and my mother was yelling, "Get out of the water now!"

While writing this book, I thought about adding more swimming into my leisure time; I spent my birthday with two close friends, and the weather was beautiful—warm enough to go for a swim, so we headed to a local river for a refreshing dip. The sun was shining, we brought a picnic and had a great afternoon visiting, swimming, and eating. It was a great way to spend a birthday.

There are so many benefits to swimming, and you do not need to be a little child to enjoy the rewards. As well as the physical benefits of swimming, there is the social aspect of spending time with others, and it reduces stress and boosts your mood. Going for a dip on a hot day is a great way to cool down and enjoy new scenery.

In an article written by Markham Heid, on *www.time.com*, *Why Swimming is so Good for You,* the author mentions: *"The exercise is also linked to many of the same life-extending, heart-saving, mood-lifting benefits associated with other forms of aerobic exercise. And it's fun, which matters. 'People tend to enjoy swimming more than running or bike-riding,' Tanaka says. While about half of people who try a new exercise program give up within a few months, people who take up swimming are more likely to stick with it, he says."* (34)

Swimming is an excellent way to exercise without the risk of too many injuries; it is easy on your joints and bones is often recommended as part of a physiotherapy program for people who have suffered injuries.

You also have the opportunity to burn a lot of calories and may not even be aware that it can be as much as running. If you tried other exercise programs without success, you might have more success with swimming. Swimming is a great physical sport because your entire body gets a workout; your heart rate increases, your muscles get toned, it adds to your flexibility, you gain endurance and build strength. When you swim, your cardiovascular system gets a great workout; your heart beats quicker, and your lungs get strong, particularly if you like to test yourself and hold your breath underwater.

You may not care what stroke you do while swimming but if you want to change it up a bit, try including any of the following strokes into your routine: freestyle, butterfly, backstroke, sidestroke, and breaststroke.

If you are recovering from an injury, have a disability, arthritis, asthma, or other health issues, swimming may be the best option for you.

If you suffer from poor sleep, regular swimming may improve your sleeping pattern. The cardiovascular workout with a change of scenery (if outdoors) and fresh air and sunshine can only boost your mood but also de-stress and make you feel calm, relaxed, and tired enough to hit your pillow and fall asleep at a faster level.

Another benefit of this sport is its affordability; swimming pools are expensive and may offer reasonable rates or free swim days. And, if you hitch a ride with a friend to a river, lake, or the ocean, the cost is free.

If you have not been swimming regularly, you want to warm up your muscles; it is critical to ease into swimming. Doing strength training is crucial—exercises such as unassisted pull-ups, squats, overhead presses, and deadlifts are a good start. If you are not sure, check with a personal trainer for assistance with your form.

Although swimming is gentler on the body, there are still risks if you are injured or have medical conditions. You want to check with your medical practitioner before beginning a brand-new exercise program.

Safety is the key when swimming, so be sure you bring a friend. Stay in designated swimming areas and if you swim during sunny days, use sunscreen and avoid the heat. Ensure you drink enough water. Make sure children get supervised when near water.

Since swimming is a social sport, this boosts your mental health as you'll often be swimming with friends and family; you may also add a picnic to gather. Many great memories revolve around the activity of swimming.

TRY THIS

TIME: With this activity, take at least 30 minutes.

METHOD: If you haven't been swimming for a long time, start small and grow with your exercises like with any sport. Ensure you do some weight-bearing exercises, flexibility exercises, and aerobic exercises as you will find it easier to swim.

You might aim for 30 minutes of swimming for your first few times and then ease up to more time; this depends on what type of strokes you are doing, how long you're doing them, and whether you are outdoors or in a swimming pool.

The next time you suffer from sleep issues, anxiety, and stress and need a great all-body workout, consider the magic of swimming. As it works your entire body, including your mind, you end up feeling relaxed and calm, an improved mood, and a night of deeper, restorative sleep. If you do not feel inspired enough to swim, nothing will motivate you.

WATER SPORTS

> "Water is the driving force of all nature." —Leonardo da Vinci

Did you know that there are over 30 popular water sports out there? If you want to be specific, there are more, and the most commonly referred to ones are activities you probably did. If you have ever gone boating, sailing, canoeing, kayaking, snorkeling, swimming, then you have enjoyed water sports.

Water sports happen in or near water. Sports include kayaking, canoeing, paddle boarding, water skiing, swimming, boating, surfing, snorkeling, windsurfing, jet-skiing, kite surfing, wakeboarding, and scuba diving, skimboarding, bodyboarding, cliff diving, and water polo. Other sports include barefoot skiing, dragon-boat racing, rafting, yachting, parasailing, powerboating, water polo, and more.

Water sports may refer to physical education camps and classes for children and teenagers or competitive aquatic events seen in the Olympics. However, for most of us, water sports are great recreational activities used to get outdoors, obtain exercise and test the limits of our fears, strength and agility, and curiosity.

There are numerous benefits of water sports. When you engage in these activities, you reduce your stress and anxiety and improve your mood. You often use muscles you might not otherwise use, and you breathe in the fresh air, strategize how to do the sport, and much more.

Other benefits of water sports are that your metabolism speeds up and burns calories without too much stress on the body.. Many activities in the water are easier on your joints, bones, and muscles.

You may experience weight loss and decrease chronic illness because you move your body and stay active.

I have always had a passion for water sports. While writing this book, I started researching to buy two kayaks to add this pastime to my spring, summer, and fall activities. I searched for kayaks for months, but due to the pandemic, everything sold out immediately, as people wanted to get outdoors.

Over the years, I rented kayaks during camping trips and other excursions, and while it was nice to rent, I wanted to own mine and have the freedom to go out kayaking when I had time.

One day, I stepped into an outdoor sports store, not expecting to see any kayaks because the store and others never had any. There were two green and blue-toned ocean-going kayaks resting on the ground in the store. I spoke to the manager, and these new kayaks had been unpacked and merchandised in the store just hours before; there were no people listed to buy them. The manager mentioned he had a six-page waitlist of people waiting to purchase kayaks, but these two new ones were not on the list.

These kayaks were what I wanted—singles with rudders and designed for the ocean and other water bodies; they were also green mixed with blue—my favorite colors. I could not believe my luck.

I have since had the opportunity to try out the new kayak with my family, and they are fast, stable, and a wonderful experience. Living on Vancouver Island offers many places to travel and explore by boat or kayak. Even if you don't live near an ocean, you probably have many lakes you can visit via a kayak.

Is there a new water sport you have noticed and wanted to try? Do you have friends who are doing the activity?

One of the best ways to try a new sport is to ask someone already doing it. Asking a sports enthusiast is your opportunity to learn about the equipment, safety elements, cost, and how to practice. Friends or family can help you save time and money to get started with the activity.

When you are considering water sports, safety is a big concern. Whether kayaking in the ocean, white water rafting, or swimming, you will want to be educated on safety and have the proper equipment to stay safe. You also will want to do these activities with others; kayaking or swimming alone is not a good idea as many unforeseen things can happen. It is always good to have a friend with you. Besides, the social aspect of water sports is another added value to doing the activities.

TRY THIS

TIME: For this escape, you will want to take an afternoon or a day to enjoy.

METHOD: If you want to add a new water sport to your list of activities, ensure you do the proper research and homework, learn the techniques and ways to engage in the water sport, and then get out there and have fun.

You might take an afternoon, day or merge that water sport into a week-long camping trip. The choice is yours.

EARTHING ENERGY

> "And forget not that the Earth delights to feel your bare feet and the winds long to play with your hair."
> —Khalik Gibran

Did you ever take your shoes and socks off and run around on the ground or grass when you were a child?

I remember running around on green grass while playing hide-and-go-seek with friends in my grandparents' neighborhood. Something was comforting about walking and running on the grass; my feet felt alive, and it relaxed me. I may have been taking a chance of landing in a mess of dog doo-doo, but I still took a chance. Generally, it was safe to be in the freshly mowed grassy yards of houses in the neighborhood as the homeowners did not leave messes on the lawn.

As adults, we probably do not have the opportunity to go barefoot often, but our ancestors often walked barefoot or wore leather moccasins while walking or running. We did not realize that they had more contact with the Earth.

You may have heard of the term earthing (grounding) to describe the action of sitting, sleeping outdoors, walking barefoot on grass, sandy beaches, or the ground—making physical contact with the Earth which transfers conductive energy to the body. The Earth possesses a giant electrical field, and humans have a bioelectrical field; researchers believe earthing puts you in direct contact with the energy of the Earth, decreasing stress and inflammation.

The Earth is like a giant battery, energized with solar radiation and lightning, creating a slight electrical charge.

Anna Medaris Miller wrote an article for *US Health & World News*, entitled *Grounding: Hype of Healing?* States: "*While the existence of Earth's energy isn't much-debated – NASA says "the flow of liquid iron in Earth's core creates electric currents, which in turn creates the magnetic field" – exactly if and how it can affect human health is less clear."* (35)

While science is still researching the impacts on people directly connecting with the Earth, one thing is sure—we feel more relaxed and energized when we spend time outdoors in nature. Whether we are relaxing on a blanket in the forest, walking along a lake, or taking off our shoes and socks and feeling the fresh spring grass between our toes, the connection with Mother Earth positively impacts us.

You may have also heard the term earthing when referring to electricity, but most people have not given it much thought unless they work in a trade or are an electrician.

Earthing (also called grounding) prevents you from electrical shock should you touch a live metal piece. If there is a fault with electrical product installation, your body may become a conductor, allowing electricity to run from live to Earth.

Earthing provides a safe path (protective conductor) so a fault current can flow to Earth. It causes a protective device (fuse or circuit-breaker) to turn off electrical currents to the faulted circuit.

Earthing has been around for thousands of years as our ancestors may have been barefoot or wore leather footwear created from animal hides. Energy from Earth could permeate their feet and travel into their body.

Newer science indicates positive effects of earthing: reduced stress and anxiety, less pain and inflammation, better sleep, and improved blood flow and mood. However, one does not need science to know they often feel better by just being outdoors in the fresh air and a change of scenery.

You may reconnect by going barefoot for at least 30 minutes or more outdoors; you might find a park or area with grass, remove your shoes and stand with bare feet. Be sure to walk on the soil, sand, or grassy areas but before you do so, make sure the area is clear of debris and anything that would pose a hazard.

It is not always easy to practice this activity, but if you go camping, walk along a park, or other beautiful outdoor areas, you may be able to incorporate a little of this practice into your day.

TRY THIS

TIME: Try this escape when you have at least 30 minutes or longer to enjoy the activity.

METHOD: Next, decide where you would like to walk, sit, or rest outdoors. Do you want to lie down on a blanket in a park? Is there a clean place where you can remove your shoes and stand or walk so you can feel the Earth at your feet?

Consider where you might be able to practice earthing. It is not so easy in a city, so it may not happen often, and you may have to travel out of the city to experience this, but it is worth it.

How can you incorporate reconnecting with the Earth? Just asking this question may open up opportunities for you. Camping or day trips to camping sites or parks will give you opportunities to get grounded and relaxed. Be creative, ask friends, look for chances to spend time outdoors.

Earthing includes lying on a blanket, walking barefoot on grass or sand, and swimming in water.

If you feel stressed, overwhelmed, and ungrounded, consider engaging in an earthing escape to reconnect to nature and the world.

STONE COLLECTING

> "Write your worries in the sand, carve your blessings in stone." —Robert F. Kennedy

Imagine being at a beach, sitting on a driftwood log, your feet buried below the warm sand. You feel the caress of a balmy breeze across your cheeks, you hear the sounds of seagulls in the distance, and you watch the incoming tide as it cascades down onto the fringe of the beach.

You watch two young brothers gathering rocks and placing them in orange and green buckets on the shore. At one point, the older boy grabs a stone and tosses it into the water, where the rock proceeds to skim across the top of the water, skipping six times before sinking to the bottom of the ocean.

Collecting stones is a simple and relaxing activity you may have done as a child. It may be time to revisit this hobby.

One beautiful summer day on a Wednesday, I was fortunate to have a day off work as it was my birthday. I took my three-year-old son to the beach to have a picnic and enjoy the sunshine and activities the beach has to offer. My other son was in school, and I enjoyed this moment with my youngest son.

We sat on driftwood logs on the beach, and then I chased my son along the water. All of a sudden, something caught my eye. It was a heart-shaped stone and virtually perfect in its design. I quickly picked it up and showed it to my son, who squealed with delight and then said he wanted to find more heart stones. We spent at least an hour scouring the beach, studying thousands of rocks in search of another perfect specimen. We did not find any more that day, but we felt like treasure hunters, and we got lost in a moment and felt relaxed after that time passed. It was such a special moment, and it triggered a life-long hobby with our family.

Stones are records of the Earth's past and may even contain fossils. There are three main rock types: sedimentary rocks, metamorphic rocks, and igneous rocks.

Sedimentary rocks cover three-quarters of the Earth's surface and include clay, limestone, shale, and sandstone. They are created when minute rock particles are deposited into lakes or oceans by the wind or rivers. These tiny pieces of rock get compressed and form sedimentary rock.

Metamorphic rocks develop with heat or intense pressure through shifting tectonic plates or volcanic eruptions, altering the minerals in the underground rocks. They get transformed into another type of rock—metamorphic.

Igneous rocks occur when molten rock rises from beneath the Earth and cools and solidifies near the surface. Erosion further adds to their current shapes. This rock includes granite and basalt.

Studying rocks is interesting as you can learn about the history of the world in a rock. The creation of rocks involves minerals.

According to an article by R. Jeffers on the WordPress blog, *www. Dr.Beachcomb, "There are more than 3000 known minerals (the number is still growing), but of these, only about 20 minerals are very common, and of these, only 9 constitute 95% of the Earth's crust."* (36)

TRY THIS

TIME: For this escape, you can take as long as you want. If you have stones in your backyard, you might take 10 minutes to study the rocks and see if you can find an unusually colored or shaped stone.

METHOD: When you take a trip and find yourself surrounded by rocks, take a few moments to find a beautiful stone that reminds you of the trip.

I have a bowl in the dining room and fill it with unusual rocks I find while hiking or spending beach time with my family. I found many beautiful stones while visiting Australia with my sister and family. I brought them home to put in the bowl. Occasionally, I will glance over at the bowl, and it triggers a memory of being on Jervis Bay Beach with family in New South Wales, Australia.

CYCLING ADVENTURES

> "Ride as much or as little, or as long or as short as you feel. But ride." —Eddy Merckx

Do you remember the very first time you learned to ride a bicycle? How old were you? Where were you when you learned to ride?

Most of us remember those first moments when we mastered two wheels and felt the rush of freedom and breeze across our faces as we pedaled our way to a new adventure.

When I was young, I learned to ride on a lime-green women's bike; the bike was too big, but I eventually learned to master it and feel confident in engaging in many riding experiences.

I took many risks, riding down steep embankments, wiping out, getting stung by a wasp while riding, hitting rocks, and flying over the handlebars; it was part of the experience as a child. I'm not as adventurous as I once was, but I still enjoy a quiet, relaxing ride on my bike from time to time.

Some people use bikes as a mode of transportation to get to work, run errands, or ride and explore new areas. Others are avid mountain bike enthusiasts that pride themselves on taking chances on challenging terrains.

Whether you like to race with your bike, explore mountain biking trails or ride in the city, cycling is a great sport offering many great escapes and health benefits.

If you are fortunate to be able to cycle to work, it's environmentally friendly and inexpensive as well as healthy. There are numerous health benefits which include improving the strength of your legs, lungs, and heart. If you habitually cycle, you lower your body fat, increase your metabolism, and build muscle. As a result, you burn more calories even when resting.

Suppose you've suffered past injuries from other activities. In that case, cycling is easier on the body as it's low impact, and you can strengthen your body core and improve your balance and coordination.

Finally, cycling can take you to new places you might not otherwise see, and it can help improve your mental health and state of being.

People realized the benefits of cycling when the global pandemic began in 2020. Around the world, people had to quarantine in their homes, and those who had bicycles dusted them off and explored their towns and cities on two wheels. Those who did not own bikes rushed to buy bicycles amidst the flurry of other interested buyers.

I spoke with bike-store owners that could not order enough bikes to satisfy the intense demand. Other retailers had backlogs of bike orders for repairs.

In my city in the last few months, bicycle lanes got added to our local streets, and I believe other towns and cities in the world have added bike lanes.

If you haven't ridden for a while, there are some things you want to do to ensure your cycling adventure is more fun.

Exercising to build strength in your legs and body care is crucial. Using weights and an elliptical machine or running or jogging may help keep you strong until you ride.

If you haven't ridden your bike in a while, take it to a bike store to get a proper bike tune-up. Maintenance is crucial. The bike frame gets checked for cracks, and the brakes may be adjusted or replaced; the bike chain may need to be cleaned or replaced, and the shifting may need adjustment and more. If you're an expert at spotting and fixing problems, you can save money on maintenance.

Before each ride, check that your helmet doesn't have cracks, your tire pressure is correct, the brakes grab, and the gears can shift. Check your wheels by spinning them to check for wobbles and ensure your handgrips and seat are comfortable.

What you wear is crucial and determined by where and how far you travel, the time of year, and the temperature.

The best type of clothing to wear is comfortable, waterproof and water-wicking, and layered; dressing this way allows you to remove layers as the temperature varies during your trip.

For longer rides, you should pack extra supplies: energy bars, water, a small bike pump, and the appropriate tools for bike repairs.

TRY THIS

For this escape, you want to have at least 30 minutes to enjoy cycling. You may cycle alone or have family and friends join you in the adventure.

If you are a serious cyclist, you'll want more time to escape on your bike; you might take an afternoon, day, or weekend to explore new terrain.

If you are not an experienced cyclist, take your time to get used to cycling again. Choose shorter routes and places to visit so you won't be too tired when you cycle.

Cycling is a powerful way to exercise your mind, body, and spirit, so get out and get cycling today!

BIRD-WATCHING ESCAPES

> "In order to see the birds it is necessary to become part of the silence." —Robert Wilson Lynd

Do you consider yourself a bird watcher? A birder? Most of us feel like our lives are busy, and we often associate bird watching with an activity that only the elderly do. Bird watching is not an activity many of us do, but we are starting to pay attention to this type of interest.

I would occasionally watch birds or revel in watching a bald eagle land on top of a tall tree in a beautiful beach cove area, but I didn't spend too much time watching birds.

My focus changed when I bought a hammock.

As I pondered how to write this mini-vacation idea, I witnessed a tiny green flecked hummingbird flitting from flower to flower in my backyard. I was resting in my blue and green canvas hammock and studying this marvelous creature who was oblivious to my existence and was buzzing around the apple tree, seeking sustenance.

I wrote over 60 percent of this book outside while I've rested in my hammock. During this time, I've seen a tiny woodpecker peck at the apple tree, a gorgeous blue jay come by for a short visit, several songbirds whistle melodious songs, crows cackle in the distance. I've seen tiny birds give themselves a birdbath of dirt by my picnic table, pint-sized hummingbirds chase each other in front of me, and much more.

Nestled against the back of my house is a birdhouse, and I have been privy to seeing two sets of bird families grow up and fly away from that tiny home. While writing this book, I saw the mother or father bird leave the birdhouse, fly away and return a few minutes later with food; the babies would be squawking loudly.

There are many benefits to bird watching. The first benefit is that you may see unusual birds or behaviors, connecting you with nature. You also slow down, remain still, and focus on something other than yourself, which is helpful for your busy mind. If you are creative, you may take a photograph, view birds through binoculars, draw or paint what you see in front of you.

Birds often reflect what is happening in the environment.

For example, you will hear a lot of singing from birds in the springtime. As summer progresses, you often will not hear bird songs if it gets unseasonably hot.

During the first-ever, unprecedented heat dome that broke temperature records on Vancouver Island, I noticed there were no sounds of birds. When the weather turned back to seasonal temperatures, the birds came back and sang.

When forest fire smoke blanketed my region, and the air quality was acrid and thick, there were no birds to be seen or heard.

Scientists often think of birds as ecosystem indicators, and they study them to determine environmental conditions and changes.

When you watch birds, you may see their playful antics, gorgeous plumage patterns, and colors and listen to their voices. There is often a lot to focus on when you engage in this activity.

Serious birders will buy binoculars, and you want to ensure you do your homework to obtain the right lenses for your experience.

If you are not as concerned about binoculars, you may use a professional camera with a telephoto lens or use your phone to zoom in and watch birds. Of course, just standing or sitting still and watching birds are also an option.

TRY THIS

TIME: For this mini-vacation, take at least 20–30 minutes to watch birds.

METHOD: How you plan to watch birds depends on you. If you are very serious about this activity, you will want to own a camera with a telephoto lens or a strong pair of binoculars.

If you are an amateur birder, you may be satisfied with using your smartphone to record photos or bird sounds. You don't even need to use equipment; you may choose to stand or sit in a park or outdoor space and wait and watch for birds. The choice is up to you.

The main thing to consider is you are using this time to calm down, slow down and focus on a creature in nature. This time outdoors will help make a positive difference in your mental state.

Happy escaping!

HAMMOCK HOLIDAYS

> "Floating in a lake lying in a hammock, playing a bit of Scrabble… that's what I'm in need of." —Karen Walker

Want to know a great way to calm down, relax, daydream, and lose track of time on purpose? Lie in a hammock; there's nothing like relaxing outdoors in a hammock.

Nothing screams the carefree days of summer more than resting in a hammock. If it's a warm day and there's a cool breeze and the sounds of birds, you may feel like you're on vacation.

I wrote at least half of this book on my old and trusty eleven-year-old laptop, a Toshiba Satellite Pro (and yes, I had to plug it in with an extension cord as the battery doesn't last). I sat in a canvas hammock tied to an apple and cherry tree in my backyard, and both trees provided lots of shade. I also benefited from a soft, gentle breeze and fresh air and heard the sounds of two owls and other types of birds in my neighborhood. Sometimes I would write for a while, close my eyes, and rest and listen to the sounds of nature.

There are numerous benefits to using a hammock; one huge plus is you immediately have an opportunity to immerse yourself in nature. As soon as you hang the hammock or lie in a free-standing one, you may feel the sunshine and a faint breeze flow across your body, and you may also feel relaxed as the hammock gently rocks back and forth.

Spending time in a hammock allows you to relax, and you may find your mind drifting as you look at the environment around you. If you're outdoors and resting, you may notice the sights and sounds of birds, bees, and other creatures.

Some research shows that the gentle rocking motion of the hammock may lead to a quicker and deeper sleep.

In an article, *Hammocks May Improve Sleep - Study: Gentle Rocking Helps You Fall Asleep Faster*, by Jennifer Warner on *www.webmd.com*, the author states, *"Researchers say the results suggest that rocking to soothe and induce sleep is an adaptive human behavior that has evolved over the years to encourage the natural oscillations that occur in the brain during sleep.*

They say the next step is to find out whether harnessing the sleep-inducing power of the hammock may be used to treat sleep disorders, such as insomnia." (37)

I never slept for long periods in a hammock, but I know many people have, and they enjoy them because of less pressure on the body and back when lying in them. The hammock may also help with muscle aches and pains. The swaying and swinging of the hammock may lull you to sleep where you have a short, relaxing nap. There is nothing better than experiencing this on a summer afternoon.

If you don't own a hammock and want one, there's no shortage of styles available. There are standing hammocks, rocking chair hammocks, canvas and nylon styles, and more. The type you purchase will depend on where you live, your lifestyle, and your plans.

For example, I own a canvas hammock under two trees in my backyard; I also purchased three portable nylon hammocks for my family. When we go on hikes, we take the hammocks and our supplies, and when we need to take a break, we set up the hammocks and rest. My favorite escape is to visit a hill by the ocean and set up my hammock; the ocean view is breathtaking, and the breeze is refreshing. Life doesn't get better than being outdoors with family and friends.

In July, a few years ago, my youngest son and I hiked to a beautiful spot by the ocean, and we set up our hammocks for the afternoon. We were shaded from the harsh sun, had a view of the ocean, and ample supply of food and water, journals, and books. It was a wonderful and simple escape.

If you live in the city and don't have a backyard, the portable hammock may be an option, as when you get to the outdoors, you can find a place to set yourself up for an afternoon. Or, if you have a balcony or porch, you may be able to tie up a hammock in the area and create your little oasis.

Another option for a hammock is to set it up indoors in the corner of a room if you have space.

TRY THIS

TIME: For this mini-vacation, take at least 60 minutes or an afternoon to enjoy.

METHOD: If you don't have a hammock, do your research to find a suitable hammock for your space. Then, take at least an hour and indulge. You might read a book, eat and drink, or take a nap.

Once you try out your hammock, you may become "hooked" and look for opportunities to regularly escape the pace. Enjoy!

A FINAL ESCAPE

> "Adopt the pace of nature; her secret is patience." —
> Ralph Waldo Emerson

The opposite of blue is green. Maybe not on the artist's color wheel; the opposite of blue is considered orange on the palette wheel. But if we use blue to represent life's pace and the stress of technology, and green to represent spending time in nature, this statement is true. Nature is a buffer to the stress of life and technology—it is the opposite.

I have forever had a deep respect and passion for the outdoors and environment. This love of the outdoors and nature originates from being a young child living on seven acres of pristine land in the Okanagan in British Columbia. This experience allowed me to engage with all types of creatures. I rescued baby birds and other animals, played with frogs, had chickens and geese, helped my parents with their large garden and two honeybee hives.

I designed and built forts outdoors using large sticks, small logs, and cedar boughs, foraged berries, and plants that were safe to eat, and much more. The appreciation I had for nature has never left me, and I feel passionate about it and our environment today.

We need to pay attention and reconnect with the natural world.

Nature has its time clock and is not hurried, rushed, or impatient. Everything happens in cycles and at the right time.

For example, if you see a beautiful rosebud and attempt to open the petals before they are ready, you will destroy the flower; it needs to open at its own pace.

The pace of humankind has been increasing with every decade. I have witnessed the advent of new technologies and the stress of our busy lives. We have become more disconnected from nature with our calendars, the technology that keeps us awake until late, and activities that distract us from the outdoors.

Some of this changed in 2020. The global pandemic forced us to slow down, stay put, and find new ways to stay sane and healthy. We began to notice how much better we felt in nature and engaged in non-technological activities. For some of us, it was an awakening—a chance to learn new skills and talents, revisit or learn new hobbies, reconnect with nature and our environment.

The sales of bikes, kayaks, paddleboards, and other outdoor sporting equipment skyrocketed as we had to stay close to home and eliminate local and international travel. We started to rediscover the beauty and importance of spending time outdoors in nature, engaging in new and long-forgotten adventures.

I bought two sea-going kayaks while writing this book, and it was the best decision I had made in a long time. My husband and I had time to reconnect outdoors while getting fresh air and exercise and enjoying new adventures.

As the world has gotten more complex, our lives busier than ever, and the news more distressing, we must find new ways to stay healthy both physically and mentally, and we need to know we have some sense of control. By taking mini-vacations every day, we may mitigate some of the stress and anxiety that living in the 21st century brings to our lives.

What are you doing to reconnect with your family, friends, yourself, and the great outdoors? Can you add energizing and fun activities to your life? What can you do to cut down on waste and help the environment? Where can you eliminate the time-wasters, energy suckers, and stressful tasks? How can you use technology to improve your life and not let technology use you? These are crucial questions you need to consider as you continue your journey.

I hope you are inspired to make changes, make mistakes, have fun, try new things, and add variety to your life. No matter what challenges you face, try one mini-escape and then another. The act of doing so will slowly add more energy and newness to your life, and you may find you start to feel more positive one mini-vacation at a time.

Happy escaping!

BIBLIOGRAPHY

CHAPTER 1

The Moment:

1. ةيبرعلاةغللاباذهضرعأ, WhyDoesTimeSeemtoSpeedUpwithAge?, Scientific American, July 1, 2016, https://www.scientificamerican.com/article/why-does-time-seem-to-speed-up-with-age/

Visualize Vacations:

2. Matt Neason, The Power of Visualization, Sports Psychology Today, August 8, 2012, http://www.sportpsychologytoday.com/sport-psychology-for-coaches/the-power-of-visualization/

Color by Crayon:

3. Dr. Nikki Martinez, Psy.D. LCPC, 7 Reasons Adult Coloring Books Are Great for Your Mental, Emotional and Intellectual Health, Huffpost, November 24, 2016, https://www.huffpost.com/entry/7-reasons-adult-coloring-books-are-great-for-your-mental-emotional-and-intellectual-health_b_8626136

Mini Masterpiece:

4. Malaka Gharib, Feeling Artsy? Here's How Making Art Helps Your Brain, NPR, January 11, 2020, https://www.

npr.org/sections/health-shots/2020/01/11/795010044/feeling-artsy-heres-how-making-art-helps-your-brain

Play-Doh Pleasures

5. David Kindy, The Accidental Invention of Play-Doh, Smithsonian Magazine, November 12, 2019, https://www.smithsonianmag.com/innovation/accidental-invention-play-doh-180973527/

CHAPTER 2

A Breather

6. Christophe André, Proper Breathing Brings Better Health, Scientific American, January 15, 2019, https://www.scientificamerican.com/article/proper-breathing-brings-better-health/

Marvelous Meditation

7. Change Your Mind: Meditation Benefits for the Brain, Ask the Scientists, https://askthescientists.com/brain-meditation/#toggle-id-1

Monotasking Magic

8. Amyh Vetter, Science Says Monotasking – Not Multitasking – Is the Secret to Getting Things Done. Here are 8 Ways to Do It: Research confirms that monotasking – and not multitasking – is the secret to getting things done, Inc., Feb 28, 2018, https://www.inc.com/amy-vetter/why-you-should-close-your-eyes-at-work-other-tips-to-achieve-deep-focus.html

Great Gratitude

9. Catherine Robertson, How Gratitude Can Change Your Life, Rick Hanson, April 18, 2017, https://www.rickhanson.net/how-gratitude-can-change-your-life/

Journal Joy

10. Maud Purcell, LCSW, CEAP, The Health Benefits of Journaling, PsychCentral, May 17, 2016, https://psychcentral.com/lib/the-health-benefits-of-journaling#1

CHAPTER 3

Musical Moments

11. Sally Sapega, Playing an Instrument: Better for Your Brain than Just Listening, Penn Medicine News, January 30, 2017, https://www.pennmedicine.org/news/news-blog/2017/january/playing-an-instrument-better-for-your-brain-than-just-listening

Sound Escapes

12. Anna Sharratt, The healing power of sound, The Globe and Mail, October 16, 2019, https://www.theglobeandmail.com/life/article-good-vibrations-the-healing-power-of-sound/

Dance Busting

13. Dancing and the Brain, Harvard Medical School, Winter 2015, https://hms.harvard.edu/news-events/publications-archive/brain/dancing-brain

Coffee or Tea for One

14. Tea: A cup of good health?, Harvard Health Publishing/Harvard Medical School, August 13, 2014, https://www.health.harvard.edu/staying-healthy/tea-a-cup-of-good-health

CHAPTER 4

Fabulous Food

15. Danny Lewis, Feeling Down? Scientists Say Cooking and Baking Could Help You Feel Better: A little creativity each day goes a long way, Smithsonian Magazine, November 29, 2016, https://www.smithsonianmag.com/smart-news/feeling-down-scientists-say-cooking-and-baking-may-help-you-feel-better-180961223/

Floral Finesse

16. Dr. Leonard Perry, Extension Professor, Relieve Stress with Flowers, University of Vermont Extension/Department of Plant and Soil Science, *https://pss.uvm.edu/ppp/articles/relieve.html*

Gratitude Journaling

17. Courtney E. Ackerman, Gratitude Journal: A Collection of 66 Templates, Ideas, and Apps for Your Diary, Positive Psychology, May 20, 2021, https://positivepsychology.com/gratitude-journal/

Magical Boardgames

18. Top 10 Health Benefits of Board Games, Health Fitness Revolution, October 27, 2020, https://www.healthfitnessrevolution.com/top-10-health-benefits-board-games/

CHAPTER 5

Escape to Nap

19. The How-To: Making Naps Work For You, Entrepreneur, March 11, 2020, https://www.entrepreneur.com/article/347512

Guilty Pleasures

20. Ellie Zolfagharifard, Science of guilty pleasures: Study uncovers how feeling bad can boost your happiness, Daily Mail, June 4, 2015, https://www.dailymail.co.uk/sciencetech/article-3111624/Science-guilty-pleasures-Study-uncovers-feeling-bad-boost-happiness.html

Like a Tourist

21. Stacey Leasca, New Study Suggests Exploring Your Own Town Can Be Good For Your Mental Health, Travel + Leisure, June 21, 2020, https://www.travelandleisure.com/trip-ideas/yoga-wellness/nature-neuroscience-study-new-experiences

Friendly Escapes

22. Kira M. Newman, Why Your Friends Are More Important Than You Think, The Greater Good Science Center at the University of California, Berkeley, July 20, 2020, https://greatergood.berkeley.edu/article/item/why_your_friends_are_more_important_than_you_think

CHAPTER 6

Try Something New

23. Harvard Health Publishing, Rev up your thinking skills by trying something new, Harvard Health Publishing/Harvard Medical School, December 10, 2015, https://www.health.harvard.edu/healthy-aging/rev-up-your-thinking-skills-by-trying-something-new

New Novelties

24. Steve Taylor, Feel like time is flying? Here's how to slow it down, The Conversation, Apr. 24, 2019, https://theconversation.com/feel-like-time-is-flying-heres-how-to-slow-it-down-115257

Superhero Day

25. Robin Rosenberg, The Psychology Behind Superhero Origin Stories, Smithsonian Magazine, February, 2013, https://www.smithsonianmag.com/arts-culture/the-psychology-behind-superhero-origin-stories-4015776/

Just Joking

26. Peter McGraw, Ph.D., The Importance of Humor Research: A serious non-serious research topic, Psychology Today, September 14, 2011, https://www.psychologytoday.com/ca/blog/the-humor-code/201109/the-importance-humor-research

Juggle Away Stress

27. Alena Hall, How Juggling Can Relieve Stress and Still Your Mind, HuffPost, December 19, 2014, https://www.huffpost.com/entry/juggling-relieves-stress_n_6356226

Making Magic

28. Sean Coughlan, Why do we like magic when we know it's a trick?, BBC News, April 10, 2019, https://www.bbc.com/news/education-47827346

CHAPTER 7

The Elements

29. How Does Nature Impact Our Wellbeing?, University of Minnesota/Earl E. Bakken Center for Spirituality & Healing, 2016, https://www.takingcharge.csh.umn.edu/how-does-nature-impact-our-wellbeing

Sunrise, Sunset

30. Kate Doyle, How to predict a good sunrise or sunset so you can brag about it on social media," ABC News, May 10, 2018, https://www.abc.net.au/news/2018-05-11/how-to-predict-good-sunrise-and-sunset/9737446

Relaxing Spots

31. Jamie Ducharme, Spending Just 20 Minutes in a Park Makes You Happier. Here's What Else Being Outside Can Do for Your Health, Time, February 28, 2019, https://time.com/5539942/green-space-health-wellness/

Relaxing Water Escapes

32. Carolyn Gregoire, Why Being Near The Ocean Can Make You Calmer And More Creative, HuffPost, December 6, 2017, https://www.huffpost.com/entry/mental-benefits-water_n_5791024

Passionate Picnic

33. Julia Plevin, Why food tastes better outside, Medium, May 15, 2017, https://medium.com/forestbathingclub/forest-bathing-essentials-part-one-snacks-16458863deb7

Swimming Escapes

34. Markham Heid, Why Swimming is so Good for You, Time, March 2, 2017, https://time.com/4688623/swimming-pool-health-benefits/

Earthing Energy

35. Anna Medaris Miller, Grounding: Hype of Healing? U.S. News, November 3, 2017, https://health.usnews.com/wellness/articles/2017-11-03/grounding-hype-or-healing

Stone Collecting

36. R. Jeffers, The insolent quietness of stones, Dr.Beachcomb, April17, 2016, https://drbeachcomb.wordpress.com/2016/04/17/rocks/

Hammock Holiday

37. Jennifer Warner, Hammocks May Improve Sleep - Study: Gentle Rocking Helps You Fall Asleep Faster, WebMD, June 21, 2011, https://www.webmd.com/sleep-disorders/news/20110621/hammocks-help-you-sleep

Printed in the United States
by Baker & Taylor Publisher Services